J. C. SSEKAMWA

History and Development of Education in Uganda

FOUNTAIN PUBLISHERS LTD.
KAMPALA, UGANDA

Fountain Publishers Ltd.
P. O. Box 488
KAMPALA

© J. C. Ssekamwa 1997
First Published 1997

All rights reserved. No part of this publication may be reprinted or reproduced or utilised in any form or by any means electronic, mechanical or other means now known or hereafter invented, including copying and recording, or in any information storage or retrieval system, without permission in writing from the publishers.

ISBN 9970 02 059 5

Cover picture: Duhaga High School in Hoima 1913

PREFACE

History of education in any country deals with the evolution of that country's educational system and the developments which it has brought about. Hence *History and Development of Education in Uganda* suits this book as a title.

A country's education system is subjected to constant reforms whenever the situation arises in order to enable the people cope with new demands.

Therefore one phenomenon a reader will notice in this book is the constant dissatisfaction of Ugandans with the nature of education at different times in the country and the attempts which have been made to address these dissatisfactions.

These dissatisfactions are always healthy; they make the education of a country ever dynamic to meet new challenges which the people face.

This book comes out at a time when there have been hectic reforms going on in the educational system as outlined by the Senteza Kajubi Education Commission of 1987.

There is a hope that this account will in some ways assist all those engaged in these reforms to realize that many educational issues tackled in this book which are a matter of concern for all of us now are not new. Therefore there will be a chance to compare and contrast the steps being taken now to address those same issues in terms of reform.

Similarly, we should realize that reforms which are being carried out through internationally funded projects should be such that once the financial assistance runs out, the country should be able to sustain the structures set up by those international bodies.

Although the citizens are welcome to play an active role in the education system of a country, the role of the government is paramount. This is why one of the definitions of education says that "education is a conscious process designed to change behaviour patterns of individuals in each society towards desirable ends as perceived by the leadership of that country."

It is the government which can view the country's educational system in its totality and thus ensure that all the country's children are brought within the embrace of education with a massive allocation of public funds and funds solicited from abroad for educational purposes.

J.C. Ssekamwa
Makerere University
1997

CONTENTS

                                        Page

1. African Indigenous Education — 1
2. The Introduction and Development of Western Education in Uganda 1877 – 1925 — 25
3. Church and State in Education 1925 – 1962 — 52
4. Literary Education in the Uganda Education System — 59
5. Agricultural Education and out of School Education — 71
6. The Development of Technical Education — 84
7. The Establishment of Private Schools in Uganda — 94
8. The Relationship Between Church and State 1925 – 1963 — 119
9. Language and the Medium of Instruction in Uganda — 127
10. Education Development 1940 – 1962 — 143
11. Colonial Education for Responsible Government 1940 – 1962 — 154
12. Development of Education 1962 – 1990 — 164
13. Effects of some Education Ordinances, commissins, committees and Education Acts on the Education System of Uganda — 191
14. Some Crucial Issues in Uganda's Education System — 202
15. A Historical Perspective of Basic Education for National Development (BEND) — 221

Index — 235

1 African Indigenous Education

Definition of Education
In books which are written about education one finds several definitions of it. All those definitions show that each society makes arrangements to see that all its citizens learn the desirable social behaviour, the necessary basic knowledge and skills for use in their daily lives so that they can be productive and useful to themselves and to the whole society in which they live.

On the basis of the above statement Ugandans educated the young and old people, before the Missionaries introduced school education along the basis of Western lines in 1877. Each tribe had an education system with aims, organisation, content, methods of teaching, teachers and places where that education was imparted.

Here are two common definitions of education:

(i) "Education is a process by which one generation purposefully transmits culture to the young, to the adults and to the old for their social, cultural and economic benefit and for the benefit of the whole society.''

In the above definition of education, culture consists of everything there is in a society which is worthy learning for the benefit of an individual and for the whole society in which that individual lives. Such things are desirable social behaviour or manners, the technical skills, customs, beliefs, values, laws, institutions and knowledge on a variety of things. We realise that culture in the above definition is not taken narrowly to mean only what was taking place before the coming of the Western education, such as old and rare African dances and songs which when performed today leave even the African audiences amazed.

The culture of a people in the wide sense of the word as described above is created continuously. Now we are creating a Ugandan culture along the lines of desirable social behaviour or manners, new technical skills, customs, beliefs, values, laws, institutions and knowledge on a variety of things. Similarly, we are discarding parts of culture which no longer fit our situation. By implication then, culture is dynamic. This means that it changes progressively. It adopts new trends while it also progressively discards old trends which stop to be useful and beneficial to society due to a changed situation.

The above definition of education is a conservative one. There are other definitions however, which directly say that education is dynamic and it is duty bound to change the nature of things in a society in the light of new changes in that society. In the light of the above statement let us look at a dynamic definition of education.

(ii) "Education is a conscious process designed to change or bring about behaviour patterns of individuals in each society towards desirable or worthwhile ends as perceived by the society or by the leadership of that society".

In the light of the above definition, governments of countries timely set up education reviews or commissions to examine the arrangement of their education systems and the curriculum to see whether both can still adequately meet the needs of their societies. This kind of action is necessary because situations in every country constantly change and demand new knowledge, new technical skills and new outlook to things. After such education reviews or commissions have discovered that there is need to change the arrangement of the education system and the curriculum to meet effectively a changed situation in a society, such a change is set in motion. This is why in the above definition it is said that, "education is a conscious process designed to change behaviour patterns as perceived by the leadership of a society."

Therefore education in a country is a useful weapon because it is used as an instrument to bring about corrective and necessary measures in any one society. The general purpose of indigenous education in each Ugandan tribe before the introduction of Western education, was to enable each member of that society to be helpful to himself/herself, to his/her family, to the rest of the members of the society and to the state. To achieve the above purpose, each member of a tribe was taught the basic knowledge, skills, desirable social behaviour, customs, history, geography, biology, chemistry, agriculture, religion, psychology, philosophy, economics and politics. The content in those subjects was not static. It changed as new knowledge and skills were discovered and those which ceased to be useful were discarded. For example, boys and girls of a tribe were taught the history of their tribe. They were taught where their great-grand fathers came from before settling in their present place. This knowledge was partly necessary because members of a tribe had to defend the ownership of the area where they were living. They were taught geography so that they knew the different seasons of the year. This knowledge helped them when grown up, to plant and harvest their crops in the right time and right manner.

Youngsters were taught the customs, desirable social behavior and laws of their tribe so that they would be good citizens. This knowledge also helped especially the boys to administer laws if they became chiefs or leaders in their tribe. They were taught many skills to help them do things and make things. For example, a boy was taught how to build a house, how to use spears, bows and arrows and shields to defend himself, his family and his tribe.

He was taught how to raise and look after cattle, goats, sheep and chickens. These helped him produce milk and meat for himself, his family and for the rest of the society in which he lived. He was also taught how to make cloths from skins and bark trees so that he could clothe himself and members of his family

CONTENTS

Page

1. African Indigenous Education — 1
2. The Introduction and Development of Western Education in Uganda 1877 – 1925 — 25
3. Church and State in Education 1925 – 1962 — 52
4. Literary Education in the Uganda Education System — 59
5. Agricultural Education and out of School Education — 71
6. The Development of Technical Education — 84
7. The Establishment of Private Schools in Uganda — 94
8. The Relationship Between Church and State 1925 – 1963 — 119
9. Language and the Medium of Instruction in Uganda — 127
10. Education Development 1940 – 1962 — 143
11. Colonial Education for Responsible Government 1940 – 1962 — 154
12. Development of Education 1962 – 1990 — 164
13. Effects of some Education Ordinances, commissins, committees and Education Acts on the Education System of Uganda — 191
14. Some Crucial Issues in Uganda's Education System — 202
15. A Historical Perspective of Basic Education for National Development (BEND) — 221

Index — 235

PREFACE

History of education in any country deals with the evolution of that country's educational system and the developments which it has brought about. Hence *History and Development of Education in Uganda* suits this book as a title.

A country's education system is subjected to constant reforms whenever the situation arises in order to enable the people cope with new demands.

Therefore one phenomenon a reader will notice in this book is the constant dissatisfaction of Ugandans with the nature of education at different times in the country and the attempts which have been made to address these dissatisfactions.

These dissatisfactions are always healthy; they make the education of a country ever dynamic to meet new challenges which the people face.

This book comes out at a time when there have been hectic reforms going on in the educational system as outlined by the Senteza Kajubi Education Commission of 1987.

There is a hope that this account will in some ways assist all those engaged in these reforms to realize that many educational issues tackled in this book which are a matter of concern for all of us now are not new. Therefore there will be a chance to compare and contrast the steps being taken now to address those same issues in terms of reform.

Similarly, we should realize that reforms which are being carried out through internationally funded projects should be such that once the financial assistance runs out, the country should be able to sustain the structures set up by those international bodies.

Although the citizens are welcome to play an active role in the education system of a country, the role of the government is paramount. This is why one of the definitions of education says that "education is a conscious process designed to change behaviour patterns of individuals in each society towards desirable ends as perceived by the leadership of that country."

It is the government which can view the country's educational system in its totality and thus ensure that all the country's children are brought within the embrace of education with a massive allocation of public funds and funds solicited from abroad for educational purposes.

J.C. Ssekamwa
Makerere University
1997

But in the old African setting, specialisation was in just a few technical skills. Therefore a person was required to learn so many skills in order to be useful to himself / herself, to the rest of the family and to the whole society. For example, a man had to make cloths for his family, build his own house, hunt game, fight wars, brew his beer, grow his food, slaughter his domestic birds and animals for meat and to do many other things which needed technical skills. Today a man may not know any of the above technical skills, yet he can live comfortably by being employed on one job for which he learnt technical skills and then use the money he is paid at his job to secure the different goods and services which he may require.

Methods of teaching
Mini Lecture method combined with instant practice and further Mini lecture.
One method of teaching was straight telling the child the knowledge which he / she should know. For example, a child was told the correct way of greeting people. He/she was then told to repeat what he/she was taught. If he/she did it correctly, he/she would be told that he had learnt it. If he/she made a mistake, the parent or any other member of the society would repeat the correct way and the child was required to repeat saying what he/she was taught until he/she got it right. After some time the parent or any other member of society would create a situation which required the child to say what he/she had been taught. If the child did it correctly, he/she would be encouraged to go on doing like that. If he/she did it badly again, he/she would be corrected and told to say it again so that he/she learnt it correctly.

To make learning interesting and easy, children were taught through plays, games, songs, rhymes and through story telling. When they were relatively old they were introduced to idioms, proverbs and riddles. The children repeated those plays, games, songs, rhymes, idioms, proverbs and riddles and stories at times alone and at other times with their agemates, and in the presence of either their parents or of other adult members of the society. These taught the boys, girls and adult persons plenty of philosophy, psychology, sociology, economics, politics, history and culture. They also taught imagination, thinking, inventiveness, shrewdness, literature, composition and public speaking.

Practical method
A second method of teaching concerned teaching technical skills of doing things or making things. Here the parent or another adult member of the society demonstrated to the child or to an adult person, the technical skill which was necessary to do something, or to make something. Then the learner was given a chance to practise that skill. This was repeated over and over again until the learner got it correct. For example, if a boy or a grown up man had to be taught

how to use a spear and shield in fighting, he was shown how to hold the spear and the shield, how to throw the spear and how to defend himself with the shield. He would then practise the necessary skills until he became good at both throwing the spear and wielding the shield in self defence, or in attacking the enemy or wild animal.

If a boy had to be taught how to get the bark from a bark-tree and then beat it out to get a bark cloth, he was shown how to get the bark from the bark-tree. He was then left to try this skill on the same bark. When the bark was being beaten out, he would do it with his father or with another adult man who knew how. Each time the necessary skill was demonstrated to him, he was straight away given a chance to practise that skill. Eventually he would learn the skill and become proficient at it.

If a girl had to be taught how to cook *matooke*, she was shown the way to hold the banana in one hand, how to hold the knife in the other hand and then how to peel the banana. She peeled the bananas together with her mother or with a grown up sister who knew how. When enough bananas were peeled to make a meal, the girl was shown how to tie the bananas in a banana leaf. She would then be left to try. At first she would not do it the correct way. But after practising several times, she tied the bananas in the leaf the correct way. Then she was shown how to put the bananas tied in the leaf into the cooking pot and how to cover the bundle with leaves. During the old days, Ugandans were cooking in clay pots specially made for that purpose. Such pots were different from those for fetching and storing water. When the food was ready for eating, she was shown how to get it from the cooking pot and how to make a mash out of it.

All these particular skills took a long time to be learnt and mastered. The girl had always to work with her mother, her older sisters or other grown up women within the society. She was constantly shown the right skills while she watched and then took a turn at practising the skills demonstrated to her.

Therefore acquiring skills of doing things or making things took a long time. Thus boys/girls had to practise those skills many times a day and for some years until they learnt the skills quite well to be left on their own. They passed the examination in the end by showing that they had acquired the particular skills necessary to do things or to make things which had been taught to them. They would then be trusted to use those skills on their own without supervision and to teach other members of the society who needed to learn them.

Exercise
  i. Try to give any definition of education and see whether it fits the African indigenous education.
  ii. What kind of stories do children tell at night in your tribe? Mention two educational values which are in such stories.

iii. If you were to teach a boy / girl how to play "omweso", list down five skills which you must teach her / him to start playing the "mweso" meaningfully. Alternatively, if you do not want to teach "omweso", think out a different game and list the basic skills which must be taught before a person can play that game.

iv. Look for seven proverbs in your tribe. Each one should show that it is teaching either philosophy, psychology, sociology, etiquette, economics, politics, the need for careful listening, or the need for careful observation.

To ease your task here, let us look at some Luganda proverbs in the above respect.

1 Philosophy: *"Bannange bangi", bw'afa wabula amukaabira.*
(A person who boasts that he has got many friends, when he dies, none cares to go to his burial). Here this proverb teaches us that we should be careful about friends.

2. Psychology: *Agenda okumala okulya, akoza avulunga.* (When a person is about to resign from office, he behaves irresponsibly. Or when a person realises that he is about to be dismissed from office, he behaves irresponsibly because there is nothing to save).

3. Sociology: *"Tunaabiwulira", tadduukirira nduulu.* (An uncooperative person in a village does not care to assist his fellow villagemates when they get into trouble.)

4. Etiquette: *Okuyitaba "Wangi", si bufuge.* (To be polite to another person does not mean that that person is your master. Even a President should be polite to other people).

5. Economics: *Nsibambi, edibya mutere.* (If you are selling your goods and you don't keep them clean, people will not buy them. Then you will blame people for not buying your goods whereas it is your fault).

6. Politics: *Ebisula byefuula, omujaasi afuuka omwaayi.*
(One philosopher king succeeds another philosopher king. Or one politician curses the previous politician for his bad ways, but after a time, the same politician behaves like the one he succeeded.

7. Need for careful listening. *"Balo embogo yamutta", ko Nnampulira-zibi nti, "Owange bw'azitta atyo".* (If a wife is told that her husband was killed by a buffalo while hunting, the wife for her poor listening may boast that, "yes, that is the way my husband kills buffaloes").

What you need to observe about the above proverbs is that they were invented hundred of years ago in situations different from the present ones, but what they were meant to teach people then, is still relevant even today. Therefore people of any tribe in Uganda which will neglect to document their proverbs and explain them along the above lines, will do a great dis-service to posterity. Such people will contribute to the death of their cultures and to a very effective method of teaching both the young and the adults alike.

Incidentally, these proverbs continue to be created daily in our languages because we are still speaking those languages. For example, see the following proverb which was invented in Buganda between 1971 and 1986: *"Olutalo lulwanirwa mu ssenta, ayagala okufuga Uganda awamba Kampala".* (A battle is fought at the centre, he who wants to rule Uganda captures Kampala). Yet a few hundred years ago one man invented the following proverb about Presidents of countries who eventually get overthrown: *"Akataazimbe, emmuli kazeetikka bukiika"*. (A person who will fail to do a job, uses wrong methods).

The curriculum of the African indigenous education

A curriculum simply means a number of subjects which have got to be taught in a course of study. For example, we talk about the curriculum in the primary schools. This curriculum consists of languages including English, Reading, Writing, Numeracy, Science and Social Studies. The curriculum in the secondary schools consists of even more subjects than those in the curriculum of the primary schools. The curriculum of the education systems of the tribes in the African indigenous education consisted of the following items.

The Environment

Children were taught how to deal with their environment. The purpose of this was that they should know how to get the best things out of it. This environment was quite difficult to live in during those days. It had wild animals and snakes which were dangerous to people's lives. The environment further had unfriendly people. At times there was no rain. There were diseases, harmful plants and dangerous spots to live in. The young people were given knowledge and skills to defeat all the difficulties in their environment and tame it so that they lived a good life.

Some environments were harsher to live in than others. By way of comparison, the environment in Karamoja was harsher than the environment in Tooro. Yet the Karimajong would not envy the Batooro for their environment. The education system of the Karimajong gave the necessary knowledge and technical skills to its people to tame their environment and thus live happily in Karamoja.

Cooperation

Children were taught how to cooperate with their friends, neighbours and the rest of the members of the society. This was necessary for living in a friendly atmosphere with other people. It also helped in taking part in creating and maintaining common services in their areas, and in defending themselves and the whole tribe. A person who did not cooperate with members of his society was looked at as a bad person indeed. When he got into trouble, nobody helped him. However, no sensible person would risk being an isolated fellow in society when the environment was so harsh that it required a person to have friends around to assist him when in trouble.

This cooperation was taught through games, plays, idioms, proverbs and folk stories such as the stories "of Wakayima"(Mr Hare).

Exercise
    i. Can you think about a story in your tribe which teaches cooperation?

ii. Can you also think about a story in your tribe which shows that it is bad not to cooperate with your friends?
iii. Can you do both things with two proverbs from your tribe?

Belonging to a group.
Children needed to be secure in their membership to a particular society. When they were adults, they were taught their clans, how those clans fitted in the whole tribe, and the places of those children in the clans and the tribe.

Consequently, children and grown up persons were taught the history and customs of their clans and tribe. This knowledge helped them fit in their clans and tribes and to defend both. If somebody tried to challenge them that they did not belong to the particular clans and tribes, they could defend themselves through the knowledge of the history and organisation of their clans and tribes. This defence consisted in speaking the language of the tribe with correct accent and intonation, through the knowledge of the history and organisation of the tribe and of the clans to which they belonged. It also required behaving according to the behavior and customs of the clans and tribe to which they belonged. All that knowledge assured their citizenship to the tribe and so they felt secure that they were accepted as members of that particular tribe. This is why clans were very strong during the pre-colonial days in many parts of Africa. For example, in Buganda, it is the clan which entitled a person to belong to the Buganda society.

This knowledge also helped members of one tribe to challenge a person who claimed that he belonged to one of their clans and the tribe even if he had learnt their language correctly. They could ask him the history of that clan or tribe to which he claimed to belong. They asked him something about their customs, behaviour and the past leaders of the clan and tribe. If he failed to satisfy them, they dismissed him as a liar and a person who did not belong to them. This was used as evidence by the rulers to dismiss such a person from their tribe or from their clan and thereby remove his citizenship from him. You can imagine the dangers to a person who was denied his /her citizenship to a tribe he/she claimed to belong. Such a person had to look for a new tribe to which to belong. This was not so easy. If another tribe accepted him / her, he / she had to learn a new language and new customs and a lot of other things and to get new friends. In fact during those old days, the knowledge of the history of the clans, tribes, and of the customs and beliefs of the tribes, assured a person of his/her citizenship and it acted as the Passport of today.

I beg the reader to share the following incident with me. There was once a middle aged man who posed as a Muganda who belonged to the Lungfish clan. He was calling himself by the name of Kiwanuka. His accent and intonation of the Luganda language were hardly any different from those of the Baganda. But there were some elderly Baganda men in the Lungfish clan who doubted that he was a Muganda and therefore his claim that he belonged to their Lungfish clan was difficult to accept. To find out whether he was a Muganda and that he also belonged to their Lungfish clan, they challenged him to tell them why his parents had given him the name of Kiwanuka. At the same time they asked him to tell them the name which they gave him to indicate that he belonged to the Lungfish clan. Unfortunately he failed to answer both questions.

Culturally in Buganda, the name of Kiwanuka has no particular clan. Any Muganda who belongs to one of the 52 Baganda clans can be called by that name. But there are four circumstances which lead the parents to call their son by that name of Kiwanuka. When grown up, such a son must be told under which of those four circumstances his parents gave him that name. Find out those four circumstances. A son who is given the name of Kiwanuka must also have a name which shows his clan.

Had the above man lived during the good old days of the African Indigenous education, he would have been dismissed from the Lungfish clan and his citizenship to the Buganda nation would have been denied of him. If he was tolerated to stay in Buganda, he would stay in it as a non-Muganda. The above example can be quoted in all the other tribes of Uganda.

Discipline

Discipline was taught to children because it was necessary for good order in a tribe. It was taught through telling the young people to obey the regulations and customs, to behave well, to respect the leaders and senior people in the tribe and to restrain themselves in pleasure, anger, pain and extreme trials in life. For example, if children were at a meal with their parents at which meat was served, they were not allowed to eat first all the meat before they finished eating the food. To do so was a sign of greed and lack of restraint in pleasure. This taught children discipline and self control.

A Karimajong friend told me one day that in their culture, the Karimajong are convinced that God created cattle for only themselves. So by that belief in that culture, their customs enjoin them to seize cattle anywhere they may be sighted in the possession of non Karimajong. But my friend told me that there is plenty of discipline in seizing cattle from non Karimajong people. There are special periods for doing so and special leaders who lead the raids. A Karimajong does not just wake up any time and go seizing cattle of non Karimajong people even when he sights such cattle and when he would like to do so. If he breaks the protocol, he is heavily punished by the elders. This shows the amount of discipline which the indigenous education of the Karimajong instils in them.

Culture

Under culture, children were taught the customs of the clans and tribe, the correct behaviour, the organisation of the tribe, the laws of the tribe and its ceremonies. They were also taught philosophy, psychology, sociology, politics, economics, history, the sciences and ceremonies. Idioms, proverbs, folk stories, riddles and children's rhymes played a key part in teaching the above items. For example, the children and adults were taught the ceremonies regarding birth, marriage, death, harvest, hunting and religion.

Exercise
 i. Tell your friends what happens when a young man goes with his friends to a home of the parents of his girl friend to announce an engagement to their daughter for marriage. ("Emikolo egy' okwanjula").
 ii. If you come from people who have got clans, tell your friends the name of your clan, the title of the head of that clan, the headquarters of your clan, the special work which the members of your clan were doing at the palace of the king or any other ruler. For example, in Buganda, the special duty of the members of the Buffalo clan was to carry around the Kabaka on their shoulders. The duty of the members of the Edible Rat (*Musu*) was to look after the sanitation in the Kabaka's palace and in the town (*Kibuga*). i.e. the suburbs of the Kabaka's palace.
 iii. Give three names which are given to girls according to your clan or tribe. If you lived before the Missionaries introduced Western education in Uganda, and you were challenged to give the information in Nos. i, ii, iii above in terms of your tribe but failed, you could easily be dismissed from the tribe to which you said you belonged. Thus you would lose your citizenship.
 iv. Think of three things which were taught in your tribe through which discipline was given to the children.
 v. Give five proverbs in your tribe which teach discipline even today.

Skills
Under skills, children were taught all the basic technical skills which they needed to do or to make things in order to be helpful to themselves, to the members of their families and to the whole society in which they lived.
For example, boys were taught skills of building houses, skinning an animal for meat, dressing chicken for eating, using spears, arrows and shields, pottery making, looking after domestic animals and many other practical skills.
  Girls were taught baby nursing, cooking food, looking after the home, growing various food crops, proper behaviour in marriage, mending clothes, making mats, baskets and plaiting hair to look pleasant and many other skills required to be known by them in adult life.

Leadership

Under leadership, boys were taught the laws of the tribe and how to use them to solve disputes among the members of the tribe. Usually some boys stayed in the residences of chiefs and other rulers. There, they observed how laws were being applied. Those of them who showed particular intelligence were later on made into chiefs to lead other members of the tribe.

Similarly, some girls were attached to the wives of the chiefs and of the kings and lived in the residences of those chiefs and kings. There, they learned the ceremonies and etiquette and taught them to the rest of the society. For example, the Bachwezi rulers of the Bunyoro-Kitara empire had very many women attendants in their palaces. They were in charge of courtly ceremonies which the citizens of the empire had to know and practise for different occasions.

When the Bachwezi rulers deserted the empire and left it to the Luos around 1380, it was these court women who taught the Luos the courtly manners and ceremonies and the central administration which the Bachwezi rulers had been practising.

Religion and medical knowledge and practice

The Ugandans knew that there is one God. This knowledge was not introduced by Islam and Christianity during the middle of the 19th century. They also had religions through which they worshipped God. There were also men and women priests who were in charge of these religions. These religions were practised in homes, in particular houses which were the churches and in holy groves.

In Buganda the churches were called "masabo" in plural and "ssabo" in singular. These words mean literally places where people go to pray to God and therefore they were churches. When the Muslims and the Christians came to Buganda, they gave the impression to the people that it is they who had introduced religion. Consequently instead of using the Luganda words "ssabo" and "masabo", they introduced their own words. The Muslims who came in 1844 used "Muzigiti", an Arabic-Kiswahili word. The Protestants who came in 1877 used "Kanisa", a Kiswahili word. The Roman Catholics who came in 1879 used "Keleeziya" a word derived from Greek which means "Assembly". The "ssabo" and "masabo" were called places of witchcraft or Satanic.

The fore-bearers of the Baganda, had through their indigenous education centuries ago created a proverb to explain philosophically the attitude of the early Muslim and Missionary teachers. That proverb if translated into English means that: once a person wants you to avoid something which you cherish, he gives it a bad name. (*Anaakugoba ku nswa nti, "tolya omulalu!"*)

Men and women priests looked after these churches. They were responsible for teaching people religion, its ceremonies and prayers. They were responsible for leading the prayers and performing religious ceremonies for the people. They were also responsible for educating and ordaining other people to become priests.

Religion was tied with the knowledge of practising medicine. So these priests knew the different medicines and how to treat the sick people. There were however, other people who were not priests but knew the different medicines and how to treat the sick people. But the greatest responsibility of diagnosing the sickness of the people and of treating the sick was upon the priests. Both the priests and those other people who knew the medicines and how to treat the sick, taught children and adults the different medicines and how to use them to treat the sick people.

Exercise
Tell your friends whether today there are still signs of the existence of the African indigenous religion in your tribe.

For Example:
(a) Do you see special houses where it is carried on?
(b) Do you see men and women priests of this religion?
(c) Do you see people who go to these priests for consultation?
(d) Do Christians and Muslims also go to these churches and to the priests?
(e) Mention three things which make people to go to these churches and priests.
(f) Do you think that the students are ignorant about the existence of the African indigenous religion?
(g) Do some of these students participate in part of this religion?
(h) What makes the African indigenous religion in your particular tribe to be discredited today?

Desirable behaviour or good manners
Through this item in the curriculum, the parents taught their children how to behave in an acceptable way. They taught them the practice of hygiene, how to greet people of different categories in an acceptable manner, be grateful, sympathetic to people in difficulties, help others, give excuse when they were in the wrong, how to welcome visitors and bid them farewell, how to sit and stand decently, eat and drink decently and many other things which show a well brought up person.

Parents also taught their children how to avoid behaving in bad ways. For example, they taught them not to sneeze in public without holding one's mouth, not to touch mucus, not to eat with dirty hands, not to belch loudly in public especially at a meal, not to spit in public, not to urinate in public or in the open even if there were no people around, not to use the toilets in a careless manner, not to shout especially when there were senior people around, not to back-bite

History and Development of Education

others, not to laugh at handicapped people such as the lame people and not to make life difficult for other people in any way, not to cheat, not to tell lies, not to steal, not to corrupt other people and not to be corrupt themselves.

In this respect, when you visit the home of a Munyoro or a Mutooro in their parts of Uganda, one aspect which will strike your attention will be the way children come into the sitting room to greet you. They all first ask for your "Empaako"- petty name. Of course if you are neither a Munyoro or a Mutooro and this is your first time to be among them, you will not have an "Empaako". But after staying with them for some time, they will give you one.

The reason why the Banyoro and the Batooro children first accost the visitor by asking for his or her *Empaako* is because their old time indigenous education teaches them that it is bad manners or uncouth to accost a friendly person without first creating a cordial relationship with him or her. Therefore under the heading of Desirable behaviour or manners, the African indigenous education taught people sensible etiquette to avoid getting on to the nerves of others.

The result of the knowledge which was taught to the young people, along with the above items was that a young person grew up with this knowledge. Then he/she was useful to himself or to herself, to the members of his / her family and to the whole society. He /she was also in a position to teach all that knowledge to other young people. The result was that people in a society had the basic knowledge, practical skills and good manners.

Exercise
  i Mention three things which parents teach their children in the home to be honest.
  ii. Think about three examples which you would give to students to show that corruption if carried on by people in responsible positions, ruins development in the country.
  iii. Mention three things which parents in your tribe tell children not to do in the presence of visitors.

Some comparisons of educational systems of Africans

The above items in the curriculum of the education systems of the tribes in Uganda, are also found in other education systems of other Africans outside Uganda. But all the sets of African indigenous education systems were usually different in aims and organisation. Those differences in aims and organisation were due to some of the following factors :
1. The composition of the population in a tribe created differences in an education system between one tribe and another. For example, in Rwanda, the population was as it is still today, composed of the Tutsi and the Hutu. The Tutsi were the rulers while the Hutu were the ruled and the working class of the Tutsi.

The aims and organisation of education in Rwanda were to give different knowledge and skills to the Tutsi children and to those of the Hutu to keep the status quo. Both attended different schools and they were taught by different teachers.

2. The historical background of a tribe also affected the nature of education between one tribe and another. For example, the Zulus in South Africa had three historical developments. They began by living in separate clans and the clan heads were the rulers of the members in each clan. Then they got kings who united the different clans under one central rule. And finally they began to conquer other tribes which were not Zulu.

During each of the above historical development, the aims and organisation of education were different. For example, during the period where clan heads ruled their separate clans, the aims and organisation were different from those when the clans had been united all under one king. Similarly, the aims and organisation of education were different during the days of empire. During the days of the empire, the aim of education was primarily to dominate other tribes in South Africa. The education was organised in special places for the boys to teach them military tactics and politics daily to conquer and to rule other tribes which did not belong to the Zulu nation. The example of the Zulu casts our minds back to what we have already seen, namely that once the situation in a country changes and demands new knowledge and new technical skills, the leadership is duty bound to review the education system and the curriculum so that the citizens can cope up with the new situation.

3. The type of government also created a difference to education between one tribe and another. For example, the Baganda in Uganda and the Ashanti in Ghana had kings. But the aims and organisation of education were different between the Baganda and the Ashanti.

In Buganda only the kingship was hereditary. Other political posts were not. One was free to struggle to get those political posts. Education in Buganda emphasised competition among the people so that the persons who excelled in knowledge, skills and good behaviour were appointed chiefs by the kings.

Among the Ashanti on the other hand, kingship and chiefship were hereditary. So men who were not sons of chiefs never hoped to become chiefs even if they were courageous, wise and had leadership qualities. The aim of education among the Ashanti was to teach obedience to both the king and to the chiefs. Also education was organized differently for the sons of chiefs and for those of the peasants.

4. The relationship between a tribe and its neighbours also created a difference between the education system of one tribe and another.

For example, the aims of the Maasai in Kenya and Tanzania were to own cattle and to prevent their neighbours from owning cattle. They taught the children that God Almighty created cattle for only the Maasai in the world. Education of the Maasai emphasized the knowledge and skills of looking after cattle well and to snatch cattle from their neighbours.

If the neighbours of the Maasai wanted to keep cattle like the Kikuyu in Kenya, the aims of the education of the Kikuyu had to teach the boys and girls war tactics like that of the Maasai and not to be compromising with them.

If other neighbours of the Maasai were few in numbers and weak and could not fight them, their education system had to teach them to hate owning cattle. This way they could live peacefully in the neighbourhood of the Maasai.

5. The national environment and resources of a tribe also created a difference in the education system betweren one tribe and another. For example, the Pygmies and the Batwa in Zaire live in forests and mountains. The aim and organization of the education of these people was designed to give knowledge and skills to live in this kind of environment.

(I owe Nos 1-5 partly to the Lectures of Prof. J. P. Ocitti which he gave to my class of History of Education in the Post Graduate Diploma in Education course for the academic year of 1979 / 1980.)

What we can learn from this comparison

Each tribe in Africa had different aims and a different education system and taught its children and adults different knowledge and skills according to the needs of each tribe and its environment. But what was being taught was arranged around nine items of the curriculum already discussed.

The above principle is applicable even today. Each country has got a different education system depending on its aims, the nature of its people, its historical development, its government or ideology of the government, relationship with its neighbours and the economic resources and environment of the country. Due to this principle, Britain, France, USA, Germany, Russia and other Western countries have each got a different education system which differs in aims, organization, content and methodology.

Another thing which we learn from this comparison is that a country should not copy wholesale the education system of another country. For example, it would be a mistake for Uganda to keep the British system of education entirely which the Missionaries and the British administrators imported into Uganda in 1877.

Why should this wholesale copying of the British education system be improper, say in Uganda? One reason is that Uganda's economic, political and

African Indigenous Education

social development is at a different level from that of Britain. Also the resources and the economy of Uganda are quite different from those of Britain. Moreover, Uganda has got different aims to achieve in her society. Therefore her education system must be quite different from that of Britain.

Exercise
  i. Which groups of people in Uganda love cattle just like the Maasai?
  ii. What was the highest political position which a common man could hope to get in Buganda during the days of the Kabakaship, before 1966, when Obote abolished the Kingdoms of Uganda ? Talk briefly about the importance of that position?
  iii. Which tribe in Uganda has got two sections of people like those of Banyarwanda?

Some comparisons of Ugandan indigenous education and Western Education brought by the Missionaries

1. The African indigenous education of Ugandans made sure that every citizen in a tribe was taught the basic knowledge and the basic technical practical skills. Both the knowledge and the practical skills helped him / her to be useful to himself /herself, to be useful to his /her family and to be useful to the rest of the society in which that person lived.

    But Western education has not so far managed to give elementary education to every boy and girl in Uganda to be useful in the above manner.Children who join and complete Primary schools where the basic knowledge and the basic technical and practical skills are taught , are about 55%. The 45% are not catered for by the present education system along the Western kind of education. Yet also this 45% need to be useful to themselves, to their families and to the whole Ugandan society. For example, a person who does not know how to read and write today may find life quite difficult in Uganda. Yet the Government demands that such a person pays taxes in the same way it demands them from those who have been fortunate to attend schools.

    Fortunately the Government of Uganda is concerned about this problem. This is why it is making arrangements so that by the year 2003, every child will be able to attend Primary education. They will thus learn the basic knowledge and the basic technical and practical skills to manage life more easily in Uganda and to assist in national development.

2. Ugandan indigenous education taught every child the culture, good behaviour, ethics and the language of the society in which those young people lived.
    In contrast, Western education which replaced the Ugandan indigenous education is quite weak on teaching cultures, languages and good behaviour in society. It is mainly teaching the young boys and girls how to pass English,

Arithmetic, Social Studies, Sciences and some other subjects at both the Primary school level and at the secondary school level. There is no such a subject as *desirable behaviour in society* in the school curriculum where such things as how to use the toilets, how to treat senior people and how to behave in different situations are talked about. In other words, our education system is weak on teaching ethics of our Ugandan society. This is one reason why we have got plenty of undesirable behaviour in our society among so many people.

3. The methods of teaching and using what was taught in the indigenous education of Ugandans was different from those in Western education which replaced it. In the Ugandan indigenous education, children learned while they were applying readily the knowledge and skills learned. So while they were learning, they were also producing useful materials and services for use in the homes and in the rest of the society. They did not wait until they left school and then start to produce useful materials and services.

The indigenous education can be called production learning. This means that the students learned while at the same time they produced, or they produced as they learned. For example, a boy in Buganda or Bunyoro or Busoga learned the skills of making bark cloths while at the same time he was producing real bark cloths which were put to different uses in the home and in the rest of the society. At the beginning as a learner, he was producing coarse bark cloths. These were used as door mats or as carpets for sitting on. As he learned further, he refined his skill and in the long run he began to produce fine, soft and smooth bark cloths fit for wearing and for sleeping in. The coarse materials he was producing in the course of his learning were not just thrown away.

On the other hand, Western education keeps children in schools for 7 years in primary schools, for 3 years in O-Level secondary schools, for 2 years in A-Level secondary schools, and for 3 –5 years at University. During all that period, these students produce almost no materials and services for use, for the use of their families and for the use of the rest of the Ugandan society. So they do not learn as they produce. Some would even think it below their dignity to cut the grass on the school compound, to sweep their classrooms, to wash their toilets, to grow the food they eat in the boarding schools and to look after the cattle on the school farm. Instead of producing materials and services, these students are using much food, materials, services and money of their old and sometimes weak parents and of the old citizens of Uganda. This is bad and wasteful. Worse still it does not give these pupils and students chance to put into practice readily the knowledge and the practical skills which they learn.

If we were to learn anything from the Ugandan indigenous education systems, learning in our schools today should be arranged in such a way that boys and girls should learn knowledge and skills and at the same time while they are using both to produce useful materials, food stuffs and services for their use, for the use of their families and for the use of the rest of the Ugandan society. The Ugandan society of course would pay for these materials and services to assist the schools financially.

You can reflect on what is happening in our schools today in the following respect.Students in secondary schools and University make experiments in laboratories and mix chemicals in test tubes and produce, say salt. After proving that what they have produced by mixing such elements, is salt, they pour away the small mixtures and nod their heads in heroic and academic satisfaction that; "yes, we have produced salt indeed". They also produce samples of manure and animal feeds in these laboratories in the same way. After producing such samples through their experiments, they throw them away yet they themselves and the society need to use them.

Allow me to tell you a story. At one secondary school in Uganda, the students who had produced salt in their laboratory between 10.30 a.m. and 12.30 noon became terribly annoyed when they went into the dining hall for lunch and found no salt in their sauce. The Head Cook saved his neck from being broken by those students, by jumping out of the dining hall through a window. The Headteacher faced a strike after supper at which salt was not again served. This incident happened in 1973 when Idi Amin had just dismissed Asian traders from Uganda and salt became scarce in the country.

Yes, indeed our great grand fathers and mothers would have looked at such an activity of producing salt in our school laboratories as most funny if not laughable, wasteful in terms of time and money which buys the chemicals and the test tubes. This kind of activity would go against the principle of students learning as they produce useful materials and services in the Ugandan indigenous education of old. Our great grand parents would say that we simply learn how to read and write and not care about society's needs.

Why not produce enough salt for the school community and for the rest of the society through our school and University laboratories as these students are learning? But our education system puts this kind of activity to the time these students will have left school and University and hopefully use the knowledge and skills learnt to produce useful materials and services for themselves and for the society at large.

To use another example, from 1972 to about 1976 after the expulsion of the Asians from Uganda, there were times when salt and soap became scarce in the country. Yet it is not our students in the schools and at University, through their laboratories, who thought out quick ways of producing salt and soap for the Ugandan society. It is the old people who had never enjoyed the privilege to experiment in school and University laboratories, who made plans to produce salt and soap in the old African way for home use.

Fortunately, in respect of producing materials and services while pupils and students are learning, some schools in Uganda have started working along "production learning". They produce food crops for food used in the schools and for sale. They keep poultry, swine and cattle for sale. They make bricks, beds, doors, windows and chairs for school and for the rest of society. But this approach is not visible in every school, nor is it engaged in by all pupils and students in schools where it is being practised. Therefore there is need that it should spread in all schools and it should be engaged in by every student at school. That way, the pupils and students will be learning while at the same time they are using the knowledge and skills which they learn to be productive even when they are still studying at school.

The suggestions of the Uganda National Education Policy Review Commission of 1987 came with the plan along the African indigenous education idea of production learning. This is expressed in the following words: "Basic Education for National Development (BEND).

The intention behind BEND is to teach children useful practical skills which they can readily use while still at school. They are supposed to use these practical skills to produce useful materials and services while still studying at school and to use them when they leave school. They will then produce materials and services for their own use, for their families and for the rest of society while they learn. Indeed these skills will be taught together with other kind of academic knowledge. This is a challege to teacher education institutions.

Our education system should also teach local languages, cultures and desirable behaviour in society. It is unfortunate for our children not to learn these things at school because we shall be looked at as 'irresponsible citizens who cannot read and write their own languages that they use to communicate daily."

Exercise
  i. Suggest five ways in which good behaviour in our society should be taught in our schools.
  ii. Point out five projects which a school can set up in which students should engage. Tell us the useful skills which they can be taught for application from such projects and how financially the school and the students can gain from those projects.

Attitude of early European and American educators to the existence of education among Africans

Introduction
Through research and various studies, we are able to speak and write confidently

today that before Europeans and Americans came to Africa and introduced the Western school system of education, Africans had their own education systems. But the early European and American educators who came to Africa never believed that Africans ever had education systems through which they deliberately educated the young and adult people. They claimed that before their arrival in Africa "all the young were left in total ignorance". Some of those however, who were keen observers of the complicated African political, social and economic systems, institutions and technical skills went a step further and claimed that the young in Africa learnt by imitating the old people.

Researches which have helped us reconstruct the situations in which the Africans were living before the coming of the white men to Africa, have proved that the claim of the non existence of education in Africa by the early European and American educators, was not correct. It would be of some interest to reflect upon why those early Western educators held such views, and the response which they got from the Africans in view of those ideas.

The following were some of the reasons why the Western educationists believed that before their arrival in Africa, Africans had no educational systems and therefore the African children were left uneducated.

Firstly, there was a conviction in the minds of the early European and American educators that ignorance loomed high in Africa. Therefore the burden of the white man was to bring light to the Africans to save them physically, mentally and spiritually. Persons who held such views could not take time off to try and see whether there was anything of value in the African situation.

Secondly, people have got tendencies to educate others as they were themselves educated, regardless of whether such people have been engaged in some educational system of their own.

Thirdly, these early Western educators viewed education from a narrow angle. They thought that education consisted in formal schools, reading and writing and in a special group of teachers. Once they saw no formal schools to which they were used, they thought that there was no education in Africa. Once they saw no literacy, numeracy and special teachers to teach them, they took it that Africans had no education systems and therefore they did not educate their young and adult people. However, the African indigenous education was non literate, it was conducted in homesteads and imparted mainly by all responsible adult members of society.

How did the Africans react to the above claim?
At the beginning, there were two groups of Africans. There was that group which readily followed the European and American teachers. They thought that indeed education had just begun among them due to what they saw. The second group consisted of those who continued to follow the African indigenous education systems, because there were few Western educators and African teachers whom

they had produced. But from about 1900, this group began to be won over to the view that before the white men arrived in Africa, there was no education in their midst. They had to go and attend schools because the political, social and economic set up had been taken over by a new power, which had declared the kind of knowledge, skills and values to give them advantages in the new order.

Let us reflect on why the first group of Africans was easily won over to the view that it was the white men who brought education to Africa.

First, the content was turned out of the familiar. In history for example, the Luos taught their young people that their ancestors migrated from Southern Sudan and eventually settled at Pakwach. Then from Pakwach they began to spread all over East Africa, some going to the empire of Bunyoro-Kitara where they were absorbed by the Banyoro after they had overthrown the empire of Bunyoro-Kitara and formed their Babito dynasty. Some remained around Pakwach and around Lake Albert as the Alur, some moved into Acholi and are the Acholi of today while others went to West Nile and they are the Jonam of today. Another group moved into Lango and mixed with the Jie people, and are now the Langi of Uganda. Others moved to the area of Kaberamaido and they are the present Kumam while others moved into Tororo area and they are the present day Jopadhola. Another group moved to the area of Kisumu in Kenya and they are the Jaluos. The African children were also taught the strong and weak leaders whom they had historically and how their political system had been evolved. For indeed this is history.

The new kind of Western teachers on the other hand however, talked about how the Vikings had invaded Britain from the north of Europe and how the British had invaded America and vanquished the Red Indians. They also talked about how the African chiefs and kings had sold to them many of their African subjects, to go and work for them in America.

In Geography, the old Africans taught their children about the seasons of their year, about the form of the land where they were, the flora and fauna, and about their lakes and rivers. On the other hand, the new Western teachers talked about the four fantastic European and American seasons of the year which are Spring, Summer, Autumn and Winter. They also taught them the coniferous trees in America, the Canadian plains, the Thames, the Mississippi, the Ganges and the Great Lakes of America. They did not know the Nile river as the second longest river in the world nor did they know Lake Victoria (Nalubaale) as the second largest fresh water lake in the world.

Indeed one could go on saying something about every subject that was introduced in the school system of education by the Western education, which had a corresponding one in the African indigenous education systems. But the point here, is that once the content in the school system looked a bit different, those Africans who were easily won to the view that education in Africa had just then begun, at once took up the view that education had come with the white man.

Secondly, formal schools and classrooms were set up. No longer was the "home-stead" the school and the "fire-place", the classroom as of old, as J. Kenyatta put it. Then in these formal schools, reading, writing and numeracy were introduced. These were new wonders by which a person could form words and even keep records out of signs.

Thirdly, professional teachers began being responsible for education. In the African indigenous education system, every adult person in a tribe was responsible for teaching the young the basic skills and knowledge and norms of the society. Now such work was being assigned to only a few specially trained people who had gone through the new Western system of schools. Those people who had not gone through the new system of schools were taken as ignorant and uneducated. And since the content had begun to be tilted outside the ordinary, not every adult person in a tribe could continue being responsible for teaching the young people. To teach others, one had to be a graduate of the new Western school system. Indeed this small group of Africans who readily became convinced that education had been brought by the white men, was joined by the rest of the Africans from about 1900 who also began to believe that education had been brought by the white men into Africa, because a new power had taken over control of the political, economic and social set-up and also demanded new knowledge, skills and new attitudes. To learn all these, one had to attend the new schools, lest one missed sharing the new power's patronage.

Questions.
1. What is education supposed to do for the children of a nation?
2. Mention three things which made the African indigenous education different from Western education.
3. Where was the indigenous education of Africans carried out?
4. What two kinds of teachers were there in the African indigenous education systems?
5. What methods were used in teaching in the African indigenous education systems?
6. Why was "Belonging to a group" necessary as an item in the curriculum of the African indigenous education systems?
7. What three things from the African indigenous education systems can be usefully introduced in our present day education system?
8. Mention five factors which tended to make one African education system different from another African education system.

9. Why did the early Western educators think that before their arrival in Africa, African societies did not have education systems and therefore they did not educate their people ?
10. Mention three things which made some Africans easily think that education had been brought by Western educators into Africa.

2 The introduction & Development of Western Education In Uganda 1877 —1925

Kabaka Muteesa I invites European teachers to Uganda –1875

A new situation arose in Uganda by 1875. It was partly responsible for making Kabaka Muteesa I invite European teachers to come to Uganda. He wanted them to teach Ugandans new knowledge and new skills which would help them and himself cope with that new situation. He also wanted those European teachers to connect him with the governments of Britain and France so that he could defend his country of Buganda more effectively against foreign invasion and annexation, especially by the Egyptians. Muteesa I also wanted to use their new knowledge to fight more effectively against his neighbours and thereby control them.

In 1844, the Arab Sheik Ahmad bin Ibrahim with a few other Arabs and Swahilis arrived at the court of the father of Kabaka Muteesa I, Kabaka Ssuuna II at Banda near Kyambogo in Kampala. These Arabs and Swahilis were traders. Besides their trading activities, they also introduced Islam in Uganda and some people began to follow Islam.

Kabaka Ssuuna II died in 1856 and his son Muteesa I succeeded him as Kabaka of Buganda. Muteesa I found the Arabs and Swahilis already teaching Islam and the Kiswahili language to some Baganda. This new knowledge impressed Muteesa I. He wanted his people to learn it so that they could widen their outlook and easily deal with foreigners who were coming to his country. Consequently, he encouraged the Arabs and the Swahilis to stay near his palace so that his people could learn any new knowledge which they had.

In 1873, Sir Samuel Baker who was employed by the ruler of Egypt arrived with his soldiers at the court of Omukama Kabalega in Masindi. He had come to take over Bunyoro kingdom and place it under the rule of Egypt. Already Egypt had taken over northern and southern Sudan and some parts of northern Uganda. Egypt planned to take over the whole of East Africa. When Sir Samuel Baker told Omukama Kabalega the purpose of his coming, Kabalega was annoyed. He ordered his soldiers who were known as Abaruusuura to attack Baker's soldiers to defend the independence of his Bunyoro kingdom. Many soldiers of Sir Samuel Baker were killed. Sir Samuel Baker and his remaining soldiers ran to Patiko fort near Gulu in Acholi. Baker never dared again to enter Omukama Kabalega's country in an attempt to annex it to the empire of Egypt. Muteesa I learnt of Baker's visit to Bunyoro and the intentions of the ruler of Egypt. He feared that his kingdom would perhaps be the next to be invaded by the soldiers of the ruler of Egypt.

History and Development of Education

While Muteesa I was in this worried mood, he was visited at his palace at Kasubi by Henry Morton Stanley. Stanley was a British explorer. He had come to East Africa to explore the high mountains, lakes and rivers of East Africa. He especially wanted to make sure whether the river Nile flows from lake Victoria on its long journey to the Mediterranean Sea in Egypt. Already John Speke and his fellow explorer Grant had explored lake Victoria in 1862 and made sure that the Nile river flows from lake Victoria at Jinja. They had even followed the river up to the Mediterranean Sea. But when they told this news in Britain, they were not believed. Therefore Stanley had been sent by the Royal Geographical Society to prove Speke and Grant right or wrong. He proved them right.

Kabaka Muteesa I welcomed Stanley warmly. In their conversation, Muteesa I asked Stanley whether European teachers could come to teach his people new knowledge and skills. He hoped that some of the knowledge and skills which those European teachers would teach his people, would help him defend his country better against Egypt and other foreigners who would wish to invade it. He also hoped that such European teachers would assist him to create good diplomatic relations with their countries.

Stanley told Muteesa I that there were many British teachers who would gladly want to come to teach his people. So Muteesa I asked Stanley to write a letter in English on his behalf inviting those teachers to Uganda. Stanley sent a letter back to England and it appeared in the newspaper called the *Daily Telegraph* in November 1875.

Kabaka Muteesa 1 of Buganda. He invited European teachers to Uganda in 1875.

Development of Western Education

Missionaries arrive in Uganda

When the news appeared in the *Daily Telegraph* in England, at once some British teachers who belonged to the Church Missionary Society (CMS) volunteered to come to Uganda and teach the people of Uganda. These were Protestants and British people. They arrived in 1877. Alexander Mackay who was however, not an ordained Pastor became the most known among these first missionary teachers of the Church Missionary Society. The Baganda pronounced his name as "Makaayi", a Kiganda name given to Baganda men who belong to the Lung-fish clan. They did this because they did not know how to pronounce British names properly. They also wanted to "Ugandanise" him by initiating him into their clan of the Lungfish. Muteesa I sent these first CMS Missionaries to live in the village of Nateete near his palace of Kasubi Nabulagala in Kampala.

A secondary school has been elected on the site in Nateete where Mackay and his CMS colleagues first lived. It is known as Mackay Memorial Secondary School Nateete in memory of this great Protestant missionary who contributed greatly to the missionary work of establishing Protestantism and Western education in Uganda.

Soon afterwards, the CMS Missionaries were followed in 1879 by the Missionaries who belonged to the White Fathers Society. These Missionaries were Roman Catholics and they were Frenchmen. Muteesa I welcomed them

Alexander Mackay

History and Development of Education

warmly too. He sent them to live in the village of Lubaga again near his palace of Kasubi Nabulagala in Kampala. So both the CMS Missionaries and the White Fathers Missionaries could easily go to the palace of Muteesa I and teach his chiefs and his servants. Indeed they were also teaching other people in their homes and compounds at Nateete and at Lubaga respectively.

Father Simeon Lourdel was the most famous among the first Missionaries of the White Fathers Society as was Alexander Mackay among the first Missionaries of the Church Missionary Society. The Baganda nicknamed Lourdel "Mapeera" – guavos because he always said "M'appel" which means in French "my name is". You need to know that these first Missionaries did not know Luganda. While they were learning it, they used to mix English or French words in it until they learnt the Luganda language properly.

Father Simeon Lourdel of the Roman Catholic Mission to Uganda.

Father Simeon Lourdel is more known in Uganda as Mapeera than as Lourdel which was his actual name. The Roman Catholic Church in Uganda has built a number of places which are either called Lourdel House or Mapeera House in memory of this great Roman Catholic missionary.

Development of Western Education

By 1879 there were three groups of foreigners in Uganda near the palace of Muteesa I. Each group had a new way of worshipping God. These were the Arab Muslims who had arrived in 1844, the British Protestants who had come in 1877 and the French Roman Catholics who had followed the Church Missionary Society Missionaries in 1879.

The new teaching and the conflicts caused
Since the reason why the British and the French Missionaries came to Uganda was to teach both Christianity and other kind of knowledge, they at once began to teach the people of Uganda. They taught them Christianity, reading, writing, numeracy, agriculture and some technical skills. The Muslim Arabs whose main job was to trade combined their trading activities with teaching people Islam and the reading of the Holy Koran.

Among the people whom all these three categories of teachers were teaching were also some chiefs and some servants of Muteesa I. These Ugandans were quite excited about the new teaching. One reason for this excitement, was that Kabaka Muteesa I supported the teaching because he knew that the new knowledge and skills would benefit his people and they would be in a better position to understand the new world developments. This knowledge would also benefit him to control his country better. Therefore the people knew that if they mastered this new knowledge and new skills, they would easily win favour of Muteesa I. He would reward them by giving them good positions in his administration. Already one student of the Arabs who was called Mafuta had learnt Kiswahili and he was acting as an interpreter at Muteesa's court and he was held with high respect.

Initially, the Missionaries and the Arabs were teaching their followers in their houses, in the compounds around their houses and in their churches and mosque. They had not yet got time to set up proper schools.

But Western education, Christianity and Islam developed in a situation of conflicts. One kind of conflict regarded the followers of the Protestant Missionaries, the followers of the Roman Catholic Missionaries and the followers of the Arab Muslims. Each group of these teachers wanted to have its own Ugandan followers. It did not want to see that its followers mixed with those who followed the teaching of another group of teachers. Each group of teachers even created queer stories about the teaching of another group of teachers. Therefore hatred and suspicions began to develop between the Protestants and the Roman Catholics on one hand and the Muslims in Uganda. The result was constant arguments and quarrels among these groups of followers and among their teachers.

The second conflict which developed was political. Each group of these teachers wanted to get political influence at the court of Muteesa I at the exclusion of the others. Each group of teachers also wanted to see that its followers were the only servants and chiefs of Muteesa I at the exclusion of other groups. This again caused much hatred and suspicions among the Protestants, the Roman Catholics and the Muslims in Uganda.

The third conflict concerned what the British, the French and the Arab-Muslim teachers were teaching their followers about God. Each group was telling its followers that what the other group was teaching was not according to the wishes of God Almighty. So the followers of one group of teachers looked at the followers of the other groups, as anti God and destined to die and live in Hell for eternity. Quarrels then broke out among these followers of the British, French and Arab teachers. They argued about this and that religious item, from the point of view of their respective teachers. Indeed they never agreed and at times they even boxed one another, some leaving the argument with bleeding noses.

Another conflict concerned what these teachers forbade their followers from doing. They told them that certain things were against the wishes of God. For example, the Arab-Muslim teachers told their followers that it was against God's wishes for Muslims to eat meat when a bull had not been slaughtered by a Muslim. So if Muteesa I gave his Muslim chiefs and servants meat which had not been slaughtered by a Muslim, they refused to eat it. This annoyed Muteesa I.

If for example, Muteesa I told the followers of the French teachers and of the British teachers to look after his Church in the palace called "ssabo", they refused. They would tell him that the British and the French teachers had taught them that it was against God's will for people to keep "masabo" and to pray in them. God wanted the Protestants to build "Kanisa" and the Roman Catholics to build "Keleeziya" and to pray in those buildings because they were holy. The "masabo" were places of witchcraft and Satan. This annoyed Muteesa I and his other chiefs and servants who were not attending lessons in the homes of the Missionaries. They began to look at the Missionaries as a disturbing element in the Baganda society.

Indeed there were many other things concerning religion which the followers of the new teachers refused to do when Muteesa I ordered them to do them. They always told Muteesa I that they did not want to annoy God because the British, the French and the Arab teachers had taught them so. However, at that time it was quite difficult for any person to refuse to do what the Kabaka told him /her to do. If such a person refused to obey the Kabaka, he/she would be easily executed on the orders of the Kabaka for his/her disobedience. Therefore the early students of the Christian and Muslim teachers must have been very courageous. They " fell in love" at once with what the new teachers were teaching them.

Muteesa I began hating the Christian and the Muslim teachers. Also his chiefs and servants who were not attending lessons of the teachers supported him. This hatred was extended to the followers of the European and Arab teachers. Lastly, was the conflict which arose from the disappointment which the British

Development of Western Education

Stanislaus Mugwanya and Sir Apolo Kaggwa some of the first Ugandans who benefited from Western education

and the French teachers gave Muteesa I in terms of politics. When he told Stanley to send a letter to England in 1875 inviting teachers, Muteesa I had hoped that this could make him stronger politically. He had hoped that these European teachers could request their home governments to assist him safeguard his kingdom against enemies from Egypt and from other countries which might want to take over his country. But when Muteesa I told the British and the French teachers to tell their home governments to assist him, they refused. They told him that they were only teachers and they were not connected with their home governments. This kind of answer disappointed Kabaka Muteesa I very much. Moreover when Muteesa I told these British and French teachers to make guns for him or to teach his people how to make guns to fight wars against his neighbours more effectively, they refused. They told him that as teachers of religion, they did not support wars since they were teachers of peace.

In 1881, a revolt against Egypt called the Madhist rebellion broke out in Khartoum, the capital of the Sudan. The Arabs in Northern Sudan hated the oppression and exploitation of the Egyptians. So they wanted to end the Egyptian rule over both Northern and Southern Sudan. This rebellion stopped the plans of the Egyptian ruler to take over northern Uganda, Bunyoro, Buganda and the rest of East Africa. This meant that Kabaka Muteesa I had no more fear from Egypt. So he could even care less for the Missionaries who had already disappointed him.

On the other hand, Muteesa I began fearing that these Missionaries were likely to make their governments take over his country. This fear arose as a result of the British Missionaries led by Mackay and the French Missionaries led by Lourdel always quarrelling bitterly whenever they met him in his palace. Each group accused the other of teaching wrong doctrines about Christianity. Kabaka Muteesa I could not understand the root cause of the quarrels of these Missionaries. He took these two groups of Missionaries as both white men - *Bazungu* and teaching the same religion of a man called Jesus Christ though the Protestants called Him Yesu Kristo and the Roman Catholics called Him Yezu Kristu, to be at least different in that minor detail.

Unfortunately Muteesa I did not know that these two groups of Missionaries were different by race despite having the same white colour, just as the Baganda are different from the Lugbara though both are black. He did not know either that the British and the French in Europe hated each other traditionally, just as Muteesa I and his subjects hated the Banyoro and vice versa. Nor did he know that deep inside Lourdel and Mackay, there was a burning desire that the country of each should be the coloniser of Uganda. It has been said with much historical truth that "the Flag followed the Cross in Africa". That is, the Missionaries of one European country came into African areas first and prepared the way for their respective countries to take over those areas as their colonies.

Additionally, Muteesa I did not know that Christianity had many sects which talked differently about what Jesus Christ had taught, and each sect disagreed with each other. For example, he did not know that there was Anglicanism, Roman Catholicism, Prebysterianism, Calvinism, Seventh Day Adventism and lots of other Christian sects, nor did he know that Protestantism and Roman Catholicism were great enemies in Europe at that time, and that all forms of Christianity hated Islam. So the Arabs, the British and the French transplanted their national and religious hatred and suspicions to Uganda without Muteesa I and other Ugandans knowing the basis of all this hatred and suspicions.

Due to ignorance of the above facts, Muteesa I wondered why these white men - *Bazungu* were always disagreeing instead of being friendly to each other in a distant foreign country, when common sense dictated that they should cooperate with each other if they were not to risk being hanged by a mighty king like himself.

Consequently, Muteesa I began fearing that these white men, Lourdel and Mackay, could one day fight between themselves and one would kill the other in his country. This could cause their countries to invade Buganda and question him as to how their citizens had died in Buganda. The consequences could be to take over his country. He therefore began wishing for the departure of these white Missionaries from his country leaving him and his people in peace which they found prevailing in Buganda. Moreover, the Muslim Arab teachers increased the confusion and fears of Muteesa I. They were always telling him that the religion of the Europeans was not right. It was only the religion of Allah as proclaimed by His Holy Prophet Muhammad (SWA), which was right.

Indeed Muteesa I was already following Islam though he had refused to be circumcised because this was against the old time Baganda customs which dictated that a Kabaka should have all his bodily parts on him. They also told Muteesa I that the European teachers were in alliance with the Egyptians who wanted to take over his country.

A story is told that in his daring characteristic, Mapeera (Lourdel) one day challenged the leader of the Muslim Arab teachers thus : He wanted Muteesa I to order his servants to heap dry wood together and set fire to the heap. Then when the fire would be burning at its highest, both Mapeera and the Arab teacher should march into it. Mapeera would be holding the Holy Cross and the Holy Bible in both his hands. The Arab teacher too would be holding the Holy Koran in his hand. One who would march out of the fire alive, would be the person who was teaching the right religion.

Of course Muteesa I shuddered at such a fantastic but dangerous idea. He definitely knew that both men would be burnt to ashes and this would be a good excuse for their countries to invade Buganda and annex her. He refused outright to have such a fire made and for both men to march into it gallantly, whatever might have been their faith in the power of their religions. He is said to have exclaimed to his chiefs in Luganda thus: *"Omuzungu n'Omulungaana bwe banaafiira muno, ensi zaabwe tunaazidda wa? Ye bannange, nga twajjirwa empalakitale z'abasajja"!* *"Omulungaana"* was the Luganda rendering of an Arab.

Due to the above conflicts, Muteesa I began hating the British and the French teachers and their Baganda followers some of whom were his chiefs and servants. He also hated the Muslim Arab teachers and their Baganda followers. Due to anger he killed three of his Protestant servants in 1883.

From 1883 Muteesa I hated the British and the French teachers so much that he no longer wanted to see them in his palace. Lourdel (Mapeera) and his group of the French teachers went to live on Bulingugwe island in Lake Victoria while Mackay (Makaayi) and his group of the CMS went to Zanzibar to avoid Muteesa's anger for the time being.

Exercise

i. Using your knowledge of the history of East Africa, what were the commodities which the Arabs and the Swahilis had come to buy in Uganda in 1844?

ii. What are the Ugandan names for river Nile and lake Victoria by which the Baganda and the Basoga were calling this river and lake in the old days?
iii. In what places was Muteesa I with his subjects attending their indigenous Baganda religion before the Muslims and the Christian Missionaries introduced "Keleezia", "Kanisa" and "Muzigiti"?
iv. Name five Christian sects which you know in Uganda.

Mwanga becomes Kabaka of Buganda

Muteesa I died in 1884. He was still annoyed with the British and French teachers by the time he died. He was succeeded by his son Mwanga who wanted to be friendly to the British and the French teachers. He called back Lourdel and his White Fathers group from Bulingugwe island. He also invited back Mackay and his CMS group from Zanzibar. Both groups returned to Kampala hoping to teach their religion of Christianity and other knowledge in peace. But Kabaka Mwanga just like his late father Muteesa I soon found the British and the French teachers troublesome. Their followers continued to refuse to obey certain orders of Mwanga. They told him that such orders were not acceptable to God because the British and the French teachers had taught them so. He said that the foreign teachers were teaching his people to disobey him.

Consequently, he ordered the killing by burning of more than thirty followers of the Christian teachers and some Muslims at Namugongo on 3rd June 1886. His chiefs who had not become students of the European and Arab teachers supported him because these followers of the European and Arab teachers had become disobedient to the Kabaka and to the Baganda customs and culture. This was unheard of in the traditions of the Baganda because the Kabaka and the Baganda culture had to be obeyed without questioning.

After the killing of the above martyrs, Kabaka Mwanga planned to get rid of the British, French and Arab teachers together with their followers. His plan was to carry all of them in boats to an island in lake Victoria and leave them there without food and boats. Some would be eaten up by crocodiles and hippos and the rest would eventually die of hunger. Thus Buganda would get rid of the troublesome new teachers and their Baganda followers. But the foreign teachers and their followers learnt of the plan and they drove Mwanga from the throne of Buganda. He went with his supporters to Ssese islands. The Christians and the Muslims made Prince Kiweewa, Mwanga's younger brother, Kabaka.

The Political and Religious Wars : Christians fight against the Muslims 1887 - 1888

Now that Mwanga had been driven away from his throne, one may perhaps think that the British, the French and the Arab teachers were free to teach their religions and other kinds of knowledge in peace but that was not so. The Arab teachers and their Muslim-Baganda followers turned against the British and the French Christian teachers and their Baganda followers. They wanted to exclude them from controlling political power in Buganda.

To achieve their plan, the Arab teachers and their followers convinced Kabaka Kiweewa to become a Muslim. Kiweewa who was not a courageous young man refused. He fled in panic and hid himself in the Kasubi Tombs in Kampala. The Muslims made Prince Kalema, another brother of Mwanga, Kabaka who was already circumcised. Kiweewa was eventually killed.

The events from 1887 which followed Kalema's becoming kabaka were terrible in Buganda's history. The Baganda Roman Catholics and Protestants on one side, began to fight against the Baganda Muslims. The Christians and the Muslims became enemies. They burnt each others' houses, looted property, and killed each other in great numbers without mercy. At that time, one could not believe that the two groups were Baganda. This was even more ridiculous because in one family some people were Roman Catholics, others were Protestants while others were Muslims. So brothers and sisters were killing each other and looting the property of each other and burning the houses of each other mercilessly because of the new and different religions which had been brought by Arabs, Britishmen and Frenchmen.

In 1888 the Roman Catholics and the Protestants defeated the Muslims and drove Kalema from the Buganda throne. He fled to the palace of Omukama Kabalega in Bunyoro. The last battle was fought at Kijungute, a village in the neighbourhood of river Kafu wl ich is the boundary between Buganda and Bunyoro. Kalema died of small pox soon afterwards in Kabalega's palace in Bunyoro. The Protestant and the Roman Catholic Christians then brought back Kabaka Mwanga from Ssese islands and placed him on the throne of Buganda.

These wars between the Muslims on one hand and the Roman Catholics and the Protestants on the other, created great suspicion and hatred between the Muslims and the Christians. Western education therefore developed in an atmosphere of hatred and suspicion in Uganda, that is why all during the colonial period, Christians suspected the Muslims and vice-versa. This did not create a good society in Uganda at that time.

The Political and Religious Wars : The Roman Catholics fight against the Protestants 1888 - 1892

Now that the Muslims were defeated, one may think that Western education would develop in peace. This was not so. The Roman Catholics and the Protestants began fighting between themselves. At that time the most important political post for a commoner in the kingdom of Buganda was that of Katikkiro. The Roman Catholics wanted their leader, Stanslaus Mugwanya to be the Katikkiro. The Protestants on the other hand wanted their leader, Apollo Kaggwa to be the Katikkiro. The Protestants and the Roman Catholics failed to compromise and so war broke out between them though both groups belong to the Christian religion. Kabaka Mwanga again withdrew to Ssese islands.

That war only ended in 1892, when Captain F.D. Lugard from Mombasa in the employment of the Imperial British East Africa Company, parted these two groups of Christian fighters by firing a canon gun into the Roman Catholic fighters and then after the fighting had ended, he invited both groups to negotiate and reach a compromise. But they had already looted each other's property, burnt houses and killed many on either side. Indeed they had sowed much hatred and suspicion, the after effects of which are still smouldering in our society today. Imagine Christian brothers and sisters killing each other for a political post in an earthly kingdom supposedly for the love of God Almighty!

The Baganda were calling Capt. Lugard "Kapere Lugadi" because at that time they had not yet learnt English to be able to pronounce English words and English names well. Capt. Lugard created two posts of Katikkiro in Buganda and he gave one to Apollo Kaggwa and the other one to Stanslaus Mugwanya. Then he called back Kabaka Mwanga from Ssese islands to resume his seat on the throne.

After this arrangement, peace returned in Buganda though the arrangement was queer and against the traditions of Buganda. To have two people as Katikkiro at the same time in Buganda, meant that there were two Kabakas in Buganda at the same time. But both the Protestants and the Roman Catholics chose to break the long Baganda traditions to satisfy their interests. Since then the Baganda have continued to abuse many of their good customs and traditions to satisfy their own personal interests.

The hatred and suspicion between Protestants and Roman Catholics was reflected in the establishment of schools and in the social life of the Ugandans during the colonial period. Though Christianity, Islam and schools began in Buganda, the same British, French and Muslim teachers and their followers spread them outside Buganda. They carried enmity with them to the rest of Uganda.

Suspicion and hatred was also reflected in the formation of the political parties when Uganda was going to regain her independence before 1962. Some people in Uganda said that DP belonged to the Roman Catholics, UPC belonged to the Protestants and Kabaka Yekka (KY) belonged to the Protestants, Roman Catholics and Muslims who were conservative.

Such was the background of all the origins of suspicions and hatreds regarding the Roman Catholics, the Protestants and the Muslims. The origins were both religious and political. This enmity was included in the Western education type of schools which were established from the very beginning to the time Uganda regained her independence on 9th October 1962. A Ugandan citizen

Development of Western Education

will notice that all this enmity arose from outside Uganda and it should not be allowed to continue dividing the citizens of Uganda.

Moreover the situation which caused the above enmity disappeared a long time ago. The Kabakaship which the Muslims and the Christians wanted to control no longer exists as a political factor in Uganda. Similarly, the post of Katikkiro over which the Roman Catholics and the Protestants were fighting is no longer a political post in Buganda. Therefore Ugandans should endeavour to see that the hatred which those political posts produced in the society of Uganda should end with their disappearance.

As regards religion, the people of Uganda have come to realise that there are many ways through which people reach God. It is futile to think that one's religion is the only correct way through which to reach God and another person who follows a different way is destined to go to hell. It is fortunate that starting with the efforts of the late Emmanuel Cardinal Nsubuga, the late Bishop Danstan Nsubuga, the late Prince Al-Haji Badru Kakungulu and by the late Archbishop Theodoros Nankyama of the African Greek Orthodox Church, Ugandans have appreciated that their destiny is the same despite the different religions they follow.

In June 1894, Britain officially accepted Uganda as her Protectorate and in August of that year Britain established her administration in Kampala. Britain would not allow Ugandans to fight any more because of the different religions which they were following and because of the desire to control political power in Buganda. From then Western education began developing in a peaceful atmosphere though the hatred which had been created during the mid 1880s and early 1890s continued to be observed in the way schools were being established and in the way pupils were being taught.

A feeling grew in Uganda that all the British people were Protestants because the first CMS Missionaries were British people. A similar feeling grew that all Frenchmen were Roman Catholics because the first White Father Missionaries were Frenchmen. Consequently, the followers of the CMS teachers were called "Bangereza", a word which in Luganda means Englishmen. The followers of the White Father Missionaries were referred to as "Bafalaasa", a word in Luganda which means Frenchmen.

When Britain took over Uganda as a Protectorate in June 1894, she decided to destroy the above erroneous feeling among the Ugandans. Consequently, she invited the Mill Hill Father Missionaries from Britain. These unlike the CMS Missionaries were Roman Catholics. This would also help to destroy the feeling of the Roman Catholics that since the British administrators came from protestant Britain, they would favour protestants at the disadvantage of the Roman Catholics. Thus the Mill Hill Father Missionaries arrived in Buganda in 1896 and they were given Nsambya near Kampala as their headquarters. So by 1896 there were three groups of Missionaries operating in Uganda all bent on teaching religion and Western education. These three missionary groups were joined in 1910 by the Roman Catholic Verona Father Missionaries or the Comboni Missionaries who spilled over from the Sudan into Uganda.

Exercise
  i. Give three names of islands in lake Victoria.
  ii. Where did Capt. F. D. Lugard set up his fort in Kampala?
  iii. Look for an old Muganda Muslim in your area and ask him to tell you about Kijungute and Abajungute.

Proper schools get established

From 1877 and 1879 people were being taught religion, reading, writing and numeracy in the houses of the Missionaries and in their compounds both at Nateete and at Lubaga respectively. A situation like this meant that those who had been following lessons at these missionary posts for a year or more could be found

Archbishop Theodoros Nankyama was brought up by Bishop Spartas. Nankyama was the head of the African Greek Orthodox Church in Uganda till his death in 1996

attending lessons together in the same group with those who had just joined the lessons. Therefore a need arose for the establishment of a system which would allow the separation of those who had just joined from those who had been attending lessons for some considerable time. Thus J. Steward of the Church Missionary Society at Namirembe wrote: "But the Bible means readers, and readers mean schools and schools mean teachers."

From 1898 proper schools began to be established. These schools were of two categories. There were those schools which were established where the Missionaries lived and there were those schools which were established in places where those Missionaries sent some of their Ugandan teachers whom they had produced by 1898 and whom they continued to produce.

Those schools in the places where Missionaries lived were better built. Each place was called a "Mission" or "Parish". It had a church building. This was intended to look after the souls of the pupils and of the other Christians who did not attend school but who went to those places to pray especially on Sundays. In the same Parish, there was a school building. This was intended to teach pupils the Bible, reading, writing, numeracy, a new approach to agriculture and some technical skills. Then in the same Parish there was a hospital or a dispensary to look after the health of the pupils and of other people.

These three buildings in a missionary Parish showed the aims of missionary education. These aims were to teach Ugandans the Christian religion and its practice, to teach Ugandans secular knowledge and skills, to look after the health of Ugandans and thus uplift their health conditions. In this last respect, the Missionaries believed that they could not teach Christianity and secular knowledge and skills to people who were unhealthy, because instead of learning both religion and secular knowledge, their minds would always be thinking about their ailments. One of their "catch expressions" was that "a healthy mind lives in a healthy body". This was at times rendered in Latin thus: "Mens sana in corpore sano".

But the imparting of Christian knowledge and Christian practice to the students took an upper hand in all categories of schools. Thus in the 1925 Annual Report of the Uganda Department of Education, the Missionaries stated in part:

> The idea that dominates our school system may be summed up clearly and concisely first and foremost, the spiritual interests of the child are paramount to every other matter and these divine interests are supreme.

The schools where Ugandan teachers were sent by the Missionaries to teach, were less elaborate. Usually there was only one building in wattle and thatch. That building served as a school on week days and as a church on Sundays. However, much useful educational work was carried on in these places where Ugandan teachers pioneered Western education.

History and Development of Education

The Structure of the Education System, 1898-1925

1. *Catechist schools:* These schools were in the majority. They were at every place where Ugandan catechists with the help of a local chief and the people he led, established a church either Roman Catholic or Protestant. These schools were meant for those people who were seeking to be baptised.

   The curriculum of these catechist schools consisted in mainly learning Christian prayers, catechism and mass cultivation. But the Protestant Church soon insisted that the pupils in these catechist schools also had to learn reading and writing. The Roman Catholic Missionaries adopted the practice of the Protestant Schools "so that their followers could vie with the Protestants in that point ". Lessons were given in the church on week days.

2. *Village Schools:* These were also at times called the following other names: "Bush schools", "subgrade schools" or "reading schools". The village schools were numerous. Each was under the management of a Ugandan teacher. They had a single building of wattle and thatch which served as a school on week days and as a church on Sundays.

   The curriculum of the village school consisted in Christian prayers and Christian practice, catechism, reading and writing, some history and geography, and mass cultivating of fields to produce food for the pupils. At the same time, the pupils learnt the value of labour. After the pupils in the catechist schools had learnt all that there was in those schools, they usually joined the village schools. The village schools had two classes which may be today called Primary one and Primary two. As time went on, a separate building consisting of two classrooms was built so that lessons ceased to be followed in the church building.

3. *Vernacular schools:* These schools were at a Parish or Mission post where there were two or three European Missionaries. They were under the management of a European missionary and assisted by a number of African teachers. These schools ran classes one to four. They were also joined by pupils in Primary three who had completed the village schools.

   The curriculum of Vernacular schools consisted in Christian instruction and its practice, reading, writing, arithmetic, history, geography, biology, agriculture and singing and games.

4. *Central schools*: These schools were at particular Parishes where there were European Missionaries. Each was headed by a European missionary. It had six classes. They were also joined by pupils who had completed the Vernacular schools, in the fifth class. A class for training teachers was attached at each of the Central School. Some of the teachers who were produced became catechists and preachers, and they were sent out to establish catechist schools in the country side. Other teachers taught in Vernacular

schools and in the lower classes of the Central Schools. This depended upon the ability of the individual teacher as judged by the European missionary who had produced these teachers.

The curriculum of the Central Schools consisted in Christian instruction and its practice, Bible history, Arithmetic, Geography, History, Grammar, singing, English and games. English was particularly taught to pupils so that they might become clerks and interpreters in Government Departments. These Central Schools were boarding schools because they drew their pupils from afar.

5. *High Schools:* These schools got their candidates from Central Schools and they were boarding junior secondary schools.

Originally these High Schools were for the children of the chiefs and of the highly placed people in society, such as clan heads and clergymen. But by 1925 these High Schools were also being joined by children of the peasants especially on recommendation by the chiefs, clan heads and Missionaries. Each of these High Schools was headed by a European missionary. The teachers were mostly European Missionaries who were assisted by African teachers in the lower level classes.

The curriculum of the High Schools consisted in arithmetic, geography, biology, drawing, music, Christian instruction and practice, English which was also the medium of instruction, drill, games, hygiene and history.

When the Uganda Protectorate government established its school at Makerere in 1922 and gave it the name "College", the Missionaries felt that the government had come in to make the people feel that their High Schools were of a lower nature. Consequently, they began calling some of their High Schools "Colleges". This is how Namilyango High School founded in 1902, Lubaga High School founded in 1908 which was later moved to Kisubi in 1926 and Buddo High School, founded in 1905 came to be called Colleges.

We need to remember that the terms High Schools and Colleges were being used erroneously at this early time in Uganda. In European and American countries where these terms originated, they meant quite different kinds of schools from those which existed in Uganda before 1925. In those countries a High School would be offering courses up to A Level. A College would be offering undergraduate courses leading to B.A. and B.Sc. Degrees.

But schools in Uganda before 1925 which were called High Schools or Colleges were offering education up to the level of perhaps today's Primary seven, though the students had ages ranging from 16 years to 20 years. Even Makerere College was not at the level of a proper High School in Europe or America – between 1922 and 1949.

Speaking of the intention behind the High Schools, Hatterslay who was at the forefront of establishing these schools on the CMS side wrote:

High Schools cater for the sons of chiefs, clergy and other influential natives with the object of developing Christian character in those who will eventually rule this country.

6. *Makerere College:* This College was opened by the government in 1922. It was the highest institution of learning in Uganda. But by 1922 its standard was not higher than the present senior two. However, its standard continued to rise so that by 1935 the first group of students sat for the Cambridge School Certificate which is the O-Level School Certificate Examination of today in Uganda.
7. *Technical Schools:* These were very few and they were supposed to serve the building needs of the Missionaries in their parishes. St. Joseph's Technical School founded in 1911 by the White Fathers at Kisubi was the most prominent. The CMS Technical School on Namirembe hill had been given away to the Uganda Company in 1903 but the CMS authorities later regretted for having done so because it stopped to serve the purpose for which it had been set up.
8. *Teacher Training Schools then called Normal Schools.*

The difference between Western education and the Uganda indigenous education

The approach to teaching in these new schools was quite different from that of the Ugandan indigenous education which existed before the coming of these Missionaries. It was carried out in schools unlike the Ugandan indigenous education which was being carried out mainly in homesteads and anywhere people engaged in economic, political and social activities. The learners in this Western education studied mainly in classrooms, while the learners in the Ugandan indigenous education followed part of their studies at night, sitting around fire-places in the living houses. This Western education had regulated hours of attendance say from 8.00 a.m. to 5.00 p.m. while that of the Ugandan indigenous education before, went on uninterrupted throughout the whole day and part of the night.

Teachers in this new Western education had to be specially trained in particular schools before they began to teach in the schools. Yet in the Ugandan indigenous education which existed before, every intelligent and responsible citizen of the society taught the young people the basic knowledge and the basic skills necessary for them to be useful to themselves, to the members of the family and to the rest of the members of the society in which they lived.

Only a few young people went to attend these new schools while every body had to go through education in the Ugandan indigenous education system. This was so because every member of the society needed to acquire the basic knowledge and skills in order to be useful in society. Those young people who did not attend these new schools along the Western kind of education were called uneducated and ignorant. They found life difficult because they had to live in a new situation where the white man had introduced new values, knowledge and skills, and he was demanding that those new aspects be acquired through his schools. A person who did not go to these new schools of the Western type to acquire those above aspects was at a disadvantage. Yet the new situation which had been introduced by the white man demanded equally that even those young people who had not joined his schools had to behave according to the new situation. Decidedly, they had to pay his taxes. For example, if a person did not know how to read and write, he could not read signs on roads or any other warning materials written in letters. When there were jobs requiring a person to know how to read and write he could not go and do them. And quite many jobs began to appear from this period onwards both in government departments, in missionary establishments and in companies which required a person to know to read and write.

While the African indigenous education was non-literate, that is, it was not through the written word, the new Western education relied very much on reading and writing. As a consequence, in most of the Ugandan languages, going to study in school is called going to read books". For example, the Baganda say, "*Asoma mu ssomero*" or "*Agenze kusoma*", meaning respectively that he is reading in school or he has gone to read in school..

The Ugandan indigenous education however, did not stop despite the presence of the Western education. It continued to be given to the majority of children who did not go to these new Western type of schools and to a certain degree to those who also attended the Western type of schools when they returned to their homes.

Pioneers in setting up schools
The Missionaries, the Ugandan chiefs and their subjects played a key role in establishing the new Western type of schools and in financing them. The colonial government at the beginning did not involve itself in establishing schools, financing or administering them.

Money for running these schools was contributed by the Ugandans through school fees and through donations by the friends of the Missionaries in their home countries. The Ugandans contributed further to the establishing of Western education by assisting physically in the building of these schools. They made bricks, cut timber from the forests and brought it to the sites where these schools were being erected, and they assisted in the actual building of these schools, the church buildings and dispensaries or hospitals.

In appreciation of the contribution to the establishing of the Western school education in Uganda by both the Missionaries and the people of Uganda, the Phelps-Stokes Commission, 1924-25 from the USA thus wrote: "An educational system which branches out into the whole Protectorate has been brought into being in cooperation with the Native Chiefs".

Back in 1913 the Church Missionary Society Board of Education which was established in 1904 had stressed the self reliance policy that schools had to be built with money from school fees or from gifts from chiefs and that church funds should not be drawn upon for the purpose of building schools and running them.

The schools for the children of the chiefs and of the most important people in Uganda

The most important schools which were built between 1900 and 1912, were for the children of the chiefs and of the most important people in the Ugandan society such as the clan heads and the clergymen. It was thought then that those children would be the future leaders in Uganda. Thus Bishop Alfred Tucker wrote:

> We felt strongly that if the ruling classes in the country were to exercise in the days to come an influence for good upon their people, and have a sense of responsibility towards them, it was absolutely essential for something to be done and that speedily for the education of their children on the soundest possible lines .

Bishop Biermans of the Mill Hill Fathers stated the aim of Namilyango College in 1901 that "many of the sons of the chiefs from that school would succeed to the Chiefships for which responsible positions they would be better prepared, after a course in an advanced boarding school".

Gradually by 1920, even children of the peasants were enrolled in these schools because of their intelligence. These most important schools were boarding schools. It was felt by the Missionaries that by putting these children in boarding schools, the Missionaries would give them new attitudes and feelings along the lines of Christian and European values. They would then be different from those who did not attend those boarding schools and so they would help create a new order in Uganda since on completion of their studies, they would return to society, and the rest of the members of society would copy their behaviour.

The desire for fashioning boarding school students into a new community, contributed to the location of such schools as King's College Buddo, St. Mary's College Kisubi, Namilyango College, Gayaza High School, Ngora High School, Nabumali High School, Busoga College Mwiri, Nyakasura School and several others from the towns.

There was also a hope that those schools would help the different people of the tribes of Uganda to cooperate. These boarding schools would be attended together by children from the different tribes of Uganda and so they would learn to cooperate. When they went back to their different tribes and if they would keep in contact with their colleagues from the different tribes and if they met at national level, they would easily cooperate. This would help bring about unity in Uganda. Thus Bishop Tucker wrote again:

> Children from Busoga, Buganda, Toro, Ankole and Bunyoro would live a common life in one boarding school, imbibe the same ideals and serve the same Lord and Master. This would help them to forget tribal antipathies and jealousies.

Another reason why Missionaries established boarding schools for the children of the chiefs and of the most influential people in the society was based on the indigenous education system of the Baganda, Banyoro, Banyankole, Batooro and Basoga which educated future aspirants to government positions through a boarding system of tuition in the residences of chiefs and in the kings' palaces. Indeed the Missionaries also had in mind the European traditions which educated children of the upper classes in different schools called the Public Schools, in Britain especially. In fact these boarding schools in Uganda were modelled along the British Public Schools and gave the same values which aimed at producing gentlemen and civil servants to work in government departments.

The following were the schools which were established for the children of the chiefs and of the most influential families by 1912. The Mill Hill Society which had come from Britain and arrived in Uganda in 1896 established Namilyango College in 1902. The White Fathers on the request of Stanslaus Mugwanya founded St Mary's Lubaga High School in 1908. This school was later moved to Kisubi in 1926 and given the name of St. Mary's College Kisubi, to get the students away from the bustle of Kampala. The Mill Hill Fathers also established Nsuube High School, a girls school intended to supply wives for boys from Namilyango College.

On the request of Sir Apollo Kaggwa, the CMS Missionaries established Mengo High School in 1903, King's College Buddo in 1905 and Gayaza High School also in 1905 for the daughters of the chiefs and of the most important Protestant families in Uganda. Girls from Gayaza High School were supposed to be married to boys from King's College Buddo after graduation and when they were grown up.

On the request of the chiefs in Busoga, the CMS Missionaries established Kamuli Balangira High School in 1912 and Iganga High School both in Busoga, nearly at the same time. The Balangira High School at Kamuli was later moved to Mwiri with the name of Busoga College Mwiri. These same CMS Missionaries established Duhaga High School in 1911 at Hoima. This school was however, transferred to Masindi as 'Kabalega High School before 1920. The CMS Missionaries also established Mbarara High School in 1905, Nabumali High

History and Development of Education

Pupils at Duhaga High School in Hoima. The year was 1913.

School around the same time, Ngora High School and Kabarole High School, all betweren 1900 and 1911.
• The Verona Fathers also now called the Comboni Missionaries came to Uganda in 1910. They were Italians and they built schools in West Nile, Acholi and Lango at a very fast speed. Besides these schools, there were numerous other schools on a smaller scale all over the country. These were feeding students to the above more elaborate schools on completion of the courses in them. From the early 1920s children of peasants began attending the high schools which were formerly intended for the children of the chiefs and the most influential members of the society. Consequently the difference between schools for the children of the chiefs and those of the peasants stopped.

It was unfortunate however, that at this early period no schools were established for the children of the Muslim parents. We need to realise that the above schools were built along the lines of religion. The Roman Catholic Missionaries built schools for the children of their followers. Similarly, the Protestant Missionaries built schools for the children of their followers.

Roman Catholic children were not allowed to attend Protestant schools. Likewise, the Protestant children were not allowed to attend Roman Catholic schools. The reasons were three. Firstly, each religious sect wanted to help its own followers. Secondly, each religious sect wanted to give its followers its separatist religious point of view. Thirdly, because of the political and religious wars already discussed, each religious sect looked at each other with suspicions.

The Arab Muslim teachers were concerned mostly about setting up Mosques and Koran schools and to teach Islamic religion and its practice. Reading and writing through the Arabic script were taught in these Koran schools together with the principles of Islam and its practice.

Due to the wars of the 1880s, Christians would not easily allow Muslim children to attend their schools. Also the schools set up by the Christian Missionaries were teaching a lot of Christian religion and practices. Consequently, Muslim parents did not want their children to be influenced by this Christian atmosphere. However, a few sons and daughters of Muslim chiefs attended some Protestant schools though they were very few. The majority of Muslim children attended only Koran schools. Muslim children began attending the Western kind of schools together with Islamic lessons after 1925 when the Uganda Protectorate government decided to set up schools for the Muslim children and when Haji Alamadhan Gava had graduated from Makerere College and determined to pioneer schools for the Muslim children.

The role of the colonial government in establishing schools in Uganda, 1900 –1920

Up to nearly 1920, the Christian Missionaries were in charge of setting up schools, running them and financing them with the help of Ugandans and the friends of the Missionaries in their home countries. The British colonial government which had been established in June 1894 in Uganda was giving the Missionaries very little money for running the schools, and it was not committed to the duty of establishing and running schools. Thus Lansdowne, the Secretary to the Foreign Office in London stated in 1901 regarding the role of the colonial government in education:

> Education is certainly our business in the last resort, but if the Missionaries will do it for us, it would be better to give them the facilities in the form of tax rebate.

One reason why the Uganda Protectorate Government left the duty of education to the Missionaries was that it was preoccupied in establishing its administration and quelling opposition to it from various rulers. For example, Omukama Kabalega and Kabaka Mwanga wanted to dislodge the British from Uganda. Both of them in cooperation, resisted with arms the British administration from 1897 to the end of 1899 when they were both finally captured in Lango. They were brought to Kampala and then deported to Mombasa. Chief Awich of Payera in Acholi resisted the British administration from 1904 to 1912. There were also several resistances in Ankole, Busoga, Lango and Bukedi. The quelling of these resistances occupied much time of the British colonial administration at the initial period of the Protectorate.

Besides, the Uganda Protectorate Government did not have much money from taxes at the beginning. It only began to have a sizeable amount of money from taxes from 1915. Any money collected was devoted to the running of the administration and education and other social services did not occupy the government's attention at this early period. Yet the few African workers the colonial administration wanted to assist it, such as clerks and interpreters, were adequately being produced by the Missionaries through their schools.

The first financial contribution from the Uganda Protectorate Government was in 1907, when it gave 100 Pounds to the Church Missionary Society for King's College Buddo. It gave nothing to the Mill Hill Fathers and to the White Father Missionaries for their educational work that year. In 1909, the Uganda Protectorate Government gave 150 Pounds to King's College Buddo, 300 Pounds to the rest of the CMS schools, 300 Pounds to the White Fathers schools and 100 Pounds to the schools run by the Mill Hill Fathers. The financial grants to the educational effort by the Uganda Protectorate Government, went on rising year by year due to the constant requests by the Missionaries for the government to assist them.

These grants small as they were, were given after real appreciation by the government for missionary educational efforts since they assisted the government to get clerks and interpreters. Thus Sir Hesketh Bell who was Governor of Uganda between 1905 and 1910 wrote as follows:

> Due to the admirable efforts of the missionary societies, the administration had been relieved of making the provision for education which in any other dependency would have been a serious call upon the government's finances.

Missionary pressure which became so insistent from 1911 for financial support from the government resulted into the Uganda Protectorate Government eventually convening a conference in 1917 of all Missionaries and to agree to terms of school operation and financial aid. After that conference the Protectorate government created an Advisory Board of Education to guide it in educational matters especially as regarded financial support to the different Missionaries.

By 1920 the Uganda Protectorate Government was forced to come in and assist the Missionaries in educational work for the following main reasons. Firstly, by 1920 the chiefs were sending their sons abroad to continue with their studies after completing the High Schools in Uganda. The number of those sons was likely to grow bigger as years would go by. Some would be going to India, some to Britain and others to the United States of America. The British colonial government in Uganda feared that on the return of those sons of the chiefs, they would not respect the British officials in Uganda and they would also start to be opposed to the British colonial rule in the country due to influences picked up from those countries.

For example, if some sons went to the United States of America, they would come into contact with the Negro Movement then led by Marcus Garvey which was opposed to the domination of the Black men by the White men. In India they would come into contact with the movement then led by Mahatma Ghandi against British imperialism because Britain ruled India up to 1947.

If they went to Britain, they would see the best part of the British life and the worst part of that life. The impression of the Ugandans of the time was that the British were a very perfect group of people judging from the way the British Missionaries and the select British officials were behaving themselves in Uganda. But in Britain where these Ugandan students would mix with every shade of British people, they would not fail to start feeling that the high regard in which Ugandans held the British people was not all that true. Therefore the Uganda Protectorate Government felt it necessary to start guiding the educational policies in the country to control this flow abroad.

It was for preventing Ugandans from going abroad for higher education that the Uganda Protectorate Government established Makerere College in 1922 with the intention of making that College into a University as time would go by.

Secondly, during the 1920/21 financial year, the Uganda Protectorate Government gave 9575 Pounds to the Missionaries for educational purposes. This was an appreciable amount of money at the time, which was even destined to rise every year. This meant that the Uganda Protectorate Government could not stand by without laying down an educational policy as to how schools were being built, administered and how the money it was granting every year was being spent.

Thirdly, the Uganda Protectorate Government wanted to put order in the development of educational facilities in the whole country and to play down the interdenominational strife that was going on in the establishment of schools in Uganda. Missionaries were using chiefs of their denominations to help build churches and schools, using free labour of people in the areas that these chiefs were administering. Thus a Protestant chief in an area made every person in that locality to build churches and schools for the Protestant Church. Similarly, Roman Catholic chiefs made all the people in their respective areas to build churches and schools belonging to the Roman Catholic hierarchy. Yet in attending both church and school, it was only the people belonging to a particular denomination that were expected to attend. As a result of this there was dissatisfaction among the people. At times in some areas, this strife resulted into burning the churches and the schools. The Uganda Protectorate Government decided to come in and put a stop to this strife which was dangerous to peaceful administration.

Fourthly, in March 1923, the Colonial Office in London established the Colonial Office Advisory Committee on Native Education in Tropical Africa. This Committee issued a memorandum on the 13th March 1925 which was the basis of the Colonial Office education policy in the colonies. This policy urged the colonial administrations in Africa to involve themselves in the direction and financing of education in their respective colonies.

Fifthly, the Colonial Office in London had invited the Phelps-Stokes Commission from the United States of America to come to Africa and examine the condition of education for the Africans. Among other recommendations made by the Phelps-Stokes Commission, was that the governments in East Africa should not leave the Missionaries to shoulder alone the educational duties in their areas. The governments should also be responsible for laying down the educational policies in each area and to execute those educational policies. Moreover each government should financially support all the educational work carried out by itself and by the Missionaries.

Sixthly, the British Protectorate government wanted to establish schools for groups of people who had no missionaries to assist them such as the Muslims to ensure equal opportunities.

The education policy that the Colonial Office in London issued in 1925, committed the Uganda Protectorate Government like any other British colonial government elsewhere to being responsible for directing and supervising educational services in the country and give out adequate financial support to education.

The missionary educational efforts however, had by 1925 established an elaborate education system which deserved praise. The Phelps-Stokes Commission in its 1925 Report put that praise concisely as follows:

> The Missionaries, both Protestant and Roman Catholic, who have played so large a part in the history of Uganda, have up to the present had practically the whole education of the country in their hands. With the exception of some recently erected government buildings at Makerere near Kampala, and of some centres where assistant medical workers are trained, all the school buildings and teaching staff belong to the missions. An educational system which branches out into the whole Protectorate has been brought into being in cooperation with the Native Chiefs, but without any supervision from the colonial Government, and until recently without any financial support. It is an educational achievement of which missions can legitimately be proud.

Development of Western Education

Questions
1. Who introduced Islam in Uganda in 1844?
2. What political threat did Kabaka Muteesa I face by the 1870s?
3. Give two reasons why Muteesa I invited Christian teachers to Uganda.
4. What were the four groups of Christian Missionaries who had arrived in Uganda by 1910?
5. What were the two names of the most famous early Missionaries in Uganda?
6. Give three reasons why Kabaka Muteesa I began hating the Christian Missionaries.
7. What did the political and religious wars betweren 1887 and 1892 bring into the social lives of Ugandans?
8. What was the purpose of each of the following three buildings in a Missionary Parish:
    (a) A church building,
    (b) A school building,
    (c) A medical building?
9. Give two reasons why the Missionaries established the schools for the children of the chiefs and of the most influential families in Uganda.
10. Give three reasons why the British colonial government in Uganda entered into education by 1925.

3 Church and State in Education 1925-1962

The establishment of the Department of Education 1925
In 1925, the British colonial government in Uganda declared its intention of participating fully in the educational work of the country. However, its intention was not to stop the Missionaries from teaching and looking after their schools which they had already set up and from building new ones. Mainly the work of the British colonial government in education was to direct the conducting of education in the country, to build and administer some schools, to make sure that its advice was being followed in the schools under the Missionaries and to give the Missionaries much of the required money to run the already built schools and to build new ones.

You need to realise however, that from 1925 to 1962, the Missionaries continued to spend quite a lot of money from their own resources on education despite the government financial support.

To carry out the above responsibilities, the Uganda Protectorate Government set up a Department of Education as one of the Departments within the administration. At that time, instead of having Ministries in Uganda, the British colonial government was organised on the basis of Departments.

For example, it had the Department of Health which today we call the Ministry of Health, the Department of Transport which today we call the Ministry of Transport and Communication, the Department of Agriculture which today we call the Ministry of Agriculture and Animal Husbandry and many other Departments which today we call Ministries. Thus the Department of Education was created in 1925 to be one of the Departments which the British colonial government had already set up.

The Organisation of the Department of Education from 1925
The Department of Education was headed by a Director Eric Hussey, the first Director of Education in Uganda. He was assisted by many officers at the headquarters in Kampala and all over Uganda at District level and Provincial level. Both the Director of Education and his Officers worked in cooperation with the Missionaries who were running and administering the old schools and who were also continuing to establish new ones, many times using money paid by Ugandan parents as fees and using financial support donated to them by their kind friends in Europe and in America and by raising money locally from income generating projects.

The government also strengthened the Advisory Council on Education formed in 1917. This council was charged with the initiation of educational policies which operated in the schools.

The Missionaries were quite adquately represented on this Advisory Council of Education.

Therefore the government's involvement in directing the educational work in 1925 was not intended to drive away the Missionaries from schools. The purpose of the British colonial government was to strengthen education. It did this by laying down common syllabi and examination regulations and the certification of candidates, by supervising the whole educational system and by providing adequate money for education. The Missionaries did not have adequate money from school fees, donations from their friends in Europe and America, and from donations locally to run the whole education system. They also did not have expert men and women to make good syllabuses and to supervise the educational system.

It may be of interest to the reader to know that the Department of Education was first located at Makerere University Campus in the building now part of which is the Students Guild Canteen and the other part of the University Bookshop. All that was the place which was directing the education activities in Uganda. It is from such humble beginnings that the present day Ministry of Education grew with its headquarters in the Crested Towers Building in Kampala. This progressive growth was fittingly depicted in the Motto of King's College Buddo namely: "Gakyali Mabaga", meaning that we are just beginning but with confidence and determination, the end result will be a wonder.

Exercise

i. Make a list of topics which you would include in the syllabus if you were to introduce in your school the following subject: *Desirable behaviour in the Uganda society.*

ii. Ask some of the old retired teachers or people who attended schools during the colonial days how many times they saw inspectors of schools in their schools in a year and how they felt when those inspectors arrived at their schools.

Benefits from the colonial government's participation in Education.

The following were the immediate benefits from the Uganda Protectorate Government's participation in education.

1. The colonial government through the Department of Education laid down a new general structure of education and the years for each section. This structure was as follows:

i. *Catechist schools:* These were under catechist teachers and the authority of the Missionaries. The Department of Education was not concerned with them by way of financing and supervising them.

- ii. *Sub grade schools:* These were under untrained teachers. They ran primary one and two. Generally it was the Missionary Education Secretaries who supervised these schools. They were usually being nursed to be promoted into the next category of schools.
- iii. *Elementary Schools or vernacular schools*: These had primary one to primary four, and were found at the Parishes where several Missionaries lived. They were being nursed to be promoted to the next category of schools.
- iv. *Full primary schools:* These had classes one to six and were under trained teachers.
- v. *Junior Secondary Schools:* These had three classes for students who had completed primary six.
- vi. *Senior Secondary Schools:* These had three classes for students who had completed the Junior Secondary Section. Some of them also ran the three classes of the Junior secondary section. By and large, the Senior secondary schools were run and taught in by European missionary teachers and were also boarding.
- vii. *Makerere College:* This was established by the Uganda Protectorate Government in 1922 as the highest school in the country and which was destined to develop into a University. It was joined by candidates who had passed quite highly from the Senior Secondary schools.
- viii. *Technical Schools:* These were joined by candidates who had completed Primary six.
- ix. *Teacher Training Schools:* These were of two categories, those for candidates from Primary six who were destined to teach in the lower section of the Primary schools and those for the candidates from the Junior Secondary section who were destined to teach in the upper section of the Primary Schools.

2. The teachers for Junior secondary schools were being produced at Makerere College. The first student teachers to join Makerere College were 25 already serving teachers and they joined in 1925. It is from this humble beginning that today's School of Education at Makerere University grew. This section of the University to date has an enrolment of 2000 students. Some of these students are under-graduates, some are postgraduate students on a one year's Diploma course in Education and others are doing M.A. and M.Ed. courses and Ph.D. courses.

3. The Department of Education also set out to organise the curriculum and the syllabi for all categories of schools.
    This point was very crucial. For example, the CMS Missionaries and the Mill

Hill Fathers both of whom had come from Britain, were following the education system and curriculum of Britain in their schools. The White Fathers who had come from France were following the French system of education and curriculum in their schools. The Verona Fathers who had come from Italy were following the Italian system of education and curriculum in the schools which they had established.

The above situation meant that there were three kinds of education systems in Uganda. Therefore it was difficult to ascertain the standard of pupils from the schools of the above set of missionary groups and to equate their educational attainment. For example, if a pupil completed Primary Six in a CMS School, it was not easy to be sure whether he was at par with another pupil who had completed Primary Six in a school run by the French White Fathers.

When the colonial government began to direct the education system, it laid down for each category of the above schools a curriculum and a syllabus for each subject, both of which were based on the British education system for all schools whether run by the CMS British Missionaries, or by the Mill Hill Fathers who were British, or by the White Fathers who were French or by the Italian Verona Fathers to ensure that all schools had similar standards.

4. The Department of Education set up the methods of examination and the certificates to be awarded at the completion of each section of the school structure.

5. The Department of Education prescribed the condition of each category of schools for example, the buildings in each school, the qualification and number of teachers in each category of school.

6. The Department of Education made a list of each category of schools all over the country so as to know their number in order to know the financial commitment of the government.

7. The Department of Education made a count of all pupils in the existing schools of every category.

8. It made a count of all teachers and their different qualifications and made arrangements to give courses in the teaching profession to those teachers who did not have professional qualifications. In this respect a course at Makerere College to up-grade a number of qualified teachers to become head teachers of prominent primary schools started in 1925.

9. It estimated the number of schools that should be built for Muslim children in a number of different areas of the country.

10. It made arrangements as to how to finance education. For example, it established the basis on which the annual financial estimates would be based such as the number of schools of each category, the existing teachers and the new schools to be built each year of each category.

After obtaining the above statistics, the Department of Education was in a good position to advise the colonial government to supervise the schools all over the country.

We need not forget however, that although the colonial govenment was now in charge of directing the educational affairs in the country, it was the Missionaries who had to carry out the actual day to day work of education in the schools. They administered the existing schools, maintained the old buildings, built new schools with some of the money given to them by the colonial government, and they carried out the actual teaching with Ugandan teachers. The officers of the Department of Education were there to inspect the schools and to make sure that the curriculum and the syllabi were being followed.

The Protestant Missionaries and the Roman Catholic Missionaries ran their own schools separately along the above structure. They also had Missionary Education Officers who worked in collaboration with the Government Education Officers. The administrative structure of the Protestant Church and of the Roman Catholic Church was as follows: The Education Secretary General headed the schools of each Church. That of the Protestant Missionaries had his headquarters at Namirembe while that of the Roman Catholic Church had his headquarters at Nsambya. These two Education Secretary Generals were very powerful people in the education system of Uganda during the colonial period. They sat on the Protectorate Government Advisory Council of Education. This Council was charged with initiating education polices to be implemented in schools. Once these Education Secretary Generals were not in favour of what the government wanted to implement in schools, such a measure was doomed to failure.

Each Diocese of the Protestant Church and of the Roman Catholic Church had an Education Office headed by an Education Secretary. Each also had School Supervisors who acted as inspectors of schools of each Diocese. The work of inspection of schools by the Education Inspectors of Schools from the Department of Education and that of the School Supervisors of the Missionaries was complementary and it helped to have a well supervised system of education. At each Parish there was in the case of the Roman Catholic Schools, a priest known as Father-in-charge of schools within that Parish. In the case of the Protestant Church he was called Pastor-in-charge of schools.

All the teachers in the schools within a Parish were under the responsibility of either the Father-in-charge or the Pastor-in-charge and other educational affairs. He was the link betweren the Parish education affairs and the Education Secretary of the Diocese. This latter one in turn liased with the Education Secretary General in Kampala from whom he took orders.

The Protectorate Government sent money for running old schools, for paying teachers' salaries and for building new schools to the Education Headquarters of the two missionary groups headed by the Education Secretary General. Then each of them allocated the money according to the educational developments of his missionary group.

The responsibility for the education of Muslim children was directly under the colonial government through the Department of Education. It set up schools for the Muslim children and took care to see to the administration of those schools. But by the 1940's through the leadership of Prince Al-Haji Badru Kakungulu, the Muslims had organised themselves in such a way that they could run their own schools just like the Christian Missionaries. Consequently, in 1948 the Muslim authorities in Uganda established the Uganda Muslim Education Association (UMEA) with its Headquarters on Kibuli Hill.

Haji Ramadhan Gava was the first and last to head the Uganda Muslim Education Association until the Uganda Government took over the control of all schools in Uganda by the 1963 Education Act. His title was that of Education Secretary. Gava had already done remarkable work in Muslim schools as a Makerere qualified teacher and as a sponsor of education for the Muslim children. His selflessness and determination contributed greatly to the development of education for Muslim children in Uganda and he deserves credit along the Christian Missionaries. He helped to establish schools all over Uganda for Muslim children and looked for teachers for these schools and arranged like the Missionaries for the supervision of those schools. There was no part of Uganda which was not familiar with his presence in his endeavours for uplifting the education of the Muslim community in Uganda.

Exercise

If you were made an Inspector of schools, list 5 items which you would look at when you would go to inspect either a Primary school or a Secondary school for which you would give advice to the Headteacher and to the teachers within that school.

History and Development of Education

Haji Ramadhan Kasule Gava 1910-1981, Father of Muslim Education in Uganda.

4 Literary Education in the Uganda Education System

Introduction

The kind of education to be imparted in Uganda taxed the sources of and influences on education policies more than anything else during the colonial and missionary period. Similarly, it continued to do so after 1962. Indeed this debate is still going on. It is an unending issue because of the constant changing economic and social situation of the country. This is one reason why studies in curriculum innovation and change have over the past decade gained so much prominence, while the independent government of Uganda went all the way to set up a whole organisation known as the National Curriculum Development Centre in 1970.

The Colonial Office through its Advisory Committee on Education in Tropical Africa was the original source of policies on the nature of education to be given. The above Committee of the Colonial Office as the source of policy on the kind of education to be offered in the British tropical colonies continued to emphasise the above stand through Commissions, memoranda and through individual education advisers whom it used to send to Uganda regularly between 1925 and 1960 when there was need. There were two prominent educational Commissions during the period under review which emphasised this policy: the de La War Commission of 1937 on Higher Education in East Africa and the Binns Study Group of 1951. The latter was backed up by the Royal Commission of 1951-55 and by the Economic Commission of 1951. Among the most prominent education advisors who came to Uganda to examine the education system and to continue to emphasize the above policy, was Dr. Harlow, Technical Assistant Advisor to the Colonial Office. He visited Uganda in 1951 to lay a firm basis for new trends in technical education development.

The Uganda Protectorate government also came in at times, as a great source of policy on the kind of education to be offered in this country. As a convenient procedure for discussing this issue of the kind of education, let us take up the literary education first.

Literary Education

From the outset, both the Colonial Office and the Uganda Protectorate government in 1925 wanted to balance literary education with practical education thus changing the status quo which was already existing. Both the Protestant and Catholic Missionaries had already begun to run the literary type of education to help produce office interpreters, clerks and teachers. But the Colonial Office drawing a leaf from the observations of the Phelps-Stokes Commission of

1924-25 felt that the Missionaries had sacrificed agricultural and technical education to literary education. The Phelps-Stokes Commission had criticised the Missionaries heavily in the following terms:

> The Missionaries have failed to relate their educational activities to the community needs of the people. The type of education has been too exclusively literary. In a country with unusually fertile soil they have made practically no provision for agricultural education.

In view of the above criticism, the Colonial Office wanted to redress the balance by insisting on a balanced curriculum. Such a curriculum would offer some literary education for office employment purposes, but for the greater part of education to be concentrated at the lower level to give a practical kind of education based on technical and agricultural skills. This latter kind of education, it was presumed, would benefit the greatest number of people in Uganda.

In this spirit the Director of Education stated at the end of 1925 that "he was poised to combat the children's view that education meant learning a little English to become clerks in offices". This point of view was in line with the Colonial Office policy which emphasised that "the advancement of the community as a whole would have to be achieved through the improvement of agriculture, native industries and the improvement of health".

Consequently the policy was to have a great learning towards the kind of activities which the majority of people in Uganda were likely to engage in after school life. In other words this was going to be adaptive education which had been very much recommended by Dr. Hesse Jones and Dr. J. K. Aggrey of the Phelps-Stokes Commission. These two educationists were drawing from their experience of the kind of education which was being given to the Negroes in the Southern States of the USA. It was termed adaptive education because it was meant to make the Negroes fit in their environment and also be happy with the conditions which the white men had arranged for them to be in.

It was unfortunate however, that despite the desire of both the Colonial Office policy and Eric Hussey, the first Director of Education in Uganda to reduce literary education from the system, the programme put forward by Hussey, was exactly the opposite of the Phelps-Stokes Commission concept. It was mainly literary with Makerere College as the desirable apex.

When Hussey was transferred to Nigeria in 1929, his successor, E.C. Morris who had been his deputy, tried to play down this literary predominance in the education system which had begun with the Missionaries. He wrote in 1930 that:

> A policy which had tended to give a purely literary training to the masses in order to serve a small minority which might benefit by higher education and qualify for semi-professional careers could, if persisted in, only lead to the creation of a discontented community divorced from its own heredity and environment with no outlet for its energies but political intrigue and the flouting of authority.

Literary Education

He went on then to blame the Missionaries and his predecessor that "an initial handicap to work such as that, was the fact that that outlook had been very largely lacking in education in Uganda", in the past.

In pursuit of this stand, Morris established in 1930 a category of schools which were named Central Schools.

These were post primary schools following a practical course for three years based on both agricultural and technical skills. They were intended to be more numerous than those other post primary schools which he termed Middle Schools, and were following a purely literary curriculum. This was also one reason why from that year there was a run down on the number of secondary schools. Thus Nabumali High School, the Verona Father's secondary school at Layibi near Gulu and Mbarara High School, were stopped as secondary schools in order to run them as post primary schools with a predominance of agricultural and technical teaching. Nyakasura School was only saved by its Headmaster, Commander Calwell, who had initiated a practical curriculum from the very beginning combining literary, agricultural and technical skills. Likewise, Buddo College had earlier on begun to include agriculture in its curriculum. With this new drive of the Director of Education, Grace, the Headmaster of Buddo even established a full set-up at Namutamba for teaching agriculture to boys who could not cope up with the literary curriculum at Buddo.

But there were strong influences in the Uganda Protectorate which were against the policy that tried to encourage practical education more especially at the expense of literary education. These influences preferred the predominance of literary education in the education system. One of these influences as indicated by the first Director of Education, Eric Hussey, were the students themselves. Hussey observed in 1925 that, "to most of the children who went to school, the learning of a little English was the coveted goal so that they might escape from the ranks of manual workers and fit themselves for some kind of clerical occupation, which they believed to be dignified and less arduous".

These students looked at adaptive education as retrogressive and meant to make them stagnant. Indeed this was also the point of view of their parents and benefactors who paid school fees for them at school. The cause for this desire for literary education at the expense of agricultural and technical education, baffled the European educators and administrators alike during the colonial days. These people looked at education as a means of helping a person to better his own situation within his environment instead of looking at education as primarily meant to make him jump out of his prevailing environment. If he was a son of a farmer and since his life was to continue as that of a farmer, education should render him more efficient as a farmer and he should be contented to be so. If he was a son of a chief who owned personal land, that son should learn agricultural techniques so that he would render his father's free-hold land more productive after leaving school. Indeed this was the whole idea behind the theory of education for adaptation on which the Colonial Office policy was based, which theory has met with much criticisms for having been intended to give a black man an inferior kind of education.

But the cause for the desire for literary education on the part of the people in Uganda is not far to seek. The colonial situation brought in new values and a person to gain out of that changed situation, had to avail himself of the literary education that the colonial masters seemed to have gone through. Comfort and the opening of new horizons meant getting away from the village routine. Therefore, no other kind of education but literary appealed to the people more because it was the road leading to a new kind of life. Education for adaptation did not excite them, and any one who preached the gospel of education for adaptation was a prophet of doom. By clamouring for literary education, the students were trying to adapt themselves to changed circumstances and to progressive ideas, as they thought.

The chiefs however, desired adaptive education for the sons of the peasants because it would then create a difference between their sons and the sons of the people whom they led. Those chiefs were no different from the post independence politicians who were loudly preaching the gospel of "back to the land", indeed not for their sons but for the sons of the people whom they were leading. Moreover, since the chiefs possessed personal freehold land, they hoped that on graduation, the sons of the peasants would go and use their land for them to get increased rent yields. If the chiefs had their own way, they could have resisted the sons of the peasants from enjoying this literary education. But by the 1920's the Uganda Protectorate government was feeling that the chiefs were extortionate to the peasants and they were inefficient. So a combination of the sons of the chiefs and of the sons of the peasants in government offices, would be a healthy thing to have. The sons of the chiefs would soon realise that the brain wavelength of the sons of peasants was not below that of the sons of the chiefs.

Moreover the chiefs were helpless in effecting this difference. Since it was the person who was financially able to pay for education that could enjoy this literary education, the peasants were also through their energies producing cash crops and animals from which they got money and then they were able to send their children to schools, from where they graduated to take up clerical jobs in the Protectorate and local administrations that required the possession of literary education.

The parents and the students were a strong influence in making literary education predominate in the educational system from bottom to top. The universal feeling of students and parents alike was that "whatever the white man might say about education, his own wisdom and administrative ability had been learnt from books."

A Church Missionary Society educator, T.C. Vincent of Bishop Tucker College, Mukono summed up this nicely in 1928 when he remarked that "parents sent their children to mission schools with the hope that they would escape from the routine of village life to which they themselves were subject, and not that they might return to it with new knowledge and ideas that would make that life acceptable and of worth to them".

During the same year at a conference at Namirembe, one son of Sir Apollo Kaggwa remarked that the chiefs "sent their boys to high schools not to learn to

Literary Education

drive bullock wagons and to look after cows, but to learn to be fitted for posts of high standing". He alleged that Canon Grace, Headmaster of Buddo then was trying to educate them for slavery work.

Implicitly, the colonial set up was also an influence working against the adaptive education policy which it was professing to encourage. The colonial set up gave white collar jobs readily to graduates of literary education and so society accorded this kind of education with high status and success in life. One who failed to reach the top and then miss the chance to be given employment in government administration, went back to the land and was taken as having failed in life. He also looked at himself as having gone to school for nothing.

Moreover the European themselves who were a reference group in the eyes of the Africans were not physically engaged in farming. Though some Europeans had plantations especially up to the mid 1930's before they joined their friends in Kenya, and the Missionaries supervised large tracts of cultivated estates, it was the illiterate Africans who kept them well tendered while the white men themselves did the supervisory work. Indeed the Missionaries had to be sympathised with. In a parish station, they had so much work to do in terms of planning policy, seeing to its being executed and supervising the people. This kind of pre-occupation usually left them with very little time to devote on actual agricultural activities. Yet there were so many Africans readily available to engage in this kind of work who only needed to be shown how things should be done and then supervised by a white Missionary. But when the Missionary played the supervisory role, also boys and girls who were going to his schools, aspired to the same role.

The educators themselves both Europeans and Africans also stood in the way of reducing the impact of practical education. They had gone through a literary kind of education back in Europe though they were supposed according to government policy to follow a curriculum imparting agricultural and technical skills with less literary over balance. With their literary education background, the kind of education which they were giving, tended in the long run to be mainly literary. That was one reason why the Central Schools failed to make an impression on society. The curriculum was practical but the teachers tended to lapse into treating it as a literary curriculum. Thus the Director of Education lamented in 1935 that the "Central Schools had been originally designed to give a three years post-elementary course, with a practical semi-vocational bias to the whole. But they had not achieved the hopes which had accompanied their inauguration".

Indeed this was inevitable. The African teachers who were charged with running these Central Schools offering a practical curriculum had themselves gone through a literary kind of course. Even before being appointed to run these schools, no attempt had been made to retrain them for their new task. Consequently, they had no knowledge and belief in an education that did not impart values of a literary nature.

Of course, failure to follow the Central School curriculum effectively should not be labelled against the African teachers only. The very directors of these courses, the Europeans themselves had no knowledge of how to give these courses, too, nor did many of them have confidence in the ultimate benefit of those courses. Thus Bishop Dr. Willis and Mr. R.S. Irvine, both C.M.S. Missionaries from Uganda, revealed at an Educational Conference in Great Britain in 1928 that, "Africans themselves were often suspicious of education in agriculture or such subjects as they thought a second best was being pushed on them. The missionary teachers too needed to believe in that type of education if they were to get Africans to believe in it too".

Even the Binns Study Group which visited Uganda twenty years later in 1951 observed that the European missionary teachers were not equipped to teach a practical curriculum nor were the African teachers whom they had trained. Consequently both groups of teachers did not have skills for teaching this practical kind of education. The Binns Study Group continued to observe that for the most part, the missionary teachers had been required to possess University Degrees. Many of them had been more familiar with town than country life and their own education had its emphasis more on literary than on practical education. Consequently with this kind of background the European missionary teachers had brought that limited experience into schools and teacher training colleges in Africa, preparing pupils and teachers for primary schools mostly in rural areas.

The literary attitude which these European missionary teachers passed on to the people was infectious. Indeed they used also to boast for possessing Degrees which they had obtained either at Oxford or Cambridge. This infection caught the Africans. Yet instead of its being blamed on these European teachers, the tendency was to blame it on the Africans. Thus the Director of Education remarked in 1929 that "there were a few natives especially in Buganda who blind themselves to the possibility to developing a system of higher education in their own country and would like to see the whole education of the country moulded on European lines and culminating in maticulation, which would qualify students to enter a European University".

During the 1950's there was much talk of decreasing literary secondary education. But this would be successful only if several agricultural secondary schools and secondary technical schools had been set up to show a good example that it was not only the literary kind of education that made a man successful in life. Two agricultural secondary schools were proposed. One in Gulu at Sir Samuel Baker (Pongdwong) and another one in Mbarara at Ntare. When the Headmaster for Ntare School was selected and put there to run an agricultural secondary school, he at once changed the curriculum of the school to purely literary lines. When the School in Gulu was set up at Sir Samuel Baker (Pongdwong), it was not even meant to be an agricultural secondary school. So both European and African teachers were not ready to see the predominance of practical education in the educational system. And indeed the suggestion of citing agricultural secondary schools in Mbarara and Gulu in the 1950's was in-opportune. The demand was for literary secondary schools at that time. And since the people in these two places for a long time were clamouring for secondary schools on the basis of Buddo, Mwiri, Nabumali and Kisubi, to cater for their areas, such agricultural secondary schools could not have been welcome to the people of those areas. So it was quite a good relief when the cirriculum of the two secondary schools was changed by the Headmasters along the lines of the already famous academic secondary schools in the country.

One reason why the Uganda Protectorate government between 1925 and 1935 was devoted to resisting literary education as a policy, was the fear of political upheaval. Governor Boudillion successor to Governor G.W. Gowers in 1931, had observed this in Asia from where he came to Uganda. He felt that literary education had done a lot to make people in those areas politically alert and disgruntled. He also felt that literary education had fitted them for nothing else but clerical jobs and agitation against the established order. Consequently there were too many clerks chasing too few jobs requiring such man-power. This made the school educated community "divorced from its own heredity and environment with no outlet for its energies but political intrigue and the flouting of authority."

Secondly, there were economic considerations on the part of the colonial administration. The nature of the economy in Uganda during that period did not show much chances for giving employment to many people so academically educated. This was of course, thinking of existing jobs. This kind of view was typical of colonial policy. It needed just a few assistants to the British officers to do the menial jobs for them. If one produced so many of them, they would be a nuisance and they would begin to demand jobs and salaries that were the preserve of the white man.

Moreover, economically, the issue for the coloniser was how to get people produce raw materials for the home market and also get sufficient revenue to run colonial services without having recourse to the British Treasury. This economic view reached a high water-mark during the term of office of Sir John Hall between 1945 and 1950. He all along blamed the educators for having failed to impress upon the African the dignity and necessity of physical toil. He remonstrated that :

> ...as education spreads, so the number of persons prepared to undertake any work with their own hands diminished in inverse ratio, and once a boy had passed through the primary school, he considered himself to have automatically joined the ranks of those who would order others to work and that any physical labour by himself would be derogatory.

Still, the uneasiness of Sir John Hall did not change the already established literary education system and the attitude of the people who revered that system. Both Sir Philip Mitchell who ran the affairs of Uganda from 1935 to the end of 1939 together with his Director of Education, H. Jowitt, had done a lot to kill the Colonial Office policy of adaptive education.

Both Sir Philip Mitchell and Jowitt were interested in literary education. Sir Philip Mitchell was particularly interested in secondary and higher academic education. He wanted to establish a large number of secondary academic schools out of which would come a flow of students to fill his College of higher learning

History and Development of Education

at Makerere. This also implied that primary education had to have a literary base to prepare students who would go to the academic secondary schools.

The support for literary education by Sir Philip Mitchell however, formalised a situation that had been made to exist by the force of parents, students and teachers since "Makerere which had been established in 1922 unconsciously dominated the Uganda system of education as far back as the first year of junior secondary education".

In a way, the above comment by the Director of Education shows how successfully the Protectorate government had been in making especially the chiefs to look at Makerere College as the pinnacle of education in Uganda. They thus stopped hankering for sending their sons abroad where the colonial administration feared, they would pick up undesirable attitudes towards colonialism.

The first schoolmasters' class at Makerere College 1925-1927
Front row: D. Mukasa, S. Kayongo, T. Damulira, P. Basajja, The Principal, The master of methods, Y.P. Mukasa, Entendere, P. Kigozi
Back row: Y. Birigenda, L. Kiyingi, E.S. Kironde, Z. Mungonya, E. Sabiti, A. Zirimenya, P. Mukedi. Middle row: S. Kasenene, T. Kibebbere, F. Muwereza, Y. Nswa, Y.B. Sempa, Y. Kityo, Elakor, S. Kiwanuka, I. Munyolo

Literary Education

During the 1950's there was much talk about trying to strike an equal balance between literary education and practical education through the influence of the Binns Study Group from the Colonial Office. The members of the Binns Study Group desired to arrest the speed of the literary trend in education by combining or integrating the literary education with the practical education in equal balance in the school curriculum. The idea of the Binns Study Group was for starting comprehensive secondary schools.

To resolve this issue, the Binns Study Group laid down the following strategy. First of all, the change had to start with training teachers who would have practical skills and who would have a belief in the efficacy of such skills. The next step would be to overhaul the school curriculum so that there would no longer be the traditional distinction of literary and practical subjects. The curriculum would be an integrated package combining both literary and practical education in one school.

Nothing so drastic and educationally healthy had ever been suggested and attempted before in Uganda as the above proposal. To draw away students and parents from the pre-occupation of literary studies, one needed to start a revolution on the above lines. But like many other good suggestions, that suggestion remained on paper. First of all, it entailed a lot. It meant beginning to experiment, retrain teachers all the way from primary to secondary schools and also change the whole curriculum in the whole education system.

The suggestion came also at a very in-opportune time when the times did not warrant experimentation but to carry on along the old beaten path and at a higher and faster speed even. The suggestion came at the time of political awareness and economic prosperity. Both those two factors demanded sending children to school to avail themselves of as much literary education as possible to get office posts that were so much available and which were becoming even more and more available as old type of expatriates were gradually leaving the country. Between 1950 and 1960 anybody who completed a full primary course was assured of a job if he endeavoured to look for it. The implication of this, is that anybody who completed a literary secondary school course was automatically given an office job since even the number of graduates at this level was very small.

Though the de Bunsen Education Committee of 1952 was in agreement with the views of the Binns Study Group, its curriculum recommendations were not along the drastic recommendation of the Binns Study Group. The de Bunsen Education Committee left the literary set up run side by side with two agricultural secondary schools, several technical junior secondary schools and technical courses at the Kampala Technical Institute leading to the acquisition of full secondary education in technical skills.

Despite this arrangement however, the period of the duration of the de Bunsen Plan, 1955-63, epitomised the failure of the policy for practical education in favour of wholesale literary education from primary through secondary education. The de Bunsen Plan itself promoted literary education from primary to secondary education and excluded practical education from the primary section which had existed all along through the school garden lessons and the handwork lessons since 1925. The reason for leaving out this aspect in the primary schools was that primary school pupils unlike during the 1920's 1930's and the 1940's, were too young to engage in agricultural and handcraft practical studies at that level. One had to talk about them theoretically in an academic manner to promote the pupils' insight. When talking specifically on agricultural education, the de Bunsen Education Committee said that agricultural education should not be concerned with practice in the routine of cultivation. Most country children were already familiar with the routine growing of common food crops before they went to school. To make those children labour in the same way to grow the same crops at school was a waste of valuable time and a most sure way of inculcating a profound and abiding dislike of life on the land.

The secondary section as of old continued to deal with literary aspects only, though however, the plan set up Rural Trade Schools, Farm Schools and Home Craft Centres for those pupils after primary six and Junior two who failed to get enough marks either to join Junior one or to Join Senior one respectively which were running literary courses. Many times these pupils lingered in Rural Trade Schools, in Home Craft Centres and in Farm Schools to gain entry to the literary Junior one or to the literary Senior one secondary schools after trying again the examinations that led to those classes.

Those pupils who remained in those Rural Trade Schools, Farm Schools and Home Craft Centres were under teachers who were not skilled in imparting agricultural and technical skills and also most of the pupils after spending in those schools two years, went to look for jobs in towns instead of going to use their acquired practical skills in bettering the situation in villages. Those who went back to the villages hardly showed any agricultural and technical skills learnt. They went about life in the same way their grand people had gone about it in the past.

The two full secondary schools along agricultural lines envisaged in the de Bunsen Plan never got off the ground as we have already seen above. Nor was the purpose for such secondary schools so different from the purpose of the already successful and famous secondary schools along literary lines to warrant much bother to set them up and run them as such. The very preamble to the establishment of these schools betrays how much literary education was influencing policy makers. The Committee members said that they had in mind "a secondary school in which the curriculum would be centred around biological and economic subjects and that the function of the school would be rather to train for higher studies in agriculture than to turn out young farmers. Even if students from these schools graduated and took up jobs in town, the members of the Committee would be satisfied that the students had received an education based on agriculture which would be as sound as any other at the secondary stage.

The eight technical junior secondary schools which got established according to the de Bunsen Plan and the full technical senior secondary at the Kampala Technical Institute never got the respect from people equal to that of the literary junior and senior secondary schools.

Literary Education

The secondary schools which endeavoured to run the literary and practical courses of education together did not help to encourage parents and students to respect practical education either. Such schools as Namilyango College, King's College Buddo, St Mary's College Kisubi and St. Peter's College Tororo, were since 1940 running commercial subjects on a practical basis. But in each of the above secondary school there were two separate groups of students: those following a purely academic line and those following a commercial and practical line of studies. The latter were not designated to enter Makerere College, the pinnacle of learning in East Africa. Indeed they were put in this section after being screened through the Primary Leaving Examinations on the basis of marks scored. Indeed their marks were below those of their colleagues who followed the academic course. Consequently those students were deemed not capable of passing sufficiently well the Cambridge School Certificate Examination after secondary six to gain entry into Makerere College. This section though was in the same schools and with the same privileges within those schools, its students faced chagrin from the students who belonged to the academic section. Since at the end of senior one, anyone who wanted to leave the commercial section and join the academic section, was allowed by passing the internal examination to the satisfaction of the Headmaster, many boys worked hard during their first year to be allowed to leave the commercial section. As a result those commercial classes used to be very small and were looked down upon.

It is a pity that the Uganda Protectorate government did not help to boost the morale of students who joined this section by raising their salaries well above those of graduates who went through the purely academic section and also make provisions to have commercial subjects at Makerere College at the time. The banks and other commercial places were full of Asians with qualifications of this nature with attractive pay. Usually such qualifications were obtained in India or in Britain where Asian parents sent their sons to obtain them.

One other influence that worked in favour of making literary education predominate in the curriculum, was the expensive nature of running practical education. The Department of Education and Head teachers felt better by avoiding that kind of education which cost more than literary education. While literary education only required books, a blackboard and a building furnished with desks, the practical subjects required much more than these.

In conclusion the colonial policy on the kind of education emphasised a mixture of literary and practical education based on agricultural and technical skills. At one time especially during the 1930's there was an attempt to make practical education as strong as the literary kind of education in the education system.

But by 1962 the literary education was in ascendancy for the following reasons. The administrators of the education system failed to produce a cadre of teachers who could teach effectively the practical kind of education and who at the same time believed in its benefits. Consequently even when the practical subjects were taught, they had a bias to literary education.

Secondly, some Governors tended at one time to encourage practical education while some others tended to encourage literary education. And since the literary kind of education was always more acceptable to both the teachers and to the students, the practical kind of education was always on the losing side.

Thirdly the majority of the students believed in acquiring literary education. These students were convinced and rightly so during the colonial period that it was only a graduate of a literary kind of education who stood a greater chance to get a white collar job and thereby get a respectable status in society.

Finally, the great expense involved in running a school along practical education, discouraged school operators from being enthusiastic for this kind of education and consequently easily ran schools which were offering literary courses. This is one reason why the pioneers of private schools whose original aim was to provide practical education in their schools eventually succumbed and also began to run their schools along the literary cirriculum as it was in missionary schools.

Emmanuel Cardinal Nsubuga (L) Haji Kakungulu (C) and Bishop Danstan Nsubuga, three religious leaders who promoted literary education in Uganda.

5 Agricultural Education and Out of School Education

The Colonial Office in London was the source of policies regarding agricultural education in Uganda and the Uganda Protectorate administration was responsible for executing those policies many times after modification to suit the particular Uganda situation. In this execution of these agricultural policies in education, the Missionaries cooperated fully. But the majority of the teachers due to lack of suitable teaching skills in agriculture and the attitude of the pupils and parents plus government oscillation between one approach and another to teaching agriculture in schools and out of schools were influences which tended to deflect the effectiveness of these policies.

Before the Colonial Office policy on agriculture was announced in 1925, the Missionaries who preceded government in the participation of conducting school education in Uganda, had already shown their enthusiasm for agricultural education vis-a-vis literary education. In this respect the Phelps-Stokes Commission which visited Uganda in 1924-25 reported that one of the Missionaries had told the Commissioners that the soil of Uganda was a veritable gold mine from which by the cooperation of Church and State, a new African society could be dug. The same Missionary had gone on to say that the chiefs' sons who possessed land through their fathers, could be encouraged to develop it after leaving school with the necessary skills which would lift up the whole of the village life around them.

Though the Missionaries had already begun to teach agriculture before the entry of government in the arena of giving education, they had failed to make an impression on society that it necessitated a person to go to school and be taught agriculture. More especially their approach had tended to make agriculture a side issue in comparison with literary education since it had been left to the chance interest of the Missionary incharge and to the necessity of producing food for the missions. Consequently the Missionaries' approach to agricultural education had not impressed the Phelps-Stokes Commission. In no uncertain terms that Commission criticised the Missionaries that:

> ...they had failed to relate their educational activities to the community needs of the people by concentrating on literary education and nearly neglected teaching agriculture.

The criticism however, by the above Commission of the Missionaries was not that of omission but of approach. The Commission was influenced by the educational philosophy of Booker T. Washington, founder of Tuskegee Institute in Alabama in the Southern part of the U.S.A. His education system was not elite-oriented, but was mass-oriented, which would give an education balanced by agriculture, literary and technical skills. It was hoped that such an education would give an individual the tools of a personal liberation so that he could become self-reliant. Such education however, had also the aims of keeping the Negro in his lowly position of "the plough, the anvil, the hammer, the broom, the frying pan and the needle".

So this sort of self reliance based on the land was not evident to the Phelps-Stokes Commission in the kind of education which the Missionaries were giving by the 1920's in Uganda. The aspirations of their disciples were inclined towards obtaining clerical jobs in already established offices of the white man, where agricultural and technical skills would not be called for.

Taken in this light even the contention of the above Missionary that the chiefs' sons after leaving school would develop their fathers' land, was a misinterpretation. Both the chiefs and their sons were not out to develop their land themselves using agricultural skills learnt in schools. They wanted to hire it out to peasants who would pay them rent after the sale of cotton and coffee grown on that land every year. Their sons after completing school would become chiefs or workers in offices, which occupation in no way connected them with the development of their land using new agricultural techniques learnt at school.

Borrowing a leaf from the recommendations of the Phelps-Stokes Commission, the Colonial Office in London went ahead and made agricultural education into firm policy when it inaugurated its Educational Policy in the British Tropical Africa in 1925. Thus ran part of its policy on agricultural education: "the aim of education should be to promote the advancement of the community as a whole through the improvement of agriculture".

It is against this background that the Uganda Protectorate government adapted its approach towards agricultural education in the education system. Agricultural education arrangement in 1925 fell under three headings: the teaching of biology in the classroom accompanied with practical agriculture through the school gardens at primary school level, the training of teachers in a agricultural skills at government agricultural institutions and the training of African assistants who were supposed to be employed in the Department of Agriculture.

Having laid down the above machinery, the Director of Education stated in 1929 that the "aim in the primary stage was to give to all primary education an agricultural bias. That bias had to be attempted by the development of the school garden and by making an agricultural course a feature of the training of all teachers in primary schools". Efforts were at once made to train primary school teachers in agricultural techniques so that they could teach them to pupils in primary schools. A scheme was therefore planned whereby every elementary school teacher attended a short course as part of his/her normal training at Bukalasa and Serere agricultural institutes.

The Missionaries who were responsible for running schools were solidly behind the Director of Education in this move and they were all the time lamenting that their approach to agricultural education might not be right and probably that was why they were not achieving as good results as would be

Agricultural Education

desirable, and they were suggesting ways and means of bettering their approach. Records in missionary schools speak eloquently on the Missionaries' efforts to inculcate agricultural values in their pupils along the lines which the Department of Education set up from 1925. Also eye witnesses are still in plenty who testify to this fact. In this respect the Verona Fathers' efforts in Gulu and in Lira at Ngetta, the C.M.S. efforts in Nyakasura, Buddo, Namutamba, Ngora, Nabumali and Gayaza, and the Mill Hill Fathers' efforts at Nkokonjeru, Nazigo, Naggalama and Nagongera to mention but a few places out of hundreds of them, come out prominently in support of the government's agricultural education policy, and also in support of the missionary practices as a matter of conviction in agricultural education.

In the face of evidence one gleans from missionary records on their efforts to establish agricultural studies and practices in the schools, one feels perturbed by comments of some contemporary people today who seem to brush away the Missionaries' efforts and indeed of all the colonial people who were engaged in giving education in Uganda.

Even the government supported the Missionaries in their efforts in this drive to teach agricultural skills in the schools. This was one reason why the Director of Education supported whole heatedly the efforts of Canon Grace, Headmaster of Buddo at Namutamba on 300 acres of land donated by Sir Apollo Kaggwa for "the Buddo boys who were less academically inclined to work out their own salvation, depending on their initiative and enterprise".

In its efforts to reduce academic education and promote practical education, in 1930 the Department of Education introduced a section of schools comprising of post primary schools known as Central Schools. The curriculum of these Central Schools was based on both agricultural and technical skills. A lot of activities on agricultural side went on in these schools. Some of the graduates of these Central Schools were expected to join the Department of Agriculture and work in its various sections but the majority of these were supposed to go back to the land and better it and also be an example to so many other people who had not been to school to learn modern techniques as farmers. During the same year of 1930 the Department of Education appointed a Superintendent of Agriculture to be responsible for the teaching of agriculture in primary schools so that those joining the Central Schools would have had already a firm base at the primary level.

But the attitude of the parents to those new schools was not likely to make them a success, " since boys whose parents could afford to pay the high fees in the literary Middle Schools would drift on to those post primary Middle Schools". The Director of Education however, felt that he had got the support of some influential chiefs who were singing the gospel of "back to the land", for it was not meant for their children but for the children of the peasants. These by going back to the land would raise the earnings for the chiefs by renting their land.

Besides agriculture being taught in primary schools through the school gardens and in the next stage of Central Schools by 1930, there were Farm Agricultural Schools belonging to each of the following missionary societies;

the C.M.S and the Verona Fathers. The C.M.S. farm school was at Numutamba, while that of the Verona Fathers was in Gulu at Layibi and the government through the Legislative Council allowed to pay a yearly grant to each one of 800 Pounds from 1933. After three years the government included them into the normal grants-in-aid system. But by and large, every mission station was a farm especially in the Roman Catholic mission stations. These were extensively cultivated estates kept up by the pupils under the direction of Nuns, Lay Brothers and Priests. Today one of the sad pictures of these mission stations are the jungles filled with furrows as a result of soil erosion arising from present day neglect that cover these once well kept areas.

The missionary cooperation and support for the government agricultural education policies sprang from several motives. One was that from the beginning the Missionaries' philosophy was that of keeping a person usefully busy to detract him/her from sin. Agricultural occupation was one of those useful things that would do that very well. Secondly, there was an economic aspect. Up to the 1950's when pupils were relatively old between their catechism classes and primary six, the Missionaries would work them on large estates to produce food and cash crops. Food produced on these estates helped to feed the pupils while the cash obtained from the sales of crops was used to solve a lot of financial problems for the Missionaries. They used some of the money to put up new buildings and furnish them and to maintain the old ones, to buy scholastic materials, to support some children of indigent parents at school and sometimes to pay teachers' wages in the numerous sub-grade schools in the villages which were not grant-aided by the government.

Moreover, the Missionaries realised the true facts that the majority of pupils attending schools had no chance of being employed in any offices for clerical jobs either in the public sector or in the private sector. So it would have been short sightedness for the Missionaries not to support agriculture studies in their schools. If they did not do so, they would be preparing the majority of their disciples for benefits that did not exist in real life. "The alternative would have been to have an increasing number of misfits, who would have gone so far on the road to higher education and yet could get no benefit out of that education in real life", as the Director of Education wrote in his 1930 education report.

The Uganda Protectorate government was supporting the Colonial Office agricultural policies for mainly four reasons. From 1912, the government policy was to develop Uganda for African peasant proprietors and thereby discourage European planters. Therefore, there was need to give agricultural education to those Africans who were joining schools to be able to better their skills as peasant agriculturalists and to act as a civilising agent among those other numerous Africans in the villages who would not come to attend school.

Secondly, the Uganda Protectorate government was engaged in a campaign of raising revenue from cash crops and it felt that agricultural education given to pupils, and agricultural propaganda through extension service given to those people out of school, would turn the inhabitants into more effective growers of cash crops for export to get revenue to run services in the Uganda Protectorate.

That is why there was such sustained cooperation of the Department of Agriculture with the Department of Education. Indeed also this would benefit the colonial power at home by getting raw materials as Dr. S.M. Kiwanuka contends that concern for the economic utility of the colonies was to maximise their resources, to keep the factories in full production capacity in Britain.

Thirdly, at the post primary school level, the government wanted to get some specialist assistants to work in government agricultural institutes and government experimental farms to do all sorts of work: to carry on guided experiments for the government at such places as Bukalasa, Kawanda, Serere, Arapai and Kojja, to mention but a few places, to help run short courses for chiefs who would go back into their villages and educate the people under them showing them modern ways of planting seeds and pruning plants, how to produce and conserve manure, how to fight against plant pests, how to work against soil erosion and how to harvest crops in the right manner especially cotton and coffee for the British industries in Britain.

Finally, behind all this there was the reality of the situation. Uganda not to mention other parts of East Africa, was and still is an agricultural country. Therefore, it was the land that necessarily would provide useful and profitable employment to the majority of the people. To teach agriculture in schools was only sensible lest the aim of the education system would have been to make those few people who attended schools to be screened off from the livelihood of 95% of the people in Uganda. To emphasise the above point the Director of Education wrote in 1930 thus:

> A policy which tended to give a purely literary education to the mass in order to serve a small minority which may benefit by higher education and qualify for semi-professional careers could, if persisted in, only lead to the creation of a discounted community divorced from its own heredity and environment with no outlet for its energies but political intrigue and the flouting of authority.

Still pursuing the idea of agricultural education in the system, in 1933 the Advisory Council on African Education in Uganda appointed a sub-committee to give views as to the best way agriculture, animal husbandry and technical education would be effectively included in the school curriculum. This sub-committee agreed that the most effective method would be to encourage the cultivation of economic crops at the village teachers' training centres, and that all this would be directed and supervised by officers of the Department of Agriculture. Student teachers from these centres, when posted to primary schools on completion of their courses were expected to develop similar experiments and demonstration plots with the aid of their pupils. These school plots were supposed to act as models of sound cultivation to the peasants in the vicinity.

During the same year, a review was made of the operation of the agricultural courses in the education system. The Director of Education was gratified at the end of the year that these agricultural courses were operating well and that the people had begun to accept them. He thus wrote that:

. the emphasis laid on agriculture in the teachers' training courses, and in the elementary schools, were having an excellent effect and that education was becoming gradually associated more and more with rural activities.

But the Director of Education and his supporters in this endeavour had great odds against which they were working to establish this agricultural inclination to education. After being in a high mood at the end of 1933, the following year he had a different story to tell. The force of literary education was almost irresistible. He thus reported at the end of 1934, five years after the establishment of the Central Schools which included a lot of agricultural education in their curriculum that "the system still seemed too academic and left the students, who were unable to continue, stranded with little knowledge of real use to them". On this, the Missionary Education Secretaries agreed with the Director of Education especially because the "Central Schools with their vague curriculum offered little attraction to pupils leaving lower schools."

One reason why these Central Schools failed to attract society and the pupils is that their teachers were not deemed capable enough. This was stated thus by the CMS Education Secretary:

> It is to be regretted that the Central Schools have not functioned according to syllabus because of the lack of suitable staff, the schools having remained largely academic.

In his 1935 Education Report, the Director of Education lamented in the same way as the C.M.S. Education Secretary had done that "the Central Schools for the most part continued to disappoint because the teachers had failed to assimilate the ideals and aims of the syllabus". But the crux of the matter was that the Department of Education established these Central Schools without having first taken steps to train teachers who would run them with the skills that were needed. Consequently the policy could not be implemented. During the term of office of Sir Philip Mitchell these Central Schools were abolished in 1938 due to their lack of popularity in society and because Sir Philip Mitchell's policy was not for stressing practical education but literary education.

However, the primary school curriculum never dropped its agriculture lessons through the school gardens and the nature study lessons. The condition for qualified teachers to attend for a year at the agricultural institutions of Bukalasa, Arapai and Serere was, however, waived because it was costly.

The Colonial Office in London still as the source of policy on agricultural education continued to play its role. The de La Warr Commision which it sent to East Africa in 1937 to recommend the upgrading of the education system gave new guide-lines for the Uganda Protectorate government to follow in strengthening agricultural teaching in primary schools. That Commission recommended three important guide-lines namely:

As regarded teaching generally, agriculture should be the core around which all other subjects should revolve to give an agricultural bias to education "since the majority of those who left the primary schools had to live by the land".

The second important guide-line given by the de La Warr Commission regarded the siting of primary schools. The Commission recommended that each primary school should be "situated near a government experimental or training farm" and such a primary school should have "its own gardens and some animals attached to it".

Thirdly, the Commission recommended that text books "should be rural in outlook, containing stories about plants, animals, farmers and markets".

To emphasise this agricultural bias, the Commission went on even to recommend to the Uganda Protectorate government that:

> ...the payment of grants to primary schools should be conditional upon the provision of facilities for gardening, rural handcrafts, and of teachers and text books suitable for an integrally rural curriculum.

Indeed though the above approach was good, it was difficult to put into practice without the text-books and the teachers trained in that kind of work. Text books used to be imported from industrial Britain and teachers had been academically trained. Again what continued to be practised was agriculture on the primary school gardens as of old and some reference to plant life in the class-room in lessons called Nature Study. The whole thing looked academic.

From the mid 1940's there was a sustained campaign to see that agriculture in primary schools was given a more prominent place especially as a result of Governor John Hall's policy to educate through mass propaganda and demonstration of agricultural techniques. Governor Hall showed annoyance for the education system to have failed to make agriculture the basis of education and teachers to "have failed to eradicate from their pupils the belief that physical labour was socially degrading".

Rather than concentrate education on agriculture in schools which tended to be purely academic, Hall emphasised that this kind of education should be run mainly out of school through propaganda and extension services and the schools should join in this campaign which would affect both the adults out of schools and the pupils within schools.

While lessons in agriculture would continue in the primary schools through the school gardens, Hall also wanted to set up agricultural schools to be joined after primary six to form an alternative to the academic kind of post primary schools. Here we see a desire to re-establish schools along the defunct Central Schools which had failed during the mid 1930's due to lack of support from the society and due to failure of government to produce teachers equipped with the skills of running them. Nothing was done first however, to change these two obstacles by Governor Hall.

However, apart from the propaganda and agricultural extension services which were carried on by the Department of Public Relations and Social Welfare and by the Department of Agriculture, and apart from the usual lessons carried on in classrooms in the primary schools, Governor Hall's plans of the above farm schools did not materialise. But the propaganda was quite impressive.

The explanation why the Central Schools, Hall's projected post primary farm schools and later on the de Bunsen's agricultural secondary schools and farm schools were bound to fail, was to run them along side the already famous academic schools both primary and secondary. The solution which we still seek now and probably which will be resolved by putting in place the recommendations of the Senteza Kajubi Education Commission of 1987, is to have a curriculum that combines academic, technical and agricultural traits in one for any school. Then the parents of the pupils would have no chance to compare and contrast schools in terms of the curriculum.

The Binns Study Group of 1951 that visited East Africa from the Colonial Office in London to advise on further educational developments, gave an advice along the above lines. It advised that a curriculum should be worked out that would integrate academic, agricultural and technical studies at both primary and secondary school levels.

The above advice was unfortunately however, not used as the basis of the guide-lines for the de Bunsen Education Committee in 1952. Instead the de Busen Education Committee continued to recommend the continuation of the school gardens at primary level "to link the theoretical lessons on agriculture in the class-room with the realities outside it". At secondary school level the de Bunsen Education Committee recommended to build a group of District farm schools at which to train students wishing to be technical agriculturists while professional agriculturists would be trained in properly established agricultural secondary schools. Therefore the idea of the Binns Study Group whereby a curriculum combining academic, agricultural and technical skills in one, was not considered.

Even the changes suggested by the de Bunsen Education Committee did not materialise fully. What came to pass was that after the de Bunsen Education Committee recommendations, the teaching of agriculture disappeared from the primary schools. First of all, because pupils were gradually attending the primary course when still very young. Consequently the school garden of the pre-1950's began to get into the back ground and biology in the classroom dominated what was called agricultural education.

At secondary school level none of the envisaged agricultural secondary schools materialised because no parents and pupils were interested in them and also because no Headmaster was keen on running such schools amidst the clamour for academic secondary education from society and the great opportunities which lay ahead for those relatively few students who went through an academic course at secondary school level. Thus Crighton, Headmaster of one of the proposed agricultural secondary schools at Ntare in Mbarara wrote:

> I did not intend to run a farm school when I knew that University men would be wanted more and could not see much future in the labour market for agriculturists with four years senior secondary but poor academic certificates.

Mr. Crighton was not even a graduate of agriculture as had been suggested by the de Bunsen Education Committee that these projected agricultural secondary

Agricultural Education

schools should be headed by such graduates. Similarly, Sir Samuel Baker Secondary School which was supposed to be run as a secondary school along agricultural lines, was not run so when it got established later after 1952.

Moreover, Makerere University College was the target of every capable secondary school candidate. Though that University College ran courses in agriculture leading to the acquisition of a Diploma and then a Degree, these courses never excited students in schools. Usually the agriculture courses at Makerere were joined each year by a couple of students, and even these were students who had followed a purely academic science course back in schools.

The success of any policy depends very much on the support the government manages to get from the people. But there was no support for a policy on agricultural education from the people. The people's view towards the aim of school education was the cause of the problem. Agriculture was not one of the subjects which they expected their children to learn at school. "Parents sent their boys to high schools not to learn to drive bullock wagons and to look after cattle, but to learn to be fitted for posts of high standing", as one son of Sir Apollo Kaggwa had said back in the 1930's.

Then the policy of teaching agriculture in schools faced the problem of teachers. Teachers did not see their role as meant to inculcate agricultural skills. Moreover they had not been trained to teach agricultural skills and the appreciation of work on farms. They had gone through a mainly literary course themselves both at school and at the training centres with make-shift agricultural lessons.

The Binns Study Group of 1951 capably wrote a comment on the attitude of the teachers themselves as follows:

> Realising the need for education in most parts of East Africa and Central Africa to be related to rural life, the authorities have from time to time prescribed a proportion of practical work to be done in all schools, and the schools have done their best to comply with the instructions thus given, in spite of the opposition of some of the African staff and pupils. We have seen children marched to a store and told to draw hoes from it and then go and dig the ground rather aimlessly while the teacher kept one eye on the clock and everybody obviously hoped for the end of the lesson.

To those of the adults who were attending school during the visit of the Binns Study Group, the above observation was so realistic that they cannot fail to credit the Group's keen observation.

The real approach to the teaching of agriculture was also discouraging. Time for agriculture could be devoted to clearing up the school compound, building a teacher's house or church and here no reference was made to any theoretical studies of agriculture that might have been talked about in the classroom.

Those of us who studied when the school garden at primary level was a widely used means of teaching agriculture, remember all this kind of thing so clearly.

We saw no difference betweren the drudgery of hoeing at home and that carried out at school as lessons.

Hoeing at school which was called agricultural education, was made worse by the fact that it made pupils dirty while they were dressed in their clean uniforms. Moreover, at times the teachers punished pupils by telling them to take hoes during the most inconvenient times of the day; either at mid-day when it was so hot and when other pupils were resting, or at the end of the day when they were all tired and had to walk long distances home late, or during the time when lessons on academic subjects were going on in the classroom. On occasions of this nature nobody ever expected to see any good agriculture practices being used or even learnt.

However, punishment of pupils by being told to go and cultivate did not necessarily make pupils hate agriculture as it has been claimed in much of modern literature of the post-independence days. It only showed pupils that agriculture was not a school subject to be taken seriously. Because while one had to solve say a mathematical problem, when it go to agriculture, one just had to apply the same kind of energy and indifference to it as one applied to that exercise back at home.

Moreover, the colonial education system undervalued agricultural education. There were weekly, monthly, termly and yearly tests in academic subjects. The pride of any pupil lay in scoring reasonable marks in those tests and indeed they were the ones that singled out a pupil as a brilliant learner and fit for joining such schools of long time academic respect as Kisubi College, Buddo College, Namilyango College, Busoga College Mwiri, Nyakasura School, Gayaza High School, Nabumali High School and St. Peter's College Tororo. Such tests never appeared in agriculture.

The colonial education system also connected agriculture with a stigma. When the de Busen Education Committee instituted numerous farm schools in 1952, such schools were to be joined by those pupils who had failed to score high marks to join academic schools of the above description. Naturally, such pupils faced chagrin from society as failures. No wonder that by 1960 those farm schools were closing down very fast for lack of pupils. Besides, the courses in those farm schools were run by teachers who were not convinced of the benefit to those pupils who joined those schools. The managers of those farm schools were being employed for a living and they had no training for this kind of education. Moreover those candidates who joined those farm schools saw no chance of being employed after school. They were being told that after graduating, they would go back to the land to initiate their own employment. Any teaching that did not show a possible opening for paid employment during the colonial days, had a very little chance of attracting pupils, parents and their fees and indeed it could hardly get any success. The pupils wanted to get away from sweated labour and the routine of village life.

If the attitude of the people is opposed to the success of a policy, it can be changed by obvious gains out of a policy. The policy of agricultural education lacked visible profits accruing from it vis-a-vis an academic kind of education. The person who followed successfully an academic kind of education easily got a paid job and began to see his economic and social status going up. If prices of crops were increased and a person could see how easily he could become rich by utilising intensive agricultural knowledge given to him in school, the attention given to agricultural education in school would have increased. But prices of cash crops were kept at a very low level. One needed high prices that would show that a person engaged in agriculture could earn more than the person who hoped to go and work in an office. Instead, the government from the 1940's was paying low prices to farmers than what their crops actually fetched from the world market and keeping the money back in a reserve fund. Yet rather than paying higher prices to farmers, the money from the reserve fund was channelled into providing other services which did not encourage farming methods, such as tarmacing roads.

Indeed this problem was not for the education system alone. Other Departments of government had to be involved to make the agricultural education a success. This is why the Castle Education Commission of 1963 remarked thus:

> With almost wearisome re-iteration people were being told that agriculture was the backbone of Uganda's economy and that in the rapid and sound development of productive forms of land-use lay the principal means of raising the levels of health, education and prosperity. Paradoxically the problems of agricultural education were not primarily education. They were intimately bound up with the solution of economic, technical, and social problems over which the Ministry of Education had no control-systems of land tenure, improved land use, finance and marketing, research and development, traditions and tribal customs being among them.

Indeed the Binns Study Group had earlier on in 1951 wisely pointed out that "the attack on agricultural ignorance had to be made simultaneously by the schools and the agencies of adult education."

Moreover, a policy to work well one needs to identify it with the general way of life of the people. The school was a separate entity within the village, teaching new values not shared at large by society. The hope expressed by Hussey in 1925 "the village school to become the centre of village life" had not materialised even by 1960. Consequently any agricultural lessons in the school were looked at as meant to familiarise the school goers with what goes on in society rather than what these people should do after leaving school. For example, even when a boy returned home and went hoeing in his parents' gardens he saw no connection between that exercise and the agricultural lessons he had learnt at school. This was due to the fact that in Africa, school education was looked at as for giving skills to be used in the white man's employment connected with office work.

A policy whose results show that one gains by following it also commends itself to the people. In Uganda by 1960, one hardly saw any progressive farmer as a result of his agricultural studies. Those people who taught agriculture and those who worked in government demonstration farms, all showed signs of prosperity which also meant a high status. But this was not due to their agricultural occupation but due to their being government wage earners. They never experienced the uncertainty a farmer experiences due to the vagaries of the weather and to the constantly falling prices. If some of them had become cultivators and showed that it could pay to be a farmer by using agricultural knowledge studied from schools, the schools would have had an easier fight to put up with to interest pupils and parents in agricultural education. But even when the plants which these workers on government demonstration farms failed, those workers' wages were not reduced.

While however, we may blame the above causes as plaguing the policy of agricultural education, we must also admit that there has been in our society on the part of so many people, failure for a desire to change. This attitude prevents people from going out of their way to try out new methods to better their situation in life. Once they get some money out of growing some small amounts of cash crops to afford to pay for the bare minimum necessities of life, they do not feel bothered any more. This is what has happened in regard to putting into practice agricultural guide, even though ineffectually taught at school and through government agricultural propaganda. Even if we consider attitudes, ineffectual teaching and low prices given to cultivators, the writer does not see why all these should have in the last analysis contributed to failure of bettering agriculture in the Uganda society. The majority of those people who attended schools during the period under review, any way had to go back to the land.

This fact was ever before their eyes. For example, between 1950 and 1960 only 8.9% of the pupils completing the primary section went on to join Junior Secondary One. This percentage was even lower betweren 1920 and 1950. So boys and girls who joined primary schools knew that it was rather the exception that escaped work in the gardens in all their lives after school.

The problem of low prices still could have been minimised by growing more cash crops instead of less and this would have come about by taking on some guide picked up from schools and from government propaganda. Even if a person's attitude is decidedly against agriculture and yet he cannot but engage in it all his life, he might as well use sensible methods, produce more and better his condition in life. This inertia for example, is seen where a person has got a plantation of bananas next to another person who possesses cattle. The cow manure is heaped in a bush and left to disappear under soil erosion or to rot away completely. Yet such a person must have heard probably unwillingly at school that the effect of such cow manure on crops is gigantic. Probably he might have seen it himself one day being used on a government demonstration farm. But such a person is content with going on with the time old methods of cultivating the land until all the good soil is washed away in his wake. Thus the Binns Study Group lamented but wrongly blamed the education system.

Agricultural Education

But in many places, even in these fertile regions, Africans are still content with a bare subsistence level because education has not yet been able to overcome wasteful habits and ineffective methods.

While all is said and done however, agricultural education efforts through schools and extension services out of school, had some impact on the people's approach to agriculture. There is evidence to show that agriculture during the colonial and missionary period did change for the better. Soil conservation was practised, crop rotation was adopted, new crops were introduced and grown extensively and pruning and pest control were carried out by a sizeable number of people in Uganda.

By 1960, a Ugandan cultivator was a better cultivator than his counterpart of say 1900, and all this was the result of agricultural education through both the agricultural extension services and through lessons in primary schools on agriculture. He was also alert to the price mechanism of crops.

6 The Development of Technical Education

The Colonial Office through its Advisory Committee on African Education and the Uganda Protectorate government through the Department of Education, were the main sources of educational policies on technical education in Uganda. The Missionaries on the other hand cooperated fully in implementing these policies. But at the same time through the approach to the problems regarding technical and commercial education, the Department of Education tended to be an adverse influence to these policies. Through its approach, it created an attitude in the pupils and in the society at large that technical and commercial education was for students who were below average and therefore incapable of coping with academic subjects.

In its policy, the Colonial Office in London in 1925 recommended the teaching of technical skills in four ways. One way had to be through government work-shops on apprenticeship basis. The second way was to be in special instructional work-shops on a production basis. The third way was through properly instituted technical schools and the fourth way was to be through primary schools where village crafts would have to be taught.

The basis for this recommendation was that there was need for self sufficiency for technical jobs in the colonies. These jobs should be done by Africans instead of relying entirely on labour of this nature imported from India as it had begun to be observed. The British officers were expected to be enough to compose the back bone of the specialised technical labour force and the local people would do the menial technical jobs under the supervision of the British technicians.

The Uganda Protectorate government interpreting the Colonial Office policy passed several supporting strategies and guide-lines as to how to approach technical education in order "to produce those native artisans to replace some imported Asians."

To achieve the above aim, three kinds of arrangements were made by both the Department of Education and by the Missionaries. One was found in existence when formal government education policies began to operate from 1925. Here the Missionaries had already set up their technical schools through which they trained tradesmen to help in the building of mission houses and in the making of furniture used in those buildings. Normally graduates from these few technical schools found ready employment in the missionary set up because at each mission station there was a workshop to service the station and its outlying feeder churches and schools. Thus the White Fathers founded Kisubi Technical School in 1911 and the Verona Fathers now called the Comboni Missionaries had Gulu and Arua Technical Schools. The C.M.S. relied on the Uganda Company having given their industrial school founded on Namirembe

Technical Education

hill in 1898 to that company in 1903 when K.E. Borup its initiator founded the Uganda Company and resigned from missionary employment to concentrate on business enterprise.

The second arrangement for technical education was carried on in government departments. The government had technical work-shops serving as schools attached to the Department of Lands and Survey, the Medical Department and to the Public Works Department. The purpose for these three technical workshops cum schools was to produce much wanted technicians with skills necessary to the running of the work carried on by the above specialised Departments. Training in these departmental schools did not stop until 1953 when all technical education was streamlined to meet all needs of the country and to stop duplication that had begun to be observable in the above three departments.

The third arrangement of teaching technical skills was through properly established government technical schools.

In 1921 the Uganda Protectorate government set up its first technical school on Makerere hill which from 1922 was renamed Kampala Technical School to differentiate it from Makerere College both of which were on the same hill. The second technical school under the government was established in 1930 at the foot of Mt. Masaba near Mbale called Elgon Technical School.

These technical schools were being joined at the initial stage by pupils graduating from primary schools. In effect these were called trade schools because they were giving a few artisan courses designed to produce an artisan whereas proper technical schools impart both manipulation skills and qualities of fore-manship. Shoe-making, tailoring, carpentry and plumbing formed the core of the courses. This situation was only changed from 1951 after the re-organization of technical courses on a new basis because of new economic demands in the Uganda society which needed other kinds of technical skills.

The fourth arrangement for technical education was included in the primary curriculum. Here a pupil was supposed to acquire the African traditional handcraft skills to produce such simple articles for domestic use as mats, stools, embroidery, baskets, brooms and ropes. Skills of this nature were encouraged because the majority of pupils did not go beyond primary schools let alone completing the primary school section. So if such skills were picked up by the pupils they would add to their worth as country side dwellers.

From 1930 in the drive to reduce literary education, the next set of schools were streamlined into two separate sections. One section was called the Middle Schools and were intended to give a purely literary course and the other section was called the Central Schools running a practical course combining subjects in agriculture, carpentry, pottery, iron work, brick making, building and typing. The fees in these Central Schools were appreciably lower than those paid in the academic Middle Schools to attract pupils to these practical Central Schools.

Some successes began to be registered as to the efforts of developing this technical practical side of education through the Central Schools. But the success of these Central Schools was short lived. In 1938 they were discontinued because they began to be unpopular as far back as 1933. Also Sir Philip Mitchell who had become Governor of Uganda in 1935 was primarily interested in academic education to produce Ugandans who could take up junior administrative jobs in the Protectorate administration.

With the discontinuation of the Central Schools, there remained two venues of producing pupils with technical skills through the education system: through the primary school course using the handwork lessons and through the proper technical schools.

The failure and closure of the Central Schools was really unfortunate. This was an experiment of certain originality. Its success could have nipped in the bud the perennial criticism of the colonial education to have been too literary. But those Central Schools could not have succeeded once run side by side with the academic Middle Schools which were literary and favoured by the top policy maker, Sir Philip Mitchell and by the parents. The salvation of those Central Schools would have come only if the academic Middle School curriculum was made part and parcel with the curriculum of the Central Schools. This way the Uganda Protectorate education system would have produced its own brand of education which the critics would have liked to see running all over tropical British areas. This would have been comprehensive education well before its introduction even in Britain during the 1950's.

When these Central Schools had disappeared, one teacher Anselm Musoke, a graduate of Bikira Teacher Training School of the 1930's ran their curriculum mixed with the curriculum of the academic Middle Schools in his own private school which he opened in 1938. It was known as Kanadda Rural Industries School, a few miles away from Wakiso off Hoima Road near Kampala. The school proved successful but being alone in the whole country, its effect was not easy to be felt where missionary schools on a different and more favourite curriculum of the academic Middle School dominated the forum.

A Director of Education of the 1950's who never knew of the practical Central Schools of the 1930's, seeing the success of this school, Kanadda Rural Indstries School, lamented that its graduates after primary education were joining mission junior secondary schools not based on the practical curriculum of Kanadda Rural Industries School and thereby lost the good principles they had picked up.

The technical schools which remained when the Central Schools were discontinued in 1938 were post primary institutions. But they were very few in comparison with the literary secondary schools and in comparison with the pupils who were completing primary schools with no opportunity to join the academic secondary schools. For example, between 1935 and 1952 there were two government technical schools namely Kampala Technical School and Elgon Technical School in Mbale. To these were added four mission technical schools: St. Joseph Technical School Kisubi run by the White Fathers, Nsambya Technical School of the Mill Hill Fathers and Gulu and Arua Technical Schools under the Verona Fathers now called the Comboni Missionaries. Any other technical education that could be obtained was that through the attached schools to the

Technical Education

Departments of Lands and Survey, the Medical Department and the Public Works Department and in a number of mission technical small schools described by the Department of Education more as workshops for producing mission furniture than technical schools.

The reason for the small number of these technical schools can be looked for from the missionary and colonial view of the time. That point of view was that the production of qualified manpower had to keep in step with the available level of paid employment in the country lest one produced a surplus which would be a disturbing factor in the society. This view and the large number of literary secondary schools, diminished the great value of technical education in the opinion of the people. Once literary education was provided for more than technical education and indeed for also agricultural education, the society had nothing to do but to value literary education more than technical and agricultural education.

The role of the Colonial Office as the source of policy on technical and agricultural education continued to be stressed through the guidelines which the de La Warr Commission of 1937 from London gave to the Uganda Protectorate administration. That Commission advised to follow what was happening in Britain by attaching workshops to primary and junior secondary schools to teach woodwork and metal-work to boys, and kitchen work, sewing and laundry to girls.

This advice of attaching workshops to schools, did not materialize until 1952. One reason for their not being established was that Sir Philip Mitchell was more interested in developing academic secondary and higher education. Consequently, he was not keen at seeing a more expensive outlay on workshops in primary schools to accommodate the advice of the de La Warr Commission of 1937. So handwork lessons continued in the primary schools and trade skills in the few technical schools mentioned above went on with no dramatic changes from what they had been before from 1925.

Though in 1944 the Chief Secretary at Entebbe set up a Technical Training Committee to shape government policy towards technical education due to the war difficulties between 1939 and 1945, the plans set up by the Technical Training Committee were not implemented. Consequently, technical teaching in the schools got less attention. After the war in 1945, the attention was turned to out of schools. Makeshift government technical training centres were set up in Gulu, Lira, Mbarara, Hoima, Masindi, Fort Portal and Masaka, to accommodate ex-service men ad consolidate the technical skills which they had learnt in the war. It was felt desirable that these ex-service men would return to civil life with these technical skills consolidated and use them for their benefit and for the benefit of the whole countryside. This exercise which was concluded in 1950 proved futile however, since "most of those ex-soldiers were illiterate or semi-literate and many of them, finding themselves unable to sustain their position as skilled craftsmen, sold their tools and lapsed into casual labourers."

History and Development of Education

From 1950 the industrial life of the country took a different turn. Small scale industries had developed and needed an increasingly large number of technicians whom the then existing set up of producing these technicians could not support. And since many technical jobs with attractive pay appeared on the scene, this changed the attitude of many young men who hitherto, "had tended to despise any form of education and training with a bias towards manual occupation". To meet this challenge, the Uganda Protectorate government set up a Technical Education Development Committee to advise government on the necessary policy towards technical education.

At the same time there was a feeling in the Colonial Office in London for the need to give a new direction to education in the British Colonial set up in Africa. In this respect, Dr. Harlow, Assistant Technical Education Adviser to the Colonial Office in London visited Uganda in 1951.

On the advice of Dr. Harlow, four developments were suggested in technical education which the 1952 de Bunsen Education Committee recommended. One was the setting up of workshops at nearly every primary school and at a few junior secondary schools depending on the availability of teachers capable of teaching some carpentry. At the primary stage, the workshops continued to serve the traditional handwork purpose for helping to produce the time old African crafts. At the secondary school level, these workshops were geared to producing carpentry articles. But by and large these workshops at primary and junior secondary schools served very little purpose. It was at only a very few schools that some useful work was done. At such schools there used to be a keen teacher interested in seeing the technical skills being imparted to pupils.

The second development was the establishment of technical schools under the names of Rural Trade Schools, Farm Schools for boys and Homecraft Centres for girls. These were post primary village artcraft schools to be attended for two years. The purpose for these Rural Trade Schools was for rounding off a pupil's primary education with tangible skills for using as a useful upcountry dweller. The skills so acquired were not meant for taking to towns to look for paid employment. On completion however, the graduates of these Rural Trade Schools rushed to towns where they had to compete with those graduates of the formal technical schools and they lost out in the competition. Of course this factor made the Rural Trade Schools unpopular and by 1960 the government was beginning to abolish them, turning them into academic secondary schools.

These Rural Trade Schools proved unpopular because apart from their failure to help a person to get a paid employment, they were supposed to be attended by those boys and girls who had failed to score high enough marks at the Primary Leaving Examinations. So they were supposed to have been failures. Many times most of the pupils who had joined these Rural Trade Schools were trying to work their way back into the system by doing the Primary Leaving Examination again which would enable them to gain entrance into the academic secondary schools.

By 1960 there were 66 Rural Trade Schools for boys and 20 Homecraft Centres for girls in Uganda. But they were attracting few pupils.

Technical Education

The third development from 1951 was the up-grading of the old technical schools: Elgon Technical School, St. Joseph Technical School Kisubi, Gulu Technical School and Arua Technical School. All these were up-graded to the status of junior secondary technical schools. Besides these old ones, several more junior secondary technical schools were established under the Uganda Protectorate and the local government administrations. Such technical schools under the government were: Lira Technical School, Soroti Technical School, Fort Portal Technical School, Kahaya Technical School in Mbarara, Masaka Technical School and Kabale Technical School to mention but a few of them.

The fourth development was that the Kampala Technical Institute at Nakawa was established as a senior secondary technical school. Students at this institute followed courses leading to the City and Guild Examination of London. Out of these it was envisaged to get students who would proceed to the Royal Technical College Nairobi which opened its doors to students in 1956 and thereafter read for degree and diploma courses.

The above sketch completes the development in technical education during the colonial days which development was also intended to reduce academic or literary education from the education system.

But there were many influences working in the opposite direction to hinder policies on technical education from producing the desired results. Technical skills at primary school level which were intended to be obtained from the handwork lessons faced two problems: the attitude of both pupils and teachers and the amateur nature of teaching those artcraft skills. By and large there developed an attitude among pupils, teachers and the public at large that education involved literary training, hence the remark by the Director of Education that "Africans thought that education had to do with only books". Practical training on the agricultural or technical side once introduced was viewed as a recreation from the exacting nature of academic studies or was meant to detract a learner wastefully from the correct route. The result was that both teachers and pupils were not keenly interested in artcraft lessons called handwork lessons at primary school level.

One cause of this attitude was the failure by the society and by some teachers alike to realise the great importance of practical skills which are productive. By this we mean skills that help to create other things tangibly such as chairs, tables and the like. One would have thought that at this early period the necessity of this would have been really realised because the above mentioned articles and others of the same nature were not easily available. Hence the echo of Stanely's letter which he wrote on the request of Kabaka Muteesa I in 1875, "it is the practical missionary that is needed".

Moreover the teachers were more of amateurs than carefully trained people who would be in schools to pass on the correct practical skills meant to be acquired. R.A. Snoxall who worked for a long time in Uganda from the 1940s to 1967, partly blamed this on the courses in the Teacher Training Colleges. Consequently, practical skill lessons at primary school level lacked emphasis, imagination and enthusiasm on the part of the teachers. Thus the Director of

Education in his 1950 Annual Education Report remarked on the teachers' attitude:

> It has become the custom to read year after year reports from the provinces as follows: 'No handwork has been done this term owing to lack of materials'. 'The teacher intends to begin handwork lessons soon". 'Handwork periods have been used for extra cultivation or cutting the grass in the compound'. Some schools in the country have specialist carpentry teachers on their staff, but it is strange with what regularity it has been reported that the carpentry master was not seen or that carpentry had to be stopped because the tools had been stolen.

Therefore due to this lack of interest and enthusiasm on the part of teachers which arose from lack of proper training and from lack of belief in the future benefit in practical skills, when a lesson for this kind of teaching began, there was a big tendency to leave pupils to practise by themselves crafts carried on in villages and which the pupils themselves knew. The pupils tended to see no educational value in this.

Above all, the examination system was such that it did no take into account this practical side of education. One had to get a first class Primary Leaving Certificate to be selected to enter into one of the famous secondary schools in the county, this practical side of education was not taken into account. It was not even examinable. Results of examinations played and still play a very important role in influencing what to emphasise by teachers in teaching in schools and to value as worthwhile content by students.

Indeed on School Open Days, teachers displayed the articles made by pupils for parents to see and even buy. But once a pupil who had made the most impressive artcraft articles did not score good marks at the Primary Leaving Examination needed for entry to a Junior secondary school, he was considered a failure rather than a pupil who had first class abilities in technical skills, and who could be a first class citizen in society as a technician or engineer.

The technical schools also suffered in the same way. Consequently, proper technical education failed to catch popularity due to the problems of people's attitude, teaching and prospects vis-a-vis the prospects which were awaiting a person who had gone through an academic course.

The curriculum of those technical schools up to the 1950s was narrow. They taught carpentry, shoe-making, tailoring, plumbing, masonry, brick-making and some mechanics courses. But then those courses tended to be the easiest to pick up even by those people who did not go to school if they got into the employment of Asians. The consequence was that a person with the above skills had nothing glamouring about him. A group of teachers in the Western Province implicitly pointed out this defect to the Binns Study Group in 1951 when they sent a memorandum to it in the following manner:

> The kind of education given to us does not make us fit to stand on our own feet. For instance, when a person leaves the Kampala Technical School he is regarded

as a person who has attained the highest technical education in this country. I wonder whether the Department of Education realizes that in the whole of the famous Kampala Technical School no one can make either a needle or a pen-nib. We would like to have a kind of technical education which will enable us to make machines (not to repair them), to make cloth (not to cut ready-made cloth).

Even the teaching failed to fire the imagination of the students that technical courses needed a lot of intelligence, imagination and inventiveness. There were many technical gadgets coming from Europe for the first time here in Africa and they were a wonder. Yet they were not being made by academicians who worked in offices. One wonders why the teaching should not have shown to society that this was where the power of the white man lay rather than in speaking his language and copying his letters with technical complicated machines made back in Europe by technicians.

One reason why the teaching of technical skills failed to fire the imagination of students is that the majority of teachers of these technical subjects were not qualified as teachers. They had been successful tradesmen in a particular trade and were drafted in to teach. "To handle tools correctly is not enough in a technical teacher". as the Binns Study Group pointed out.

Alfred Wallace Wood, in his study of the Educational Policies and Social Change in Uganda, points out that teaching in technical schools was left to amateurs - usually European former army corporals and bridge mechanics, who might have got some mechanical skills back in Europe. Also for lack of technical teachers, African technicians who had shown success at things in the field such as in masonry, brick-making, carpentry, shoe-making, were brought in to teach. But such people were good only at one kind of trade and yet they were left to run different courses of the curriculum for students and without having been given before hand any teaching methods. Therefore they had no patience to stick to a syllabus.

Because of this kind of approach to technical education, "many school boys failed to appreciate as did their headmasters, that a real craftsman must be intelligent as well as having manual skills and that the openings for such people were many and the pay attractive."

Social attitudes also acted as an adverse influence to technical education. There had been a prevalent conviction in our society that carpenters, shoe-makers and builders could not become rich. This indeed implied the low nature of their earnings arising from the low nature of their training and skills acquired from the technical schools. This also implied lack of business acumen on the part of people technically trained. During those days of Asian presence in Uganda, the majority of the technical graduates were being employed usefully for the enrichment of the Asians with business acumen. Asians were running prosperous furniture marts, selling articles made by graduates of those technical schools whom the Asian businessmen locked up at the back of their workshops to produce those articles. This also implies the lack of connection between education and real life, initiative and imagination.

Then the Asian and European technicians in both private and public sectors tended to hold the most attractive technical jobs. So the African technicians were held in the third category whether they had better education or not and their pay was consequently low. Thus the African technicians were always in a subordinate status, or were assistants to the European or to Asian technicians. Indeed this was the status quo during the colonial days even for any person who had gone through an academic course and held an employment. But this made those boys going through these technical courses feel that they were not being trained up to the standard. On the 28th February 1956, Honourable J.B. Babiiha touched on this question which had been simmering for a long time when he asked in the Legislative Council as to "when it was expected to train fully qualified engineers in Uganda to stop being assistants to Asian and European technicians".

The feeling that the courses in technical schools were not up to standard made the students in 1957 at Kampala Technical Institute at Nakawa to go on strike. The students wanted to be called full engineers on graduation rather than assistant technicians. This contention was disallowed by the Commission of Inquiry which the Uganda Protectorate Government set up to inquire in the courses at Kampala Technical Institute. The students were told that they could be given such status only after going through the Royal Technical College in Nairobi.

This state of affairs left a lot of dissatisfaction in the minds of boys joining technical schools in Uganda for they continued to feel that their courses were not up to standard and consequently the majority of boys went to those technical schools after failing to get access to academic secondary schools which offered chances to an entry into Makerere University College. Since there had been no attempts to create a powerful department of technology at Makerere to give chance to students with a technical bias, students continued to feel that they were being made to follow inferior courses in the technical schools.

Indeed the de La Warr Commission from the Colonial Office in 1937 had advised the Uganda Protectorate Government to create a competent department of technology at Makerere. But this had not been heeded and indeed failure to heed that advice lost a very good chance of enhancing technical education in Uganda. Of course the operators of Makerere College were graduates of British traditional Universities where technical education tended to be considered as belonging to a different kind of education system. For example, the course of engineering that had been running at Makerere from its very inception in 1921 was dropped by Turner, Principal of Makerere College early in the 1940s because he had no faith in producing "narrow specialists". He contended that the world had never been ruled by specialists but by men of broad studies in humanities. In the above contention of Turner, he was only emphasising the line of thought of British Universities at the time and before that time which Ashby said:

> The industrial revolution in Britain was accomplished by hard heads and clever hands. Men like Arkwright and Crompton had no systematic education in science or technology. Britain's industrial strength lay in its amateurs and self-made men. In this rise of British industry the English universities played no part whatever.

Technical Education

This comment of Prof. Ashby fits well the Katwe artisans in Kampala.
But the above view applied to Makerere College wrought disaster to the success of the technical education in the education system of Uganda. This meant that as the academic secondary schools were ever bettering their courses to produce students to enter into Makerere College, the technical schools were not doing the same. For example, St. Mary's College Kisubi had as long a life as St. Joseph Technical School Kisubi, each in the proximity of the other. But the courses of the latter school remained static while those of the former developed from Junior to Senior and to Higher Secondary school status.

Those boys who failed to get enough marks for joining St. Mary's College Kisubi at Primary School level, were the ones who were sent to St. Joseph Technical School. Old boys who have gone through St. Mary's College Kisubi have had a long tradition of listening to chagrin remarks by the students of St. Mary's College passed on to the students of St. Joseph Technical School. The inferiority complex that those remarks developed in the boys at St. Joseph Technical School was enough to keep one's son from contemplating taking up a technical career.

In conclusion, while there was a consistent education policy towards the provision of practical education during the colonial days, this kind of education was relegated into second place, and the teaching staff for this kind of education was not as properly trained as that for literary education. This made the courses weak and since the recipients of these courses were considered weak, they faced chagrin from society. Since the pay for technical graduates was relatively lower than that for graduates of literary schools, this led to low status in society of technicians. Consequently technical education attracted less attention in comparison to literary education in Uganda.

7 The Establishment of Private Schools in Uganda

Introduction

The term private schools was applied in Uganda to schools which were not run by the Missionaries and by the government. But we need to realise that missionary schools were also private since they did not belong to the government. This set of schools first appeared in the country in 1925 on the initiative of African teachers. These schools were getting no assistance from the colonial government in terms of money, professional supervision and advice until 1953. Until that year, they developed under great opposition by the Missionaries.

Today the existence of private schools in the education system of Uganda is taken for granted but the rise of these private schools during the colonial period was a stiff struggle which merits a full account for us to appreciate the determination and struggle of the pioneers of these schools in this country.

Reuben Ssebbanja Mukasa who in 1937 founded the African Greek Orthodox Church in East Africa was the first teacher to open up a private school in 1925 at Degeya near Bombo in Luweero District. He trained as a teacher at the Mukono Teacher Training School which was then being run by the Church Missionary Society in Uganda.

On graduation at Mukono Teacher Training School in 1911, Ssebbanja Mukasa taught in several Protestant primary schools under the Church Missionary Society. But by 1925 he decided to break with the Church Missionary Society authorities in Namirembe and start his own schools. These schools would have no connection with the Education Secretary General of the Protestant Church at Namirembe. In the hope of getting financial assistance from Europe, Ssebbanja Mukasa was ordained priest in the Greek Orthodox Church in 1937 as Father Spartas and dropped the name of Reuben. From that time he established the African Greek Orthodox Church all over East Africa and schools and hospitals like the Roman Catholic and the Protestant Missionaries. He became a Bishop in 1968 and died in 1976.

Chwa II Memorial College at Namungoona about eight Kilometers away from Kampala along the Kampala-Hoima Road is the most famous private school in Uganda which Fr. Spartas founded. It is still going strong together with a beautiful church and a good hospital under competent management. Indeed Fr. Spartas helped to establish other private schools under the African Greek Orthodox Church in Uganda and in the rest of East Africa.

Dr. Ernest Balintuma Kalibbala joined Fr. Spartas in establishing private schools in Uganda. He was also a qualified teacher from Mukono Teacher

Private Schools

Training School. He taught in several schools of the Church Missionary Society. In 1927 he went to study in the United States of America at Tuskegee Institute in the state of Alabama. He returned to Uganda in 1930 with a B.A. Degree. Kalibbala was subsequently appointed Education Officer at the Education Headquarters of the Church Missionary Society at Namirembe. But he resigned after working there for a few years and opened up his own private secondary school, called Aggrey Memorial School at Bunnamwaya about 15 Km from Kampala on Kampala-Entebbe Road. Kalibbala's followers founded in 1942 a sister Primary School known as Aggrey Memorial Primary School near the Kabaka's lake at Mengo. Kalibbala returned to the United States of America in 1939 for further studies and got a Doctorate in Philosophy. But his secondary school at Bunnamwaya continues to exist up to the present day.

Anselm Musoke was the third pioneer of the private schools in Uganda. He had qualified as a teacher at Bikira Teacher Training School near Kyotera in Rakai District which was under the management of the Roman Catholic White Fathers.

On graduation, Anselm Musoke taught in several Roman Catholic schools. But in 1938 he broke away from the authorities of the Roman Catholic Education Secretary General at Nsambya and went to establish his own private school at Kanadda Village, a few miles away from Wakiso on the Kampala-Hoima Road in the neighbourhood of Ttemangalo, close by the home of Dr. Samson Kisekka.

These private schools and those which were established later by others were famous for enrolling even students from Kenya, Tanzania, Malawi and Zambia. Registers of Chwa II Memorial College and of Aggrey Memorial School at Bunnamwaya had no less than 3500 students every year from 1955 to 1962.

Nearly half of the students came from the above countries. This shows how popular these private schools became all over East Africa and Central Africa. Those which were founded after these early private schools were no less popular and they were similarly enrolling nearly the same number of pupils from Uganda, from the rest of East Africa and from Central Africa. The best representative of them is Light College Katikamu near Masuuliita in Mpigi District founded in 1948 by Kiberu, Kivumbi and Yake Musoke.

Many people who subsequently held important posts in Kenya, Tanzania, Malawi, Uganda and Zambia after these countries had regained their independence had their education in these private schools because the missionary and government schools in those countries were not enough for the nationals there.

Why some Ugandans began to establish private schools
The following were some of the reasons why some Ugandans pioneered the establishment of private schools in Uganda.

The Protestant and the Roman Catholic Missionaries did not give chance to the Ugandan teachers to have a say in the direction of the schools such that

Ugandans who had good and progressive ideas as to how education should be in this country, had no opportunity to suggest their good ideas and to make sure that those ideas were put into practice in the schools. "We were tired of being called and treated like boys," Bishop Spartas told the writer when interviewed in 1969. Dr. Kalibbala added:

> I was the only person who had a Degree in the Offices of the Education Secretary General at Namirembe. But when the white Missionaries came from the Districts for advice, they always by-passed my office and went to ask for advice from their fellow white men,

Secondly, the above three men were dis-satisfied with the curriculum which the colonial system was following. That curriculum emphasised too much reading, writing and arithmetic at all levels of the education structure.

Consequently, a student qualified in those schools run by the Missionaries without any other skills which he would use on his own to do things or to make things. A graduate of those schools left them and went to look for jobs in government departments and in company establishments usually owned by Asians who despised the Africans, as Dr. Kalibbala stated. Such graduates had no skills to stand on their own.

When questioned about their determination to open their own schools when the majority of Ugandans at that time thought that it was only the White men who possessed knowledge, the pioneers told the writer that they were annoyed at seeing Ugandan graduates from schools going to look for jobs in the Indian shops, and they said that an education which made a person to seek jobs in the establishment of another person in the presence of so many opportunities for making things, was meant for making Ugandans slaves. Therefore these men never respected the education which was being given in the schools of the Missionaries.

"When could we ever make a needle or a pin with this kind of literary education?" Mr. Anselm Musoke wondered when being interviewed by the writer one day at his home in Kanadda in 1969. "When I saw that the missionary education was taking the Ugandans nowhere, I took the curriculum and banged it on the table of the Education Secretary at Lubaga in whose schools I was teaching and told him that I had left his employment to go and start my own schools," he continued to tell the writer.

Therefore those pioneers of private schools in Uganda began to set up schools determined to teach practical skills combined with academic knowledge to pupils and students. Anselm Musoke's private school at Kanadda-Wakiso ran a curriculum which combined both the academic and practical parts that even impressed the Department of Education as a school based on original ideas and quite progressive. But the Director of Education lamented in his 1948 Annual Education Report that the good work done by Anselm Musoke was being spoilt by the mission schools because when the boys left his school and joined secondary schools of the Missionaries they had to follow literary education and the skills which had been acquired in Musoke's school were not improved on.

Unfortunately however, these early pioneers of the private schools failed to make into a reality their hope of running schools which combined both academic and practical subjects and their pupils preferred education which would give them white-collar jobs in offices. So these pioneers of private schools and those others who joined them later in establishing other private schools were forced in the end to follow the curriculum taught in schools which were under the management of the Missionaries and of the colonial Department of Education.

Thirdly, the early pioneers of private schools wanted to provide further educational facilities for the children of Uganda. Though the Missionaries were building schools assisted financially by the colonial government, those schools were never enough just as it is today. There used to be very many children who could not get access to these schools, therefore private schools filled up this gap.

These pioneers of private schools were later joined by other people in Uganda. By 1950 these private schools were many and they were running side by side with schools run by the Protestants, the Roman Catholics, the Muslims and the colonial government.

The colonial government eventually appreciated the contribution of these private schools to the development of education in the country. The de Bunsen Education Committee which was appointed in 1952 by Sir Andrew Cohen, then Governor of Uganda, was loud and clear in the praise of these private schools. Following the advice of the Binns Study Group in 1951, it said that private schools were a demonstration of people's determination for Independence and for a desire of increased educational facilities which were not adequate at the time.

Consequently, that Study Group advised the colonial government to set up a section within the Department of Education headed by an experienced Education Officer to deal with private schools and advise the owners of those schools to put them in line with the schools under the Missionaries, the Uganda Muslim Education Association and those under the direct administration of the colonial government. Thus in 1953 Mr. Chesswas was appointed in the Department of Education to advise the private schools and he did quite commendable work in bringing them in line with the above schools.

Fourthly, the pioneers of private schools hated being belittled by the European Missionaries. They were men with ideas and vigour along with determination to pursue to a logical conclusion of what they had decided to do.

But the European Missionaries never accepted that Africans had the ability to start anything and to manage it efficiently. Of course the attitude of these European Missionaries like that of the colonial administrators was designed to create dependence of Africans on Europeans. But these pioneers of private schools could never accept this subordination.

Dr. Kalibbala told the writer that, " I could not stand being so belittled and led by such a batch of incompetent white men. So I resigned to start my own school at Bunnamwaya", he concluded.

Those people who did not know Dr. Kalibbala may be interested to know that he was a tall person with an imposing personality and very proud that he was a very intelligent man. When he left Uganda a second time to pursue his studies in the USA in 1939, he never returned to Uganda untill 1961. After he had got his Doctorate he was employed in the offices of the United Nations Organisation in New York untill 1961 when he was retired and then he returned to Uganda.

On his return to Uganda, his two schools, the secondary school at Bunnamwaya and the primary school at Mengo near the Kabaka's lake were in different hands and they had already departed from the original ideas on which he had founded them. Any way he was no longer interested in education unlike his two fellow pioneers of private schools Bishop Spartas and Mr. Anselm Musoke who were still running their schools. Dr. Kalibbala was now aspiring to becoming a politician and become the President of this country. But he was too proud and lacked the shrewdness of a politician to work with other politicians smoothly and he eventually lost out. He became a private citizen engaged in philosophical thoughts which he used to express to the public on Radio and TV in the programme known as Brain Trust. He died in 1979.

Fifthly, the strict moral code which the Missionaries applied to both the teachers and the students was another reason why these pioneers started their own schools. In their drive to cement Christian principles in the country, the Missionaries demanded quite a strict adherence to the Christian practice by the teachers and by the students. The teachers had to act as a good example to be followed by their students and by the public at large. For example, a teacher had to attend Church services on Sundays and on Holy Days and also receive Holy Communion. His home was supposed to be an example of Christian practice to all people. He was not supposed to drink beer and at the same time appear in public looking a bit tipsy. If he was married, he had to have married through the Church and not to practise polygamy. If such a teacher was a female teacher, she was not expected to become pregnant without being married in Church. If not properly married in Church, when she became pregnant, she would be stopped from teaching until she delivered and then only be allowed to teach again one year after delivering.

Indeed there were many other aspects of a strict moral Christian code which were applied to teachers in missionary schools. Many of those aspects were quite irksome and difficult to keep. Consequently, many qualified teachers were losing their teaching jobs in missionary schools for failure to keep these aspects of the Christian moral code.

Private Schools

The pioneers of private schools felt that there should be a separation between a teacher's private life and his or her professional responsibilities as a teacher. The Missionaries were looking too much into a teacher's personal and private life. Therefore they set up private schools so that good teachers in terms of their profession could have alternative schools where they could teach without the employer looking into their personal and private lives.

As regards the students, many used to be dismissed from schools for failure to follow the strict Christian moral code as demanded by the Missionaries. The Missionaries had a good system of monitoring students dismissed from one missionary school for failure in this respect so that they would not be enrolled in another one. It was the same for a teacher dismissed for moral turpitude. The pioneers of private schools felt that this kind of student and teacher dismissal made many brilliant teachers to lose their jobs. The students who failed to stick to the strict Christian moral code in mission schools should have alternative schools to attend and teachers to teach in. Consequently, many teachers and many students who failed to keep the strict Christian moral code as required by the Missionaries joined the private schools.

Sixthly, these pioneers of private schools did not support denominational education. They contended that denominational education was a cause of disunity in Uganda. Roman Catholic, Protestant and Muslim children were made to look at themselves as if they were not belonging to one country by attending separate schools in terms of their religions. Therefore the pioneers of private schools wanted to play down this disunity based on denominational education by allowing children of different religions to attend the same schools together.

Seventhly, the pioneers of the private schools like the rest of the society realised that it was necessary for the Ugandans who joined the schools to learn English as soon as they joined school. This would help them to understand the white man. But the Missionaries were insisting that English had to be taught from Pimary five onwards. They contended that the pupils would learn English better if they mastered first their vernaculars. Moreover they were fearing that if Ugandan children learnt English in so many numbers they would be proud and therefore difficult to control. During those early years the majority of the pupils attended school for a few years and then dropped out. Consequently few were reaching Primary five and fewer still were completing the whole Primary section of six years.

The contention of the pioneers of the private schools was that English should be taught right from Primary one. So at whatever stage a pupil dropped off, he should have picked up some English, thus echoing the remark of the first Director of Education, Eric Hussey: "To most of the children who go to school, the learning of a little English is the coveted goal".

Private Schools Flourish

The Second World War period (1939-45) and after was a period when private schools increased very much in Uganda. There were several key reasons why this happened. One of them was that there was a rise in the demand for school education because the war period and especially after it, was a time of rising prices for the farmers' crops. Therefore many parents had money to send their children to school. Also ex–service men on their return from the war had savings some of which went to pay school fees for their children and for those of their relatives on the basis of extended family relationships. Yet due to the war, there was a marked stagnation in the development of schools under the Roman Catholic and the C.M.S. Missionaries. Missionaries were not readily coming from abroad because they volunteered for war service in Europe while others in Uganda left to fight in the war. Figures of schools built show a decline during the war time. So the gap could well be filled by private schools especially in Buganda. After the war these schools continued to increase even though missionary educational activities were stepped up. The movement of opening up private schools spread also to Busoga during the 1940's.

The second reason for the growth of this movement was that there was a growing spirit among some Christians to be independent of Missionaries, a factor generated by a feeling that the Missionaries were not revealing the full range of knowledge to the pupils. Some parents believed that schools run by fellow Africans would reveal everything necessary to uplift Africans from their non-industrial way of life. There were complaints that Africans were not being taught, for example, how to manufacture such simple things as safety-pins and the like and that such simple manufactures had to be imported from Britain. Some of the ex-service men had learnt some skills such as making guns, and on their return they began to make these guns and a black-market of illegal guns flourished especially in Buganda. These guns were nick-named *Magezi ga Baganda*, the result of the intelligence of the Baganda.

Before 1962 there were complaints that if the education system was right, those going to school should have been taught the industrial skills and so all manufactures could have been made by the people in Uganda as a result of school education because the students had the intelligence to learn the techniques. But the people forgot that it was they themselves who had refused to see that practical education took the upper hand in the education system way back in the 1930's when they refused to send their children to the practical Central Schools at junior secondary school level.

The feeling that the Missionaries were not doing all what was possible to show their students all the knowledge was commented upon by the Director of Education in his report of 1950 thus:

Private Schools

There are now in Uganda about 200 private schools containing about 10,000 pupils. The majority of these are in Buganda. To some extent private schools have grown up because the schools of the grant-aided system are insufficient or do not take children far enough. Even more, they apparently spring from the desire of many Africans to manage schools of their own; they think that private schools may be providing something which the official schools do not provide or even which is being deliberately withheld in them.

The third reason why there was an increase of private schools during and after the Second World War was due to the teaching of English from primary one. The Inspectorate of Education insisted that English should be taught beginning with primary five in the grant-aided schools. The Missionaries supported the government believing that students should first learn the grammar of their mother tongues and the 3R's before beginning English. They feared that if students began learning English too early it would make them proud. But parents still wanted to see their children learn English as soon as they joined school to understand the white man. Indeed the refusal of the Missionaries to teach English as early as possible made some parents suspicious that there must be many other things which the Missionaries were purposefully withholding from the children. So to send a child to a private school was a wise course to take.

Moreover private schools provided space to which pupils dismissed from mission schools for supposedly bad behaviour could run. Others did not favour the compulsory Church services on Sundays and on Holy Days of their denominations. Some pioneers of private schools however, were devout practising Christians such as Fr. Spartas, Mr. A. Musoke, Mr. B. Kakinda of St. Bernard Kiswera Secondary School and Mr. Kiberu and Y. Musoke of Light College Katikamu in Mpigi District.

Private schools arouse the concern of Missionaries

Private schools in Uganda developed in stiff opposition put up by the Missionaries who had pioneered the introduction of Western education in the country.
The Missionaries wanted the education field to be their own preserve. There were several reasons for this opposition.

Firstly, the Missionaries had taken it as their duty to give education to Ugandans which should be Christian and denominational in character, while they were being supported by government financially. These Missionaries for the above reasons were always also resisting the Protectorate government from establishing its own non denominational schools.

Secondly, a feeling began to develop among some people in Uganda that they should be independent of the Missionaries because of political feelings which had developed. Especially in Buganda CMS Missionaries had annoyed the Baganda traditionalists by supporting the remarriage of the Namasole, the mother of the late Sir Edward Muteesa II in 1942. Custom had it in Buganda that a mother of the Kabaka never remarried once her husband had died. So the Missionaries felt that if this spirit of independence could have a system of schools to strengthen it, the magnitude of its results could never be measured in terms of opposition to the missionary factor in Uganda.

As a result of the uneasiness of the Protestant and the Roman Catholic Missionaries over these private schools, there used to be many accusations against private schools. First of all, these two missionary bodies viewed the owners of these private schools as rebelling against their own respective denominations. Secondly, qualified teachers who had been dismissed from the mission schools either opened their own private schools or went to teach in the private schools already set up. Thus the disciplining of teachers in missionary schools was becoming less effective than before. The Director of Education reflecting the Missionaries' fear wrote in 1950 thus:

> In the case of the men teachers many more than on the women's side are able to live down their moral lapses and after a time either are able to return to employment in the mission schools or to work in private schools where generally speaking such a strict code of morals is not demanded. It cannot be said that many of the teachers dismissed or suspended by the Missions who take up service in private schools are men of outstanding character or ability nor have they any real stake in the private schools in which they teach.

The same report went on to state:

> In recent years a number of privately owned African schools have grown up, almost entirely in Buganda. Some of these are worthy of admiration, being owned and managed by Africans genuinely interested in spreading education on progressive lines. More often however, others are started by teachers who resigned or been dismissed from Mission schools, and do little good to their pupils.

Moreover though some owners of these private schools were genuinely interested in giving education on progressive lines, some particularly after the Second World War in 1945 looked at the exercise as a commercial affair so that they ignored the rules of a healthy school establishment. In some schools a classroom was made to take as many pupils as offered themselves, whereas the educational rules then limited the number to 25 pupils. So the Missionaries took examples of a few of these to be the rule and condemned all the private schools and the goverment tended to follow missionary thinking. For example, the Education Report of 1950 further reported:

Private Schools

These private schools are maintained for the private profit of their owners. They do not get Government financial assistance: few of them deserve it any way.

The private schools approach to education was not approved by the Missionaries. For example, they opposed teaching English so early to pupils, abhorred the absence of a Pastor to care for the spititual life of the pupils in these schools and they complained of classroom overcrowding and they hated to see that these schools were interdenominational. So they looked at the whole movement of the private schools as educationally unsound and usually they sought occasions to discredit these private schools. For example, during the 1949 disturbances in Buganda spearheaded by the Bataka Movement, the Missionaries declared that Aggrey Memorial School boys at Bunnamwaya were very active in acts of arson, looting shops and in comitting other atrocities.

The campaign of the Missionaries against the private schools movement was intensified by placing under religious disability Christians who established private schools, or those who taught in them, or who sent their children to them and the students themselves. For example, the Missionaries refused them to receive the Sacraments until they disassociated themselves from the private schools movement. Some few ones heeded the missionary sanctions. But the majority of teachers and parents and students did not heed them.

However, not all the clergy were agreed in condemning the private schools and their owners. For example, there was a strong difference of opinion between Bishop Dr. Joseph Kiwanuka, then Bishop of the Roman Catholic Masaka Diocese and Bishop E. Michaud then in charge of the Roman Catholic Lubaga Diocese. The latter was strictly opposed to Roman Catholics founding private schools. Dr. Kiwanuka on the other hand was of the opinion that if such Roman Catholics appeared, they should be encouraged and perhaps they would in the end call in the help of the priests who would come and incorporate the laymen's activities in the mission educational activities. Dr. Kiwanuka particularly wanted to see the initiative of the Roman Catholic laymen in all fields and to see that the Roman Catholic laymen's initiative was part and parcel of the Roman Catholic activities in his Diocese. He particularly encouraged Mr. B. Kakinda in his determination of founding his private school of St. Bernard Kiswera Secondary School in Masaka District during the early 1950's.

These private school owners were faced with the problem of getting the firm confidence of the society in terms of examinations. They went around this problem by instituting a recognised Primary Leaving Examination system of their own. Up to 1953, each denomination, that is the Roman Catholic denomination, the Church of Uganda (C.M.S.) denomination and the Uganda Muslim Education Association, each set the examinations for its respective primary schools, marked them and awarded the Primary Leaving Certificates. They would then send these results to the Department of Education for record.

None of these organisations would accept pupils from private schools to sit for their Primary Leaving Examinations. In this way, the Missionaries hoped to squeeze out these private schools because parents would not readily allow their children to study and complete their primary education and yet graduate with no recognized certificates for their academic attainment. This would prevent private school children from proceeding with further studies or even securing jobs, for by the 1950's pupils graduating with Primary Leaving Certificates were usually over fifteen years of age, many of them used to be employed by government and private firms immediately or they were allowed to enter Teacher Training Colleges to train as Primary school teachers. So the possession of a Primary School Leaving Certificate was a very valuable asset then.

The owners of the independent private schools formed the Buganda Private Schools Union in 1942 to face the challenge of this examination problem and other problems of interest. One lady teacher of Gayaza High School whom they approached for advice as to how they could approach the goverment to allow their pupils to sit for either the Primary School Leaving Examinations of the Roman Catholic or C.M.S. schools, advised them to institute their own examination system, mark the examination papers and award their own certificates. They took the advice and it worked. Their Primary School Leaving Certificates were accepted by society and even by the missionary schools because many pupils possessing them would win places in missionary secondary schools. This again encouraged the private schools owners and it also won faith from the parents.

As for the Junior Secondary School Leaving Examination, the government easily accepted students from those private schools which began to give lessons leading to that examination. Chwa II Memorial College of Fr. Spartas was the first in this category followed by Aggrey Memorial School Bunnamwaya and Light College Katikamu near Masuuliita.

The attitude of the Uganda Protectorate Government to the Private Schools

The Department of Education tended to have no well worked out policy towards these private schools from the time they first appeared on the scene in 1925 until 1951. This was due mostly to the fact that the government thought that the movement would soon die out as running schools was quite difficult and expensive. It was concerned with watching the standards of the mission schools and a few government schools on which government money was being spent. When it realised that these private schools were determined to co-exist side by side with the mission and government schools, it tried somehow to weaken them or to drive them completely out of existence.

According to the 1927 Education Ordinance, any school had to be registered with the Department of Education to have a legal existence. The owners of the private schools took care to register their schools to safeguard their position and that Department recorded them well knowing that they would soon disappear from the scene.

Occasionally officers from the Department of Education would visit these private schools to see how they were doing and order any of them to close if the health situation was not considered satisfactory. Such schools would often reopen soon after the departure of the Inspectors.

Some of the owners of such schools who were interviewed by the writer lamented that the Inspectorate of the Department of Education used to measure the standards of their schools against the standards of the government and of the mission schools which were getting government financial assistance and free gifts from abroad. So it was unfair if they were told to close. They suggested that they should have got government help to better their standards, after all these schools were also assisting the children of the Protectorate.

Government attitude towards these private schools was quite negative. A more positive attitude would have been to establish standards which these schools had to achieve in order to win government financial assistance. This had been the policy which the government applied to the mission schools. Had the government not done so, some mission schools would have been in as bad a condition as many of the private schools.

A more reasonable policy would have been to try and separate the good from the bad by offering government grants as an inducement for excellence. But the stand of the government was to let these private schools develop so long as they did not cause trouble though they were looked at as undesirable for they would never achieve the standards which were desired by the School Inspectors.

In 1949 the government sought to weaken the private schools by encouraging the mission schools to introduce English in their Primary Schools from Primary one so that people who were keen on sending their children to private schools due to English would stop. It is interesting that a policy advocated for long by the private schools was ultimately adopted by the government. Thus the Director of Education wrote in 1950:

> It is as yet too early to see what will be the effect of the new regulations for the teaching of English in grant-aided schools. Hitherto private schools especially in Buganda have drawn pupils from the Missions by the inducement of English taught from class one upwards. Now that the Missions are also entitled under certain safeguards, to teach English in classes beginning from one to four if they think fit, some private schools may find themselves much less popular and be compelled by financial straits to offer themselves to the African Local Governments.

The private schools were not to be destroyed so easily, however. Some parents had become firm supporters of these schools. Furthermore, the mission schools could not cater by the 1940's to all those children presenting themselves for education. In addition, the missions did not respond wholeheartedly to the freedom the govrnment gave them in 1947 to introduce English at a lower level.

The 1951 Education Report stated sadly that:

> In the 1950 Department Report it was suggested that private schools might no longer be so attractive by reason of their teaching more English than the grant-aided schools. This year there is considerable evidence that the attraction of English, however badly taught in private schools, is still powerful. The owners of grant-aided schools have been most restrained in availing themselves of the Department's permission given in 1947, to teach English below Class V. Both Missions (i.e. the C.M.S. and the Roman Catholic) have imposed severe tests on vernacular teachers wishing to give English lessons, while in very few schools, and those mostly girls' schools with European Headmistresses, is any English taught below Class III. So the private schools still lure the ignorant.

The government now adopted new tactics to stamp out the private schools and cater at the same time to the growing demands of especially the Buganda government to possess its own schools. They proposed that local governments should be persuaded to take over these private schools. By the recommendations of the 1940 Education Committee, local governments were charged with the responsibility of financing the primary schools run by the Missionaries although they did not have their own schools then. But by the end of the 1940's, some started to desire to own their primary schools even though they would continue to finance those of the Missionaries as this would show the people the usefulness of the local governments by directly taking part in the provision of education which was so much demanded.

The Buganda government was very much desirous of owning its own schools because it could not direct or control the policy of the mission schools even though it financed them. In 1949 it even appointed an officer who would be responsible for a programme of setting up its schools. When the Protectorate government suggested that the local governments should try to take over the private schools, the Buganda government welcomed the idea warmly. The provision was that the owners of the private schools taken over by the local governments would be left to continue as salaried Headmasters and they would besides each year receive 10% of the proceeds from their schools. Thus the Annual Report of the Department of Education of 1947 stated:

> This represents an interesting development, particularly in the province of Buganda where private schools have been much more popular than elsewhere, for it may be that the owners of private schools, who usually find their development a great strain on their financial resources, may prefer the alternative of handing them over to the Native Governments as the owners, as a condition of the schools receiving grants from their own or other public funds, would have to abide by the regulations and to employ only qualified teachers, which is far from being the case at present in the great majority of the private schools.

Private Schools

Some private school owners suspected this move by the government regarding their schools. They believed that this was a trick by the government to take over their private schools and to kill the movement. They did not readily come forward to accept control by the local governments. The Director of Education suspected this and wrote at the end of 1948 thus:

> The hope expressed in the 1947 Report that private schools would be willing to come under the African Local Governments has not yet been fulfilled.

There were some few private school owners however, who accepted the Buganda government's control. And indeed all who did so were gradually pushed out as Headmasters and eventually their schools became proper Buganda government schools. Other private schools taken over by that government were after a time abandoned by the same government as being on unsuitable sites which could not allow for further development. This also destroyed those private schools because their initiators had already taken to other interests.

Two owners who nearly lost their schools to the Buganda government made an effective row. Anselm Musoke drove that government out of his school of Kanadda Rural Industries School in 1956 and sued it for destroying his school by changing its practical curriculum. Musoke had made that curriculum since the establishment of the school in 1938, and he had developed a school which was academic, agricultural and technical. The Buganda government had turned it into a purely academic school and replaced him with its own Headmaster. The case went to the High Court of Uganda in 1957 and dragged on until 1962 when the Buganda government was finally forced to pay Shs. 120,000/- to Musoke as damages. That was quite a lot of money by that time because one could buy a Benz Saloon Car at 30,000/=.

However, Musoke's school eventually closed because after 1962, the students particularly wanted academic education to get jobs which were so much available after Uganda had regained her independence. At the same time Musoke became very much involved in politics and he even won a seat in Parliament in 1961 on the DP card.

Fr. Spartas was another one who drove the Buganda government out of his Chwa II Memorial College at Namungoona in 1957. When that government had built a very good building as a secondary school block, he started to suspect that the Buganda government would try to get him out of the way because it had also brought in its qualified teachers to help improve the standards of the school. He himself had refused to step down as Headmaster. In 1957 all teachers were served with a Buganda government circular to sign a bond that they belonged to it as its employees and not to Fr. Spartas, and any one who would not sign the circular would not get his salary. Fr. Spartas and his assistant, Fr. I. Magimbi who was the

Secretary of the African Greek Orthodox Schools, influenced their teachers to refuse to sign the bond. Those teachers who had been brought in by the Buganda government feared to lose their salaries and they signed the bond. Those who had been recruited by Fr. Spartas and Fr. Magimbi refused to do so.

Fr. Spartas and Fr. Magimbi retorted by reorganising the constitution of their African Greek Orthodox Church schools. They officially made Fr. N. Seryazi the Education Secretary of all the schools founded by Fr. Spartas all over East Africa which now began to be called the African Greek Orthodox Church Schools. Now Fr. Seryazi held the same position as Al-Hajj Ramadhan Gava of the Uganda Muslim Education Association (UMEA). Fr. Spartas wanted to have a system which was similar to that of the Roman Catholic and the Church of Uganda Educational Organisations and of the Uganda Muslim Education Association. He then declared that Chwa II Memorial College was a mission school like any other mission school, so the Buganda Government should have no say in the management of the school.

The Buganda government realised that Fr. Spartas and Fr. Magimbi had been too clever for it. It pulled out its teachers and began a school in the Kabaka's Lubiri (palace) at Mengo hoping also to take most of the pupils from Fr. Spartas' school. This was the origin of Lubiri Secondary School which was moved to its present site in 1967 after, on Obote's orders, the Uganda Army had stormed the Lubiri in 1966. But Fr. Spartas' school was not shaken, it continued to go from strength to strength.

Anselm Musoke and Fr. Spartas' episodes were the two incidents which were prominent in the take over of private schools by local governments. Other private school owners who from the beginning adamantly refused to have any dealings with the Buganda government or with any other local government prided themselves for having foreseen the danger.

After these two incidents the Buganda government was not any more keen on taking over private schools. It concentrated on building its own schools. Yet the movement of the private schools each year got stronger and stronger as more enterprising people went into the school business because more pupils were finding that they could not secure places in mission schools. By 1950 these schools were no longer concentrated in Buganda and Busoga, they were opening up in nearly every district of Uganda.

The Growth of Private Secondary School
It was in the provision of Secondary education that the independent private school movement got widespread support both in Uganda and in the rest of East Africa, Malawi, Zambia and Namibia. In the 1950's secondary education became more in demand as primary education gradually lost its status as a minimum qualification for employment or for further training for a good paying profession.

Private Schools

Yet government and mission secondary schools did not increase appreciably enough to satisfy this increased demand.

Secondary schools for Africans in Kenya, Tanzania, Malawi and Zambia were even fewer. While all European and Asian children could get enough places in their secondary schools, Africans had very few of these schools and they were not allowed to study in the schools of the other races even if they had vacant places because during the colonial period races were segregated in education.

In 1953 the independent private schools in Kenya were closed and banned by the colonial government because they had become a breeding ground for nationalist resistance to the pro-settler colonial government in Kenya. So even this outlet for Africans in Kenya was closed down.

Tanzania did not have private schools, nor did Malawi and Zambia have such schools. The result was that many pupils desirous of getting secondary education but who could not be accommodated in the government supported secondary schools in those countries, came to Uganda to attend private secondary schools. The mission secondary schools in Uganda would not take them on. Firstly, because there were not even enough places for Ugandan children in the mission schools. Secondly, these pupils had been rejected by their secondary schools back at home as a result of the selection process using the Primary Leaving Examination. Indeed some had become truculent pupils in those countries and they had been dismissed from the education system as it used to be in Uganda. Thus the Director of Education in Uganda had this to say about this issue in 1957:

> Private schools continue to be popular in some parts of the country, notably in Buganda. Primary classes during 1957 were conducted at 154 such schools with an enrolment of some 13,000 children while there were 63 private schools offering some form of secondary academic education with 7,000 students enrolled. Many students of these private schools particularly on the secondary level, come from Kenya and other East African territories; they do not appear to be deterred by the comparatively high rate of fees charged, poor accommodation in most cases offered, and poor examination results of such schools.

The report in another place continued to say:

> Uganda is the one territory in East and Central Africa which permits the existence of a substantial number of private school; as a result a large number of rejectees from the state-financed system in other territories come to Uganda for education in such schools. The legal, administrative and professional problem here is the extent to which schools meeting the needs of such children should be controlled; the Uganda government has taken a very liberal attitude in this matter and tries to hold a reasonable balance.

Because it was not paying much to run primary sections of these private schools, consequently the owners of these schools tended to hand over these sections to the local governments and so concentrate on running the secondary sections where students paid high fees. Those new people who started to establish private schools from the late 1950's did not even envisage to include primary sections onto them at all. They started straight away with secondary classes because this is where big money could be made.

All records of these private secondary schools and information from those people who were running them show that from the mid 1950's up to 1965 students from outside Uganda were nearly equal to those from Uganda. Chwa II Memorial College, for example, had students from 1958 to 1965 who were ranging between 900 and 3000 each year, half of them were from outside Uganda especially from Kenya.

Unfortunately, though these schools enjoyed a good attendance and charged appreciably higher fees than the mission and government secondary schools, the management of their finances was usually bad by their proprietors who tended to use the money from the school fees for purposes other than those concerned with bettering the schools. For example, Fr. Spartas was using part of the fees for maintaining his clergy and for running many operations of the African Greek Orthodox Church. The result of using some of the collections from the private schools for other purposes was that by independence time in 1962 when there was an even bigger upsurge of students seeking secondary education, it was mostly the recently established Asian private schools that were better set to receive these students. The traditional private schools were rather dilapidated and were in financial difficulties arising out of poor financial management. Aggrey Memorial School was eventually handed over to the government in 1965 to save it from collapsing.

One interesting aspect of these private schools is that they did not develop into political hot-beds ready to play a nationalistic role against the colonial government. Since these private schools began as an instrument of oposition to the domination of Missionaries in education, who were at the same time backed by the colonial government and as the Missionaries opposed the establishment of these private schools, there were elements in the movement of private schools which could have created a spirit of nationalism to oppose the colonial government. Moreover many of those people who opened up these private schools and others who taught in them were politically minded and they belonged to political movements which began to spring up from the 1940s and even played an active part in those political movements. For example, Fr. Spartas of Chwa II Memorial College was one of the leaders of the Bataka Movement which was so prominent in the riots of 1949 opposing the colonial administration and the presence of the Asians in the country. He was even rusticated by the colonial government in Karamoja together with a number of other political leaders of the time.

Private Schools

Secondly, when the two national parties emerged in 1961-DP and UPC with a factional party, the KY- many of the private school owners and their teachers were found in the ranks of these three political parties playing an active part.

Thirdly, since the students in these private schools were rejectees from the well financed mission and government schools, one would feel that such students would have a grudge and seek a chance to strike a blow at the colonial government. Yet nothing of the sort happened unlike in Kenya where students in private schools played a remarkable role in the *Mau Mau* Movement which raged from 1951 to 1960.

Then why did these independent private schools unlike in Kenya not become hot-beds for nationalistic ideas and activities? One reason was that the proprietors were engaged in a struggle to establish the legality of their schools. So if they had gone on to give them the spirit of opposition to the colonial government, their schools would have been easily closed . For example, there were teachers who had been dismissed from King's College Buddo in 1942. Some of them reopened Kalibbala's Aggrey Memorial School which had been closed by the Inspectorate in 1941 on health grounds. Others founded a primary school as a feeder to that secondary school at the side of the Kabaka's lake at Mengo. These teachers initially found it difficult to get permission from the Department of Education to re-open the secondary school at Bunnamwaya and others to open up a primary school section of it in Mengo. The reason was that it had been imputed that they were against the interests of His Majety King George VI. It was alleged that it had been due to their advice that the students at King's College Buddo had broken the picture of King George VI in their opposition to having two pictures of kings in their school, one the newly crowned Sir Edward Muteesa II and the other, the King of England. If such men carried on their nationalistic attitude after the reopening of Aggrey Memorial School, the school could have never been allowed by the colonial government to operate.

Secondly, as we have already pointed out, from mid 1950's, these private schools concentrated on secondary students half of whom were foreign students. These had come to get education with the hope that they would return home with their chances bettered to get jobs. So such students were not the sort to be interested in Uganda's nationalistic movement even if the owners of these schools and their teachers would have tried to interest them in it. Any attempt to interest these students would be considered by them as meant to detract them from their main concern for which they were paying a lot in money and in personal discomfort.

Moreover students in the private secondary schools were working under an inferiority complex vis-a-vis those who were in mission and government secondary schools having been themselves rejected by such schools as failures. So the main concern of the students in the private secondary schools was to overcome this inferiority complex by showing that they were comparable to the secondary school students in the government and mission secondary schools. They could show this only by concentrating on studying what those students in government and mission secondary schools were studying but not by engaging in political activities.

The desire to do well at their studies usually led students in private secondary schools to go on strike against the management of their schools, because by comparing notes with some of their friends from government and mission secondary schools, they found out that some of their teachers were not capable of giving them the necessary preparation to enable them pass their Cambridge School Certificate Examinations.

The life especially of the foreign students was most times hazardous. Due to the publicity which the owners of private schools were making about their schools in the press in Kenya, Tanzania, Malawi and Zambia using high sounding titles such as "colleges" and "high schools", students from those countries used to come with high hopes about these private secondary schools. They were thinking that these secondary schools compared with the mission and the government secondary schools back in their countries. On arrival what they found was disappointing in many aspects. The majority of their teachers were unqualified. The schools had scanty facilities and make-shift buildings. Living accommodation was hard to get and the school fees were higher than those at the subsidised mission and government secondary schools which were so well provided for.

Landlords and land-ladies in the neighbourhood of these private secondary schools used to capitalise on the presence of these foreign students by putting up mud-houses covered with iron sheets and rented narrow rooms to these strangers. Those near townships had an advantage because they were near private accommodation of a better sort. That is why such schools like Chwa II Memorial College Namungoona, Aggrey Memorial School Bunnamwaya, Luwule Secondary School near Mukono and a few others had a high influx of foreign students.

But the chances of students in the private secondary schools to pass the Cambridge School Certificate Examinations were quite meagre not because those students were dull as many people have tended to think, but because the tuition was in hands of teachers the majority of whom had no qualification to teach at the secondary school level. The Director of Education remarked on this phenomenon thus in 1957:

> The standard of all but one or two of the private schools is considerably lower than that of the grant-aided schools, as must be expected when far too much is attempted with inadequate staff. A private school recently opened in Kampala advertises as

taking children from the age of six years up to Cambridge School Certificate and its only qualified teacher is its proprietor.

The difficult life which these students had to live in rented rooms also made private study difficult at night. However, these students were never deterred by these difficulties. Moreover they were free to repeat the classes as many times as they wished so long as they had money to enable them to keep in these private secondary schools.

Usually also the registration of the students in the private secondary schools was at fault. Many private school owners did not understand the educational systems of Kenya, Tanzania and of the rest of Central Africa. The Primary section for example, in both Kenya and Tanzania had two parts: one was called lower primary and it stretched from primary one to primary four. The second one was called upper primary and it stretched from primary five to primary eight. At the end of each part there was an examination. But it was the certificate obtained at the end of the upper primary Section which entitled a pupil to join a secondary school if he had passed well within those countries. But when students from those two countries presented certificates obtained at the end of the lower primary Section, they were also enrolled together with those who had obtained the certificates at the end of the upper primary section without the proprietors being aware of this fact. Where they were aware, they valued the money.

Some pupils even from Uganda had no Primary Leaving Certificates allowing them to start secondary school work. With a convincing excuse that their certificates had been lost, the owners of these private schools could enrol them. So one could find many students in these private secondary schools whose academic attainment was not meant for secondary school work. This made teaching difficult and chances for passing the Cambridge School Certificate Examinations very small. Numerous students from these private secondary schools used to enrol for the Cambridge School Certificate Examinations each year but only a few could manage to pass them and usually in the third class.

Finding that such a great number of students were wasting the examiners' time, the Cambridge Examination Syndicate in England had to request the then Uganda colonial government in 1956 to constitute a qualifying test for all private secondary school students intending to enrol for that examination. It was only those who passed the qualifying test who were allowed to qualify for enrolment. This was officially called the qualifying test by the Department of Education.

Indeed there were other factors militating against students in the private secondary schools doing well in the Cambridge School Certificate Examinations. There was the question of attending regularly. Students' attendance was irregular sometimes because they had to work for food when their food, usually maize flour, which they had brought from home at the beginning of term had been exhausted, or when their money with which they were supposed to buy food had all been spent before the end of term. Other times they were sent out of classes because their school fees had not arrived in time or had got lost in the Post Office. In other cases they would decide to go home early before the term closed while others would take holidays within the term because they had no parents or relatives to control them.

Such big failures in the Cambridge School Certificate Examinations made many people during the colonial period wonder whether education in independent private schools was worthwhile. But up to the early 1960's all students in East and Central Africa who were attending the official secondary schools were relatively few. So even those who failed their Cambridge School Certificate Examinations were easily taken up for further training or they got jobs in government or in private firms. So from this point of view, the private secondary schools were helping to give secondary education which brought into the reach of these students further opportunities of training. All over East and Central Africa one used to meet with graduates of these private secondary schools and many of them were well employed and they remembered Uganda's private secondary schools with gratitude.

The usefulness of these private secondary schools became apparent to the Uganda Protectorate Government as early as 1950. That government realised that they were providing educational opportunities which otherwise many children could not get, given the small number of mission and government secondary schools. This realisation was backed by the Binns Study Group which visited Uganda in 1951 to enhance the situation of education in Uganda and recommend new developments in the education sytem. On the advice of the Binns Study Group from the Colonial Office the de Bunsen Education Committee of 1952 recommended that private schools should be included in the education system because they showed initiative, a sign of desire for independence and because they were supplementing the educational facilities provided by the Missionaries and the colonial administration. The Department of Education then appointed Chesswas one of its officers to be in charge of private schools. He got an assistant, Joseph Magoba, a seasoned teacher to work with him. Both Chesswas and Magoba competently advised the proprietors of the private schools and won their confidence. Those who willingly followed their advice were recommended to get financial assistance from the government to better their schools. However, there were some who refused to cooperate fearing that allowing too much government involvement in their schools might in the end lead to their schools being taken over by the government.

The advice given to the private schools proprietors concerned having sanitary or hygienic school plants, having a certain minimum number of qualified teachers and licencing after being tested those who were not qualified, having an ideal number of students in a classroom instead of having very large numbers hard for a teacher to manage effectively. Chesswas and Magoba began to supervise and inspect these private schools on the same basis of the mission and government schools.

By 1960, these private schools were running properly and were accepted in the education system as another channel through which pupils and students passed to acquire primary school and secondary school certificates. And many young men and women from Uganda, Kenya, Tanzania, Malawi, Zambia and Zimbabwe got these education cerfificates which enabled them to go for further studies abroad. All these people played a useful role in the early days of independence and afterwards. In fact, many of them even now are holding important jobs in all the above countries.

After Uganda's regaining her independence on the 9th October 1962, the politicians began to eye the mission schools and Asian schools with uneasiness for four reasons. Firstly, these schools were run on religious and racial lines. This was viewed as continuing to divide the citizens of Uganda while there was a clarion call for unity in the country.

Secondly, the politicians feared that the Missionaries and the Asians using their religious and racial bias would prevent the government from achieving its manpower targets because a school belonging to a certain denomination or race could refuse a deserving student a place while the schools of the denomination or race to which such a student belonged lacked a place for him or her.

Thirdly, the politicians feared that mission schools would not easily allow to teach the government ideology of "African personality" and "African identity", treating it as funny if not laughable. Yet the government had launched a drive for instilling confidence in its citizens that they had taken their rightful place in the comity of nations. During the colonial period, colonial and missionary education had the tendency of making the students to feel that they did not measure up to the level of the white man.

Fourthly, the politicians could not tolerate white Missionaries and Asians controlling the education system with all their superiority complex when the white colonial administrators had been replaced by Ugandans. This would not reflect well the fact that Ugandans were then in full control of their affairs.

The end result was the passing of the 1963 Education Act which brought all the former mission schools and Asian schools under the control of the government. Because the private schools could not be accused of any of the above four disabilities, the 1963 Education Act did not put them under the control of the government and therefore they remained independent of goverment control.

The post independence period saw a greater increase in private schools especially at secondary school level. We need to remember that due to the shortage of qualified personnel at the time Uganda regained her independece, the independent government stepped up the increase of secondary schools to produce men and women who could safisfy the demand for secondary schools. So the private schools endeavoured to fill up the gap.

In 1963, the Castle Education Commission had recommended that pupils in primary seven and those in eight would do the same Primary Leaving Examination at the end of 1966 so that in 1967 all pupils would be selected for Senior Secondary one and Primary eight would be phased out. So 1967 saw a great number or pupils who were seeking senior one places. The government secondary schools could not even take on half the number of pupils qualified for entry into senior one. Many enterprising people and adventurers established private schools and joined those other proprietors who were already in that business.

Ironically, the Roman Catholic Church and the Church of Uganda which were great opponents of private schools during the colonial period, began also to open up private schools after the passing of the 1963 Education Act. Having lost the control of their former schools to the government, those two churches felt that they still had a role to play in education. So they cooperated with some of their followers and set up private schools known as Parents Schools mostly at secondary school level. These schools were really Church schools disguised under the above name lest the government suspected that the discriminatory and denominational schools of the colonial days were being reintroduced in the country. These Parents Schools were being built on church land in church parishes where no secondary schools existed before.

However, this step of the Roman Catholic Church and of the Church of Uganda had the praiseworth result of increasing secondary schools. Moreover these schools were no longer denominational and discriminatory. They enrolled any student regardless of the religion to which such a student belonged. If we take Mpigi District alone, the government never set up any new secondary school in the District. It only continued to support St. Mary's College Kisubi, Trinity College Nabbingo, King's College Buddo and Ggombe Secondary School.

Yet the following secondary schools have been developed over the years as Parents School: Nkozi seconday school, Kibibi secondary school, Mitala Maria secondary school, Ggoli secondary school, Matugga secondary school, Masuuliita secondary school, Kiziba secondary school, Naddangira secondary school, Mende Kalema secondary school, Kasengejje secondary school, Nabbingo secondary school, Nsangi secondary school, Jjungo secondary school, Our Lady of Good Counsel Gayaza, Magezi Ntakke Wampeewo secondary school and Nnabitalo secondary school, Kiwenda.

However, because these Parents Schools were financially difficult to run, and because their owners wanted to enhance the status of these schools by being called government supported schools, their owners eventually began to hand them over to the government during the 1970's. However, in the end they had to lament for their having handed their schools to the government. They had hoped for financial assistance to these schools. But they got very little and many times coming too late. Yet the government was many times using these schools to appoint to them its Headteachers whom it wanted to reward with Headships, a thing which irked their proprietors: that is the Church of Uganda and the Roman Catholic Church and their respective followers. To help these Parents Schools out of their financial difficulties, these schools used the device of the Parents Teachers Associations which they had devised as we shall see later.

The great upsurge in the number of private schools during the 1960's was accompanied by some opposition, nevertheless. Some adventurers who looked at the exercise more from a financial point of view than from an educational standpoint, began to establish private schools in all sorts of buildings including abandoned former cotton ginneries and abandoned former bakeries. At times some of them would collect the school fees and disappear from the students. Or they were hardly teaching the students adequately and providing in their schools adequate scholastic materials.

The above phenomenon was one reason why the government passed the 1970 Education Act which require even upto now any person intending to open up a private school to seek permission first from the Commissioner for Education. Also because there was a rapid development of Parents Schools and Private schools owned by Asians, the government feared that the discriminatory Church and racial schools were likely to re-appear on the scene. So another reason for passing the 1970 Education Act was to restrain Churches and Asians from opening up private schools which might in the end become discriminatory on the basis of religion and race. However, the Parents Schools and the Asian owned private schools were no longer discriminatory and denominational. They were enrolling any student capable to pay the school fees regardless of his or her religion or race.

Today the private schools are accepted as educational institutions in the education system of Uganda as an important aspect of the initiative of Ugandans in the education field.

These private schools have added lustre to their existence by many of the proprietors running many of them as institutions which give technical and practical skills in the form of polytechnics to enable the students to become job creators rather than job seekers, thus following the spirit of Anselm Musoke, one of the pioneers of private schools in Uganda who opened up his private school at Kanadda in 1938 in Mpigi District with the name of Rural Industries School.

Now at the time of writing in 1995, there are 630 government sponsored secondary schools in the country while there are 409 private secondary schools. The implication of this is that were it not for the existence of private secondary schools in Uganda, thousands of students would miss attending secondary

History and Development of Education

schools because the government is not yet in position to provide enough such schools.

The race of establishing private schools has now reached University level. At the time of writing, five private Universities have been established namely Ndejje University in Luweero District, the Uganda Martyrs University at Nkozi, Bugema University, Nkumba University, Seguku University and Musa Body University in Katwe, Kampala. All these are a result of the initiative and cooperation between the Roman Catholic Church and its followers and the Church of Uganda and its followers, and purely private citizens with no connection with the above churches.

Serunyiigo Kasolo one of the veterans of Private Schools in Uganda, now proprietor of Kampala grammar Secondary School

8 The Relationship between Church and State, 1925-63

The role of the Uganda Protectorate Government in education vis-a-vis that of the Missionaries was the other important issue in education. From 1925, the Uganda Protectorate officials wanted to direct all educational affairs in the country. But the Missionaries looked at the government role as meant for only assisting them with funds and to leave every educational matter concerning the management and the direction of education to the Missionaries.

But the Protectorate government saw its role wider than the Missionaries tried to make it: it should include opening up of schools and run them side by side with schools belonging to the Missionaries. It should also take over some mission schools and run them. Eric Hussey, the first Director of Education had originally proposed that the Protectorate government should start by taking over some of the mission schools called Middle School which were Junior secondary schools. He felt that when such schools developed into fully fledged secondary schools, the Missionaries would have no academic know-how and funds to manage such schools.

The Missionaries opposed this move of taking over of some of their Middle Schools and also the government's intention of building and running its own elementary schools. This they felt would jeopardise the religious outlook which they wanted to implant in the schools. They would even lose the chance to influence the elite who would be their strong support in the future. The Missionaries wanted the Protectorate government to run some technical schools like the Kampala Technical School which it had already any way set up in 1921. They also agreed to the Protectorate government's establishing and running a few schools for groups of people who would not like to join Christian schools such as the Muslim children. Such schools under the government would definitely be very few and if the education influence of the government would be there at all, it would affect only a few people in Uganda.

If the Government was left free to establish many of its schools, the Missionaries feared that the Government schools with plenty of money would be more prestigious than the mission schools. Even the government could deliberately give less money to the mission schools in order to retard their growth. Consequently pupils might prefer to attend Government schools. This would again make the Missionaries miss educating the future elites who would support them and influence society in terms of their point of view.

To show their determination to limit government participation in education, the Roman Catholic hierarchy in the Lubaga Diocese under Bishop H. Streicher, a White Father Missionary had formed a Board of Education in 1924 at the time the Uganda Protectorate government was planning to direct the educational affairs of the country. This Board like the C.M.S. Board of Education formed in 1904, had on it the most respectable Roman Catholic chiefs in Uganda. Both of these two Boards were poised to prevent the government from going beyond the limits which the Missionaries thought were proper for it. They opposed all the implications in the 1927 Education Ordinance which gave too much power to the government in respect of missionary educational activities. Because of their alliance with the Missionaries, the chiefs who had helped to build many schools and were still continuing to do so, supported the Missionaries in their struggle to keep the Government to the proper level as defined by the Missionaries. Eric Hussey, the first Director of Education had hoped originally that the public would support him against the Missionaries. He even wrote:

> As to which method of expansion would be adopted, the aiding of more mission schools, or the establishing of new government schools, the natives themselves would be the ultimate arbiters.

In his optimism, Hussey underestimated however, the hold which the Missionaries had by then on the minds of the Ugandan public. And indeed the natives themselves did not support him in opposition to the Missionaries. Hussey had assumed that the public would at once appreciate the benefit of the government's entry into the directing of the educational development of the country. He assumed that the government had all the potentialities to bring about an educational development which the Missionaries could not do. But to the people, the limitations of the Missionaries who were white like the government Education officers, were not obvious. The public thought that the Missionaries had unlimited sources of funds and that they had all the professional qualifications to lead Uganda's educational development to the highest limits. However, after the Education Officers of the Protectorate government had realised that like themselves, the Missionaries wanted to establish Western values in the country, they tended to leave the Missionaries to have their own way in many things regardless of government policies.

Sir Philip Mitchell who took over the Governorship in 1935 indicated that he would leave the Missionaries to do what they felt like doing despite government educational administrative polices. He thus wrote in his book remembering his service in Uganda:

> At this time (1935-1940), there were aspects of missionary educational practices and policies which seemed to be open to objection. But I was convinced that a departmental, secular school system, was not a suitable way of doing what we had to do and equally convinced that the Missionaries had an indispensable contribution to make, for in the case of a people recently converted or in the process of

conversion to Christianity, their schools must be such as to confirm and strengthen their belief, must in fact be actively Christian schools.

Therefore the Missionaries were given a free hand to influence any government education policy in the name of strengthening the people's belief and practice in Christianity.

The Colonial Office in London through its de La Warr Commission on Higher Education of 1937 was uneasy about giving this large freedom to the Missionaries to disregard government administrative policies. That Commission advised the Uganda Protectorate government to take a firm stand with the Missionaries in all administrative matters. It feared that this great latitude left to them by the Protectorate government officials, would in the long run turn to naught any of its educational administrative policy provisions. It therefore recommended that "the task of the Government should not be to supplant the Missions but to take steps to see that the work of the Missions was regulated, endorsed and carefully controlled".

Influenced by the above de La Warr Commission, the Uganda Protectorate government appointed an education committee in 1940 to consider many of the views expressed by the above Commission which entailed a change in the operation of some of the stipulations of the 1927 Education Ordinance and which also implied expansion of the education system with a view of "regulating, endorsing and carefully controlling the missionary freedom in education".

Some lay members of the 1940 Education Committee though quite Christian in principle and in faith, wanted like the de La Warr Commission to see that it was time to start loosening the missionary denominational administration of schools and outlook. This would begin by opening up inter-denominational secondary schools under government control on regional basis starting such a school for example in Gulu. But the missionary stand especially that of the Roman Catholic hierarchy was quite opposed to this kind of idea and the proposal fell through.

Eventually what came to be decided as a unanimous stand by the Committee through missionary influence, was that Christian principles were to be the basis of education administration denominationally. The Protectorate government would establish and administer only those schools for Muslims where there was enough demand for them. Thus the Missionaries used the existence of the 1940 Education Committee to make their feelings of 1925 vocal and writ large as the principles of administration of education in Uganda. By way of commitment to this principle, the Education Committee wrote in its preamble thus:

> We must respect and favour the educational establishments and machinery we find, not because education executed by missionary societies may be cheaper, but because the highest public interest demands the incalculation of the Christian values.

In a spirit of this nature the Missionaries were quite free to turn any government administrative educational policies to their point of view. For example, the stipulated Boards of Governors created by the above Education Committee were intended to make the people influence the administration of schools. But the Missionaries filled the Boards with themselves and with people who had to support the missionary point of view. The Chairman had to be from the Foundation Body. One government representative and the above three members plus the Chairman elected six other members who naturally belonged to the Foundation Body. The Boards of Governors of such very prominent schools as King's College Buddo, St. Mary's College Kisubi, Namilyango College, Busoga College Mwiri, St. Peter's College Tororo, Gayaza High School and all Teacher Training Colleges and Technical Schools, all were chaired by the Bishop of the Foundation Body.

The missionary strength in overshadowing the government influence in education was further demonstrated through the de Bunsen Education Committee of 1952. There was in the Committee some members who felt strongly that the denominational nature of education in Uganda should be stopped because it led to divisions of people and to making children walk long distances past schools because they did not belong to the denominations which owned those schools nearer their homes. Such members were Messrs Y.K. Lule, later on President of Uganda for two months in 1979, S.W. Kulubya and Miss Senkaatuuka. These members even produced a Minority Report to emphasise their stand, that denominationalism should stop in Uganda's education system.

The Minority Report however, was a cry in the wilderness. It was tantamount to stopping the increase in the missionary schools, missionary finances and missionary administrative practices in the education system of Uganda. Even the Uganda Protectorate Government could not accept this proposal fearing to lose missionary support of its role in partially directing the educational affairs in the country and in heavily financing the education system.

This lay opposition however, to missionary hold on educational administration was beginning to be vocal in Uganda by the 1950s. It was observed in the local press and in the remarks made by the Directors of Education of this period. This was one reason why the private schools gained much support during this period though there was the shortage of room in missionary and government schools. To keep the reading short on this, let us quote a few observations here. One is by the Director of Education who observed in 1947, "that there seemed no doubt that there was a growing desire for secular education which was becoming increasingly evident in the Acholi District of the Northern Province, Buganda and Toro". Speaking of the existence of private schools and their rapid growth, the de Bunsen Education Committee Report observed that "private schools were a natural outcome of the desire for independence from missionary hold and increased educational facilities".

In the Legislative Council meetings in the 1950s there were repeated attacks by African unofficial members on the missionary hold on education administration and predominance in all educational matters. But the government could not accept the attacks of the public and of the Legislative Council members on the Missionaries. In answer to the above attacks of the Legislative Council members, the Director of Education said in one session in 1951 thus:

> The Missionaries have got an honesty and self denial and devote more time to education than lay people could have done. The Churches pour into education directly and indirectly an amount of money which I am quite incapable of estimating, and therefore, an attack on the Missionaries from any quarter is difficult to support by the government.

He was saying the truth. During the same year a group of teachers in the Western Province wrote to the Binns Study Group complaining against the missionary hold on educational administration thus:

> The teaching career is not inviting to many people in Uganda partly because most schools are controlled by Missionaries, and so the ordinary teacher is mistaken for a missionary who is determined to sacrifice all for the Saviour's sake.

To the above, the Provincial Education Officer for the Western Province remarked in disapproval of the attitude of the teachers towards the Missionares. He thus wrote:

> The remarks made about Missionaries are cruel and thoughtless. Do the writers not realise that, but for the unselfish sacrifice of thousands of Missionaries, there would have been no education in Uganda? I cannot understand people who, owing their education and livelihood to Missionaries, are so bereft of all sense of loyalty as to make derogatory remarks about their benefactors.

From the Northern Province the Provincial Commissioner for Education supported the Missionaries and commended their efforts in furthering educational development in the area. He thus concluded his 1956 annual report:

> It is, therefore, depressing that there should be so much ignorant criticism of the Missions' work both in education and in social advance generally and little appreciation of the great debt owed to the Churches' leaders.

Indeed all the above shows that the dominance of Missionaries in educational administration was an established fact in Uganda and highly appreciated by the colonial Protectorate government. Thus Dr. M.S.M. Kiwanuka observed:

This predominance of mission education seemed to have been taken for granted; neither the British government nor the Missionaries themselves saw anything odd in it.

The stand of the Missionaries can be appreciated. The Missionaries had come to Uganda to establish Christianity and to consolidate its practice in the country through Churches, schools and hospitals. While the Uganda Protectorate Government did not endeavour to direct their Churches and hospitals, why should it try to control and direct their schools? Indeed the government wanted to control the schools because the schools had demonstrated themselves as the most potent instrument to influence the people of Uganda daily from their earliest formative years. Therefore the Missionaries could not give away this instrument easily to the government.

The Missionaries however, were quite positive in their resolve to control and direct education in Uganda. They stretched their physical and financial means to the utmost in this endeavour. They used to solicit for funds from friends and from their families abroad, they solicited for funds from Ugandans, they collected very small amounts of school fees from the pupils and they got grants-in-aid from the Uganda Protectorate government. Having done so, they spent every shilling on education with an honesty which will ever stand as an example which should be admired and worthy emulating by the Ugandans especially by the officials in the Ministry of Education from the Minister of Education and Sports to the District Education Officers and by the Headteachers of our schools. Embezzlement of school money was never heard of during the missionary era.

Many Missionaries stretched their financial means and they paid school fees for students of poor and deceased parents. In this respect, Fr. Spartas, leader of the African Greek Orthodox Church was similar to the Missionaries. Indeed thousands of Ugandans who have been prominent in the Uganda society at various levels from the grass roots to the top were orphans or sons and daughters of very poor parents. Had it not been for the presence of these Missionaries and Fr. Spartas, such people would have never been raised to such status. Therefore the Missionaries had a justification to insist on the control of their schools. The Uganda Protectorate government could have never played the role which the Missionaries played so admirably.

Fortunately, though we have seen some few Ugandans who were criticising the missionary role in education, the majority of the Ugandans appreciated and continue to appreciate even today the role which the Missionaries played in the educational system of Uganda. These people were in agreement with the following comment by the Director of Education, Mr. Jowitt in one of the sessions of the Legislative Council of 1951:

> The Missionaries have got an honesty and self denial and devote more time to education than lay people can do. The Churches pour into education directly and indirectly an amount of money which I am quite incapable of estimating, and therefore, an attack on the Missionaries from any quarter is difficult to support by the government.

Indeed Sir Hesketh Bell who was Governor of Uganda between 1905 and 1910 had already passed a similar comment on the role of the Missionaries in Uganda thus:

> Due to the admirable efforts of the Missionary Societies, the administration has been relieved of making the provision for education which in any other dependency would have been a serious call upon the government's finances.

The Phelps-Stokes Commission in respect of the missionary role in education had made an observation in 1925 which did not change much by 1960. That observation in 1925 ran as follows:

> The Missionaries, both Protestant and Roman Catholic, who have played so large a part in the history of Uganda, have up to the present had practically the whole education of the country in their hands. With the exception of some recently erected government buildings at Makerere near Kampala, and of some centres where assistant medical workers are trained, all the school buildings and teaching staff belong to the Missions. An educational system which branches out into the whole Protectorate has been brought into being in cooperation with the Native Chiefs and until recently without any financial support from the colonial government. It is an educational achievement of which the Missions can legitimately be proud.

In respect of the above observation which was made in 1925, considering secondary education, by 1960 Uganda had 28 secondary schools. Out of these 28 secondary schools the Uganda Protectorate government had only eight secondary schools while the Missionaries had 20.

The secondary schools which were under the Uganda Protectorate government were as follows:

1. Makerere College School under the Makerere University College Council.
2. Ntare School in Mbarara.
3. Kigezi College Butobere in Kigezi.
4. Kabalega Secondary School in Masindi.
5. Mvara Secondary School in Arua.

6. Sir Samuel Baker Pongdwong in Gulu.
7. Lango College in Lira and
8. Teso College Aloet in Teso.

At primary school teacher training institutions and technical school levels, the government fared even less prominently in founding and controlling such educational institutions. Besides, the Missionaries were "pouring into the building, maintaining and administering those educational institutions directly and indirectly an amount of money which the Director of Education found quite difficult to estimate". Therefore the observation of the Phelps-Stokes Commission made in 1925 still held good by 1960. Indeed Uganda's education system owes a lot to the selfless devotion of the Protestant and Roman Catholic Missionaries in its formative years and to the pioneers of private schools to a lesser extent.

Sir J. Hathorn Hall, Governor of Uganda up to 1951

9 Language and the Medium of Instruction in Uganda

The Colonial Office was the source of policies on language and the medium of instruction. In its policy of 1925, the Colonial Office in London stated that:

> ...the study of the educational use of the vernaculars was of primary importance and that scholars should be aided by both government and Missionaries in the preparation of vernacular text-books. That policy also stated that English should be taught in the top classes of the primary schools so that in post primary classes, students should have a fair knowledge of English to benefit by instruction through that language.

In its implementation of that policy the Uganda Protectorate administration at first followed the Colonial policy as stated above. But when it seemed as if Uganda would be administered politically as part of the East African Federation, the Uganda Protectorate government brought in Kiswahili, a language which was not native in Uganda, and the Colonial Office had to come in to reverse the trend of things along its already stated policy of using local vernaculars at a lower level and English at an advanced stage.

By the time the Colonial Office declared its policy, the Missionaries however, had already begun to work along the lines of what the Colonial Office passed as policy in 1925. They had already learned the languages in Buganda, Busoga, Bunyoro, Tooro, Ankole, Bugisu, Teso, West Nile, Acholi, Lango and the number of languages was increasing as the Missionaries were getting into more contacts of other people in Uganda. Besides they were using such languages as media of instruction and also writing text-books in them for use at primary school level.

Luganda which by government policy of 1912 had been encouraged to be the official language in Buganda in government business besides English, had tipped the scales because of the large number of people who were speaking it in Buganda and outside. Since it was spoken in the area where all the Protectorate administrative headquarters had been established, many other people besides the Baganda had to be in contact with that language. And since the first African teachers and the British colonial collaborators in terms of chiefs were Baganda, they had helped to spread Luganda outside Buganda, making it a language for both long distance trade and education.

Moreover it is very similar to all other Bantu languages in Uganda so much so that other Bantu non-speakers of Luganda easily learnt it. So the Missionaries had already made Luganda by 1925 a medium of instruction in vernacular schools in Buganda, Tororo area, Busoga and Bugisu. Likewise text-books written in that language and religious books, were being used both in schools and churches in those mentioned areas.

Runyoro-Rutooro was being used in Bunyoro and Tooro, while Runyankole-Rukiga was being used in Ankole and in Kigezi. Luganda would not be easily acceptable in the other kingdom areas because their traditional kings were as jealous of keeping the source or the treasury of their culture as the king of Buganda was in terms of Luganda.

In the north, that is Lango and Acholi, Luo was being used, while Ateso was being used in the central portion of the eastern area. The Comboni Missionaries who had spilled over into Uganda from Southern Sudan from 1910, were battling with learning Lugbara, Kakwa, Madi and Luo in West Nile and beginning to use those languages as media of instruction and languages for vernacular text-books. But since Lugbara and Luo tended to be more widely understood in West Nile, Acholi and Lango, those two languages tended to be adopted as media of instruction and languages for text book production in West Nile, Acholi and Lango. Ateso was being used in Teso and Karamoja.

Therefore, by 1925 the Uganda Protectorate government comfortably fitted in well with the Colonial Office policy on language of developing some of the African languages as media of instruction in schools and teaching English as "a means of uniting Africa with the great civilisations of the world".

To facilitate the use of Luganda as a medium of instruction and for using it in the preparation of textbooks, the Uganda Protectorate government appointed a committee to establish a common orthography for that language because pupils attending Roman Catholic schools spelt it differently from those who were attending C.M.S. schools. Consequently, a common orthography would stop confusion. This issue of the orthography, however, remained unresolved for none of each Christian group would give up its hard worked out system of writing Luganda. The issue was only resolved in 1944 after an expert on African languages, Dr. Turner, from the Sudan, was seconded to the Uganda government by the Colonial Office to set up a practical orthography for all African languages which were being used as media of instruction in Uganda. The new orthography for the vernacular languages which was then worked out, was enforced by the examination system and separate spellings of not only Luganda but also of other languages which were Runyoro-Rutooro, Runyankore-Rukiga, Luo, Ateso and Lugbara were enforced.

Educational policy regarding language as a medium of instruction became an issue of great concern and heated debate from 1927 and eventually petered out by 1937 through the advice of the de La Warr Commission from the Colonial Office. It became an issue because in 1927 the then Governor of Uganda, Sir W.F. Gowers suggested that Kiswahili should begin to be used in government business and as a medium of instruction in schools, an issue that had been shelved in 1912. In 1927 there was talk from the Colonial Office wishing to administer Kenya, Tanganyika, Zanzibar and Uganda as one political unit. This was then referred to as Closer Union which however meant federation. This idea of federation excited the Governors of Kenya, Uganda and Tanzania.

As a first step towards the realisation of this ideal, Sir. W.F. Gowers abruptly issued a policy statement in Uganda regarding language. He declared that

Language and the Medium of Instruction

Kiswahili should replace Luganda in government business in Buganda, Busoga, Tororo area and Bugisu and in schools at the lower level as a medium of instruction in those areas. He blamed his predecessors for having encouraged Luganda since 1912 instead of Kiswahili. He thus stated:

> A policy by which a local dialect is encouraged (Luganda) at the expense of this widely-spread alternative language, (Kiswahili) can no longer in my opinion be maintained. The range of Luganda is in my opinion far too restricted for it to be regarded as a dominant union language.

Sir W.F. Gowers contended that since 1912, the favour given to Luganda in preference to Kiswahili had not helped Luganda to develop quickly in all parts of Uganda while Kiswahili though set "at a disadvantage", was developing on its own. The Governor had the following assumptions. He thought that Kiswahili would facilitate the development of education in a country where there are so many small vernacular languages. Since, Kiswahili was being used in the rest of East Africa and in Burundi and Rwanda, the production of text-books in it would be cheaper and communication easier.

Since Kiswahili is a Bantu language, the Bantu people who made up the greater part of Uganda, would easily master it. It would be only a few Nilotic people who would find some comparative difficulty in learning it. But even this, he contended, was not a formidable problem, since it was they who had already begun to master it up instead of mastering up Luganda.

Since Kiswahili belongs to no tribal group in Uganda it had the advantage of arousing no animosity among people in Uganda for having been picked on while another alternative local language in Uganda had been left out.

Above all, Kiswahili would save the Uganda Protectorate officers from learning a multiplicity of vernaculars on their constant transfers from one tribal area of Uganda to another. Gowers therefore concluded that "Kiswahili had been discarded in favour of Luganda for reasons which appeared by 1927 to any unprejudiced observer to be wholly inadequate".

Governor Gowers' policy statement on language and the assumptions behind it, caused so much uneasiness both in educational circles and administration that the `Protectorate government was between 1927 and 1937 obliged to issue several statements to clear the situation about its language policy in the country. Opposition came from the Missionaries, from the Uganda elites, from the traditional kings of the south and from the general informed public, primarily down south.

The Missionaries based their opposition to Kiswahili on two grounds. Firstly, they contended that it was closely allied to Islam, and therefore to encourage it through their schools, would be facilitating the spread of Islam and its influence. Earlier on, Bishop A. Tucker, the powerful C.M.S. Bishop, had opposed the use of Kiswahili in schools vehemently which partly helped Luganda being declared an official language in 1912 in Buganda, Busoga, Tororo area and Bugisu. He had insisted that "Kiswahili was too closely related to Mohammedanism to be welcome".

The second ground for opposing Kiswahili by the Missionaries was based on the fact that it belonged to no people in Uganda and that Luganda which belonged to Uganda could be developed instead of Kiswahili for both administration and educational purposes. Moreover, it was a contradiction to tell the Missionary educators to endeavour to preserve African culture and at the same time be told to destroy people's languages. Thus the missionary point of view was partly expressed by Rev. R. Rowling as follows:

> We are daily urged to retain all that is most valuable in African life and customs. Now if any African vernaculars at all are to be retained for school work, 'Luganda deserves a place in the first seven languages in Uganda on its own merits, and as a most valuable educational factor in itself.

Indeed the support for Luganda by Rowling and by other Missionaries both Catholic and Protestant, had also ulterior motives. Rowling for example, with a few other C.M.S. Missionaries had been involved in a lot of serious study of the language and in translational work into Luganda for the C.M.S schools. Similar efforts were being expended by the White Father and Mill Hill Father Missionaries. Consequently these Missionaries did not like to see their efforts die so naturally like that. And in fact by studying Luganda so deeply, these Missionaries had cultivated a very great liking and admiration for its rich vocabulary and viability.

There was also confusion as to whether the introduction of Kiswahili in schools, meant ceasing to use vernaculars in schools at all levels. The Missionaries got this impression though wrongly, from what was happening in Tanganyika. Kiswahili was the medium of instruction in disregard to many vernaculars there spoken even over a wide area such as Luhaya in Bukoba and Chagga in Chaggaland. Consequently, as a *lingua franca*, Kiswahili was destroying other local languages together with the cultures to which they were allied.

The Missionaries here were developing a keen interest in the study of nearly all African languages whose people they were getting into contact with. As they were doing so, they were teaching those people especially catechism through their languages thereby to get a more sympathetic attitude from those people and respect. In their dual purpose of spreading both Christianity and school education, the Missionaries felt that to touch the minds of the Africans more deeply, one needed to learn their respective languages and cultures so that one could talk to them through them. Therefore, on this basis, they resisted the government policy of introducing Kiswahili as a subject in schools which eventually would become a medium of instruction in schools and a lingua franca for Uganda. To clear this confusion, the Director of Education had to state in 1928 thus:

> The policy with regard to language, initiated by His Excellency the Governor and outlined in the last report, has been successfully pursued. The mother tongue is taught in the first stage of the elementary vernacular schools and followed during the final years by Swahili in all provinces of the Protectorate with the exception of Buganda

Language and the Medium of Instruction

The Missionaries were supported by the traditional rulers in preserving the vernaculars spoken in their areas and in opposing the use of Kiswahili as a medium of instruction. This support, however, was more evident in Ankole, Buganda, Bunyoro, Tooro and in Busoga. The support by the traditional rulers in Buganda, Bunyoro, Tooro, Ankole and Busoga, sprang at least from two motives. One was that as traditional rulers, in the politics of indirect rule, it behoved them to safeguard the customs and traditions of their respective peoples. At least this was strictly one of the major raison d'etre for the justification of their existence in the eyes of their peoples. To withdraw official recognisation of their languages in the system was the first serious step to abolishing their existence and the embodiment of their cultural pride, a thing which had already begun to develop in Tanganyika.

After a long drawn discussion of the issue in the Great Lukiiko of Buganda in 1929, Sir Daudi Chwa II Kabaka of Buganda issued the following objection to the Kiswahili policy to the Governor of Uganda:

> I am entirely opposed to any arrangement which would in any way facilitate the ultimate adoption of the Swahili language as the Official Native Language of the Baganda in place of or at the expense of their own language, since I feel convinced that such a course will assuredly bring about the loss of our tribal status and nationality among the native tribes of Africa.

But Sir Daudi Chwa II did not rule out the teaching of Kiswahili as a subject in Buganda schools if such a step would enable his subjects to serve the Protectorate administration more effectively, "If especially called upon to act as Swahili interpreters in districts where Luganda was not understood".

Sir Daudi Chwa's point was taken up by the Governor who assured him that Kiswahili would not be enforced on the Baganda and that it would be taught in Buganda only if the Baganda so wished: hence the Director of Education's statement that efforts of teaching Kiswahili in all provinces were being pursued with the exception of Buganda.

Other traditional rulers raised also similar objections, the most vocal of them coming from Kasagama, the then Omukama of Tooro who wanted to see neither Kiswahili nor Luganda adopted in the Tooro Kingdom. He wanted to retain the use of Runyoro-Rutooro both in the schools and in government business and the teaching of English to his people.

The opposition to Kiswahili by the traditional rulers together with that of their chiefs was strengthened by the fear of the Closer Union of East Africa which they disliked. Thus Dr. A.B.K. Kasozi contends:

> The Kings realised, like the Presidents of the late 1960's, that in an East African Federation they would become very small fishes in a very big pond whereas in their tribal kingdoms they would be sharks. It was realised that if Swahili became the medium of instruction all over East Africa, then the obstacles to an East African Federation would be reduced.

Then there was the opposition of the elites mostly from Busoga and from the kingdom areas. This opposition is best epitomised by the four men whom the Uganda Protectorate government sent to London to give evidence to the Joint Select Committee on the Closer Union of East Africa in 1931. These were S.W. Kulubya then Treasurer of the Buganda Kingdom, Samsoni Bazongere, a Ggombolola Chief in Buganda, Yekoniya Zirabamuzaale, a Ssaza Chief of Kigulu in Busoga and Kosiya Rabwoni, a Ssaza Chief from Bunyoro. Kulubya, Bazongere and Zirabamuzaale, were in favour of using Luganda and English because English opened wide horizons for their people while Luganda was their national language which should not be lost. When he was asked by a member of the Joint Select Committee as to which foreign language should be introduced and used in Uganda, Kulubya eagerly answered: "English, of course, my Lord, which is the key to everything, as it is".

Rabwoni of Bunyoro however, while insisting on the keeping of Runyoro in Bunyoro as a matter of course, expressed that he had no objection to seeing Kiswahili being taught as a subject but not to be used as a medium of instruction in "schools and the people being forced to speak Kiswahili in their native courts".

The elites were also supported by the prominent British educationists of the time, famous of them H.M. Grace, then Headmaster of King's College Buddo who expressed the view that English was the vehicle of knowledge.

To the opposition of the above people in terms of the reasons given, Kiswahili as a language suffered a social disability in the southern part of the Protectorate. This social disability is only diminishing slowly now. The man on the street in this southern part of the Uganda Protectorate, viewed Kiswahili as a language of people without a real background, the Swahili. Moreover, the first people who came to Uganda from the coast speaking Kiswahili did not inspire much confidence and respect in many seriously minded people "who considered the Swahili people to have low standards of morality and thought them as a serious temptation to the young and the unstable".

Granted that at the court of Muteesa I, Kiswahili gained a respect and the first Missionaries had to use it, the people who introduced Kiswahili as a language, the Arabs and Swahilis, were at times irresponsible, double-dealers and that the few Ugandans who learnt the language, tended to be connected with this kind of behaviour. For example, such Ugandan people would hide their duplicity by speaking Kiswahili to conceal their true identity. "*Omuswayiri*" in Bantu languages in Uganda, had the connotation of a person who was canny and hard to trust and a double-dealer. It was worse if a woman spoke Kiswahili. Many people would take her for a widely travelled person who had met a lot of other people of dubious character. Therefore to impose upon people a language with no local origin, which language was so connected with this kind of disability to replace other Ugandan languages whose owners respected, was looked at as an outrageous decision made by the Uganda Protectorate government.

In the absence of good speakers of Kiswahili in Uganda, also people had the impression that it was a language without grammar and anybody could devise a way of speaking it anyhow. As a result one heard all sorts of constructions of

Language and the Medium of Instruction

Kiswahili. Since the Asians used Kiswahili more than any other people in Uganda when talking to their customers and employees, then Kiswahili became most funny if not laughable. And since the Asians were employing mostly illiterate or semi-literate people especially for sweated labour, who also tended to speak Kiswahili of all descriptions, the people down south, tended to associate Kiswahili with low paid illiterate labourers who did sweated work. The sum total of all this, made many people even if not belonging to the elite group down south, to look down upon Kiswahili. The first impression created by an African who spoke Kiswahili, was that of an African who had not gone to school.

Having gathered all the opposition from the people, Bishop J.W. Campling, Vicar Apostolic of the Upper Nile of the Mill Hill Mission, Bishop A.L. Kitching of the C.M.S. in Teso and Bishop H. Streicher of the White Fathers of Lubaga, produced in 1931 a 9 points opposition to the adoption of Kiswahili as a medium of instruction and for use in government business in Uganda. That document summed up all the feelings of the Missionaries, the elites, the traditional rulers and of the informed public.

The Bishops finally supported Luganda because it was spoken by a very large section of the people not only in Buganda. It was also akin to all other Bantu languages in Uganda and nearer to the other people speaking different non Bantu ethnic languages, than Kiswahili which was foreign in the country.

But the Bishops of the Verona Fathers mission and of the African Inland Mission both of whom were working in the Northern and West Nile Provinces, did not attach their signatures to the above memorandum. One explanation for this, is that already Kiswahili had caught on in those areas and it was helping to solve the problem for Missionaries regarding the use of a multiplicity of languages within small areas. In fact since the time it had been declared a medium of instruction in the north from 1928, enrolment of pupils had increased in primary schools as the Director of Education contended in his Education Report of 1928.

With the confidence that opposition to Kiswahili in Uganda was primarily concentrated in the south of the country, the Director of Education frowned at the above exposition of the Bishops for trying to "disassociate Uganda from the accepted policy of using Swahili as the lingua franca for East Africa, and to use one of the local tribal vernaculars as a lingua franca of the Protectorate".

Despite the Director's lashing at the Bishops, their influence was such that it should not be ignored by government. The Advisory Council on African Education in Uganda on which all the Bishops sat together with the Kabaka himself or his nominee, though the Council was chaired by the Director of Education, it revised government policy as regarded Kiswahili. The line taken in that revision was mostly intended to allay the fears in Buganda from where the greatest opposition to Kiswahili seemed to be. Thus ran the Council's statement:

> The Advisory Council wishes to express very strongly the view that in Buganda Province the medium of instruction should always be Luganda. Kiswahili, however, might be introduced as a subject at a later date, if the Baganda desired to and teachers were available.

That the teacher trainees at the Government Teacher Training at Nyanjeeradde near Makerere, should be trained for teaching in Kiswahili at the K.A.R., the Police schools and selected elementary vernacular schools in the mixed linguistic areas. That grant-aided mission teacher Training Schools at Nabumali, Ngora, Arua and Gulu should teach Kiswahili to the Teachers in training.

That in the mixed linguistic areas Kiswahili should be taught as a subject in elementary vernacular schools as soon as teachers qualified to teach are available from those Teacher Training Schools, but the local vernaculars should remain the medium of instruction.

That in the Government Technical School in Kampala which will cater for boys from all over the Protectorate, Kiswahili should be taught.

But since Kiswahili was not allowed to be taught strictly in Buganda, the idea of its gaining a firm foothold in schools would hardly succeed else where. With the opposition of both the Missionaries down south and of the Baganda to it, Kiswahili had no chance to flourish in Uganda's education system. Luganda with so many other people speaking it besides the Baganda, had also the added advantage of possessing a rapidly growing literate society and a fast growing written literature.

The Missionary efforts to translate many religious and educational works in Luganda was accompanied by efforts in original compositions by some Missionaries, by some Baganda and by some other speakers of Luganda. To this was added three popular newspapers in Luganda which were by the 1930's being published every month, namely Munno by the White Fathers, Ebifa by the C.M.S. and Sekanyolya published by some Baganda elites based in Nairobi.

As far as some Missionaries and their supporters were concerned, the battle had been won. Kiswahili would not be a medium of instruction in Buganda and in Busoga but only taught as a subject like any other subject in the academic section of the educational system. They also realised that with the African growing clamour for learning English and with the scarcity of Kiswahili teachers, the chances for the success of Kiswahili even in other areas would be very little for Kiswahili to eventually become a lingua Franca at the expense of their contention that a local language had a greater claim to being developed for that purpose and not Kiswahili.

The Missionaries however, cooperated in teaching Kiswahili according to the above decision of the Advisory Council. Especially in the grant-aided mission primary schools and in the teachers' education institutions in the North and part of the East, there was a remarkable progress. The efforts in the Teacher Training Colleges in the North and the East were supplemented by those in the Kampala Government Teacher Training School at Nyanyeeradde near Makerere. To help introduce fluency in grammatical Kiswahili, visits lasting for three months were every year being arranged for the teacher trainees in those colleges to stay at the coast in Mombasa.

At the end of 1932 the Director of Education showed satisfaction at the way Kiswahili was gaining ground as a subject and in some cases as a medium of instruction outside Buganda. He thus reported.

It is quite clear that the people in the East are on the whole in favour of the use of Kiswahili in preference to Luganda as the second language of instruction, and the very fact of the discontinuance of Luganda might help them to stand on their own feet and provide from amongst their own people both their political and spiritual mentors. In the Northern and Western Province the change also seems to be universally popular.

But the Uganda Protectorate Government ceased to be too keen on the Kiswahili policy after the issue of the Closer Union was shelved after 1933. Even the Joint Select Committee on the Closer Union of East Africa had recommended a gradual change from Kiswahili to English more especially after the views put to it by such men as Kulubya, Rabwoni and Zirabamuzaale mentioned already above.

Though efforts after 1933 continued to teach Kiswahili in schools in the North and in the East, there were no more efforts on the side of the Department of Education to press for the teaching of Kiswahili and to see to its spread. For this there were a host of reasons. One reason was that teachers of Kiswahili were too few and to produce them was quite expensive. For example, a three months stay in Mombasa by teacher trainees who were supposed to teach Kiswahili to gain fluency, was not cheap.

Secondly, the Central Schools which had been planned on a practical basis and which had a large content of Kiswahili were discontinued after 1938 due to lack of support from society for their practical curriculum which people saw as having a limited scope for the pupils who wanted to continue higher up the academic ladder.

Thirdly, on the arrival of Sir Philip Mitchell as Governor in 1935, the emphasis was on secondary education and Kiswahili was looked at as a retarding agent in this direction. Since English had to be used as a medium of instruction in secondary schools, the pupils needed to master it while they were still in primary schools and Kiswahili would retard their mastering English whose relative usefulness could not be compared to that of Kiswahili.

By 1937 even the Government Kampala Teacher Training School at Nyanjeeradde near Makerere, whose mission had been to train teachers of Kiswahili and teach it at national level closed. One reason for its closure was lack of support for teachers trained in it by the Missionaries. Since the government had only a few of its own primary schools, it was finding it difficult to post teachers from that teacher training school. The Missionaries preferred teachers who had been brought up according to their own point of view through their denominational teacher training schools.

Fourthly, Hussey and Morris both of them Directors of Education between 1925 and 1934 and who were keen supporters of Kiswahili in the educational system, got transferred to other British territories. Also the Governors under whom they worked and who had been fervent supporters of Kiswahili, Governors Gowers and Boudillion, were both by 1934 transferred from Uganda. H. Jowitt who became the Director of Education and Philip Mitchell who took over the governorship from 1935, were both not in favour of Kiswahili. With these two top government officials not being committted to the Kiswahili policy and with a strong unfavourable attitude to the language in one large section of the Uganda society, the Kiswahili issue was on its way to decline.

To the above reasons then came the advice from the Colonial Office that its original policy of 1925 should be reverted to. Consequently the government had to restate the new status quo as regarded the policy of language in the educational system. Thus Jowitt, the Director of Education stated that policy as follows: Vernaculars had to be the media of instruction except "in a very few primary schools where the students were drawn from diverse and unrelated linguistic groups where there was no dominant vernacular".

After vernaculars as media of instruction, English would take their place in the post primary educational institutions. To emphasise Jowitt's policy statement, the de La Warr Commission from the Colonial office in 1937 added that "it would be a mistake to delay the teaching of English in primary schools for the sake of Kiswahili". This then meant that English had to start being taught early in primary schools so that students proceeding there from could learn through it as medium of instruction at post primary level.

After the departure of the de La Warr Commission in 1937, there was no more serious effort expended on the teaching of Kiswahili in schools let alone to think of it as one day becoming a medium of instruction in schools and a lingua Franca in Uganda. It however, continued to be taught in the Police schools, in the K.A.R. and in some primary schools in the northern and the eastern provinces. But since Jowitt dropped Kiswahili from the curriculum of the teacher training schools both in the north and in the east, there was then a dwindling number of teachers who were involved in teaching Kiswahili in the above mentioned areas.

When the Colonial Office sent the Binns Study Group here in 1951, it continued to stress the above policy on language. It emphasized the need to use vernaculars as media of instruction in teaching at primary school level because it had been proved through research that one's own native language was the most natural instrument for acquiring knowledge at that early age.

The Binns Study Group in retrospect restated the ideas of the Phelps -Stokes Commission way back in 1925 and the ideas which the Missionaries and other educators were by then fostering. Those ideas were concerned with using the schools to preserve African culture by fostering the use of selected African languages. Already the Uganda Protectorate Government had selected the following languages in Uganda as very viable to serve large areas educationally: Luganda, Luo, Lugbara, Runyoro-Rutooro, Ateso and Runyankore-Rukiga. The government had also had the orthographies of those languages worked out and standardised in 1947 by Turner, a linguistic expert from the Sudan.

Production of books in these languages was being encouraged for use in primary schools through local education committees backed by government. The East African High Commission, was committed to publishing books in these languages once the material was vetted as good by the language sub-committees of the Education Committee in each language area. And already in these languages, history, proverbs, folk tales, riddles and infant rhymes, were being taught in schools because by so doing one could see the philosophy that lay behind African culture. The adoption of Luganda as a subject examinable by the Cambridge School Certificate Examination Syndicate, enhanced this side of approach. All this was endorsed by the 'Binns Study Group in 1951 as being in agreement with the Colonial Office view on language which contended that:

> ...the mother tongue was the most potent to awaken the dawning imagination of the Africans through songs, stories, nursery rhymes, folk tales and proverbs and that it helped the Africans to select the best from the spiritual strength of Western culture.

The Binns Study Group further discouraged the teaching of Kiswahili in the Uganda schools because Kiswahili stood in the way of teaching the selected vernaculars and English.

The East African Royal Commission of 1953 again from the Colonial Office, also advised the Uganda Protectorate administration against teaching Kiswahili in schools. The members regarded the teaching of Kiswahili as a second language to children whose early education had been in other vernaculars, as a complete waste of time and effort. In terms of knowledge, Kiswahili was not taking such children further than their own vernaculars. The members of the Royal Commission then lashed at the practice which had developed whereby in the Police and Army schools Kiswahili was the medium of instruction, saying that "the last thing that was desired was a Police Force using a language different from that of the people among whom it worked. There would develop a rift between the Police Force and the people," an observation which was not divorced from experience.

But the Uganda Protectorate government had a problem over this one. The Police Force and the Army were being joined by all members of the different tribes in Uganda who had to be posted any where in the country mostly outside their tribal areas. The majority of the recruits used to join those Forces when already familiar with Kiswahili.

Those who did not know it, easily picked it up from fellow recruits which was not the case with English. Moreover, Kiswahili of a sort was more commonly understood in all parts of Uganda unlike English. Besides, to use one of the Uganda vernaculars in the Police Force, would have invited animosity from those other members whose language it was not. Therefore the practical way for the Uganda Protectorate administration was to use Kiswahili in the Police Force.

The efforts of encouraging Kiswahili in Uganda's schools in the face of all the above opposition definitely failed though however, there still remained some signs of its being taught in some schools in Uganda so much so that by 1956 a casual observer wrote in the Journal of Africa that:

> Swahili had not entirely disappeared from Uganda especially in the Northern Province where, at least during the forties, there were still some teachers left who

had been trained in Swahili at the Kampala Government Teacher Training School twenty years before.

Indeed the North preserved the flicker of light of Kiswahili and its respect up to independence time. Kiswahili in Uganda tended to be popular in Karamoja, Lango, Acholi, Teso and in the area traditionally called West Nile. This was a bit peculiar because the peoples in these areas do not speak Bantu languages and therefore one would have expected Kiswahili to have been more difficult for these peoples than for those in the southern area where the languages are of Bantu origin like Kiswahili.

Several reasons can be advanced to explain this phenomenon. One reason was that the peoples in the areas Kiswahili tended to be more popular, did not view Kiswahili as competing with their own languages. Secondly, the peoples from those areas were very interested in working in the Police and in the Army Forces as a career, and since Kiswahili was compulsory, they learnt it and they saw it as an advantage to learn it before joining both the Police and the Army to pass the interview very easily. Also the Asians who employed most of the labourers knew Kiswahili of a sort. So Kiswahili helped these peoples moving all over Uganda and even to Kenya to easily be employed by Asians and saved them from the trouble of learning a multiplicity of other Bantu languages.

The 1970's were years when Kiswahili was resurrected with stronger cards to be established firmly and expanded in Uganda than during the colonial period which ended on 9th October 1962.

The following were those stronger cards. Firstly. On the 25th January 1971, Apollo Milton Obote and his first administration were overthrown by Obote's right hand man, Idi Amin Dada. At once Kiswahili came into the lime-light because it was the language of the army people who were at the helm of power. At once there was an order from the army leaders for news in Kiswahili to be read on the Uganda Radio and on the Uganda Television, ostensibly for the army men to understand the news.

The man on the street began to realise that it was advantageous to know and speak Kiswahili to be on easy talking terms with the army leaders and their rank and file. So Kiswahili began to gain status in the Uganda society though the school elites still treated it as a language of the unschooled.

Secondly, in 1972 the army leaders forced a Bill through Parliament and Kiswahili was made a national language. But unfortunately no efforts were made to teach it briskly in schools so that it would eventually become a medium of instruction and also gain a greater respectability among the students who were the future leaders in the country.

Thirdly, in 1972 Idi Amin Dada's administration expelled the Asians from Uganda to enable Ugandans to complete the cycle of regaining their independence by controlling the economy of Uganda since they had taken over the political control in 1962.

Language and the Medium of Instruction

The expulsion of the Asians from Uganda led thousands of Ugandans into business. Kenya which has got numerous industries in East Africa was the immediate country where Ugandan business men and women went to import industrial goods for Uganda. A knowledge of Kiswahili and fluency in it was necessary to do business easily in Kenya. So Ugandan business men and women got out of their way to learn and speak Kiswahili to facilitate business dealings with Kenyans. And indeed the low status of Kiswahili in the eyes of many Ugandans began to decrease.

Fourthly, in April, 1979, Uganda lost her independence to Tanzania. In that month and year Obote's guerrillas assisted by the Tanzanian soldiers overthrew Idi Amin's administration. Uganda came under occupation of the Tanzanian army up to 1981. Uganda was then being ruled on the orders of President Julius Kambarage Nyerere from Dar-es-Salaam.

In regard to Kiswahili, the above period saw a great enthusiasm for that language on the part of the man on the street. Kiswahili was the language of the swarms of Tanzanian soldiers who spoke it with such gusto and intonation which easily made a great impression on the man on the street. So the Tanzanian soldiers set up a standard to be followed by the man on the street. All this helped to boost the status of Kiswahili in the Uganda society. Though the Obote II regime 1981-85, cared less about Kiswahili, the low status which was accorded to that language prior to Uganda's regaining her independence in 1962, waned greatly.

The National Resistance Movement which took over power in January 1986 after the fall of the Obote II regime and of the Okello Lutwa administration was not opposed to the Kiswahili more so because it came into power by the use of armed forces whose language is Kiswahili. The National Resistance Council decided that Kiswahili besides English would be one of Uganda's national languages, a decision which had been already passed by the regime of Idi Amin way back in 1971.

But the Uganda National Education Policy Review Commission which was appointed in 1987 by the National Resistance Council and chaired by Prof. W. Senteza Kajubi recommended to tow a line in education regarding Kiswahili and other languages which was similar to that which existed between 1931 and 1962.

Thus in part that Commission recommended:

> As a general policy, the Commission considers that the development and use of all Ugandan languages should be encouraged both in formal and non-formal education programmes at the level of basic education. This encouragement should particularly recognise the key role which language plays in cultural expression.

As a general language policy in education,

The Commission further recommended that:

a. The mother tongue be used as a medium of instruction in all educational programmes up to P.4.

b. English should be taught as a subject from P.1. From P.5 onwards, English should become the medium of instruction.
c. The area language (a language of wider communication) should be taught as a subject in primary schools. The area languages are Luganda, Luo, Runyakitara: Runyoro-Rutooro and Runyankore-Rukiga, Ateso/Karimojong and Lugbara. These languages should be examinable subjects in the Primary Leaving Examination.
d. From S.1. students will be required to take, in addition to English and their area language, another Ugandan or foreign language, English continuing as the medium of instruction.
e. The teaching of Swahili should be strengthened at secondary level in order to prepare for the training of teachers of this language.

The Government White Paper on the implementation of the recommendations of the Senteza Kajubi Commission however, was more bold on the Kiswahili issue. It thus said in part:

> The potential for Kiswahili to promote the badly desired national unity is far greater than that of any other Ugandan languages. Point number 3 in the NRM Ten Point Programme provides for the consolidation of national unity. The education system will, therefore, be making its contribution through emphatic teaching of Kiswahili, towards the attainment of this goal of national unity. For, with its high potential, Kiswahili will be spread rapidly throughout the country through this policy. Its rapid development at national level will contribute to the faster eradication of illiterary, and the establishment of permanent functional and developmental literacy in the whole country. It will facilitate cheaper, easier, and faster development and production of reading instructional materials for literacy, post-literacy, adult and life long education for the various categories of the people of Uganda. This in turn will facilitate the spread of knowledge, constructive values and skills. And the above developments will certainly lead to faster socio-economics and cultural development and to the reduction of differences and elimination of animosity between people of different social groups, regions and nationalities in this country. It is also likely to promote amity between civilians and security forces-the latter who are already more accustomed to the use of Kiswahili.
>
> Kiswahili and English will be taught as compulsory subjects to all children throughout the primary cycle, in both rural and urban areas. Emphasis in terms of allocation of time and in the provision on instructional materials, facilities and teachers will, however, be gradually placed on Kiswahili as the language possessing greater capacity for uniting Ugandans and for assisting rapid social development.

After the publication of the Government White Paper in April 1992, the public picked up the issue of the language policy in Uganda. One point of view was that Kiswahili should be selected as a national language and a medium of

Language and the Medium of Instruction

instruction because since it belonged to no tribe in Uganda, it would arouse less animosity among the tribes of Uganda. Moreover it offered wider opportunities for Ugandans to communicate more easily with Kenyans, Tanzanians, Rwandese and the citizens of Burundi and Zaire.

Another point of view however, utterly opposed the adoption of Kiswahili as a national language because it is foreign to Uganda though it is an African language. If there was any need for choosing a national language which should be even a medium of instruction in schools, at least a Ugandan language should be selected. This point of view was however, vehemently opposed from several quarters because the obvious language was Luganda which is understood and spoken in all parts of Uganda and it is akin to all Bantu languages in the country.

Another point of view was that both Kiswahili and Luganda did not offer wide enough chances for communication outside Eastern Africa. And both languages are limited in terms of educational applicability. Therefore to get out of the tangle, the only way out is the use of English as a national language and as a medium of instruction in education. Ugandan languages should be taught and used at primary school level as the Senteza - Kajubi Education Commission had recommended. And Kiswahili should be taught as a subject as a means of assisting communication with Kenyans, Tanzanians, Rwandese and the people of Burundi and Zaire.

This debate is still going on. But the point of view of leaving English as the official language and as a medium of instruction after Primary Four, would be a more viable proposition in terms of national unity, international communication and economy. Thus we would be reiterating Kulubya's statement of 1931 when interviewed by the Joint Select Committee on the Closer Union of East Africa in London, "English, of course my Lord, which is the key to everything, as it is".

Looked at from both a national and a world perspective however, Ugandans should aim at securing a means of oral communication universally at national level and at international level beyond the confines of East Africa. Therefore it is the acquisition of fluency in English which should pre-occupy the minds of Ugandans besides developing their indigenous languages for cultural preservation.

AD 2003 has been earmarked for launching universal and compulsory primary education in Uganda. If every child goes to school for at least eight years, after fifty years from AD 2003, every Ugandan will be fluent in English. He or she will then be in contact with all the economic, social, political, cultural and scientific knowledge of every country in the world for his /her benefit and for the benefit of Uganda.

If English is adopted as a medium of instruction from primary five through tertiary institutions and as an official language, the issue of language in Uganda and educational instruction will be dynamic. English will prevent the development of emotionalism, sectarianism, reactionary and prejudice which hinder progress.

Besides, regional co-operation comprising East Africa, Central Africa and Southern Africa and Pan-Africanism will be better served by English than by either Kiswahili or any Ugandan indigenous language. English will help Uganda's capacity to participate in international affairs and to share relatively cheaply in the rich world wide educational and scientific developments of every kind. Uganda will also be in the new world order which is fostering and endeavouring to make Europe one village, America one village, Australia one village, Asia one village, NewZealand one village and Africa one village and eventually the whole world, one village.

This will foster national unity, regional cooperation, Pan-Africanism and internationalism per excellency which Uganda is now seeking to achieve through its language policy by way of medium of instruction in her education system and by way of an offical language. Therefore the eventual adoption of Kiswahili as a medium of instruction through Uganda's education system and as a national languages does not have the above advantages for Ugandans. To reiterate Kulubya's contention of 1931 that English is the key to everything as it is, would serve Uganda best of all. Adopting Kiswahili or any Ugandan indigenous language as a national language and a medium of instruction would be only postponing the problem and wasting much of the scarce resources of the country. English will eventually prevail in the face of the trend of things of reducing the whole world to one village.

But this should not be interpreted to mean that the Ugandan indigenous languages should be neglected in the education system. They should be encouraged and developed because they are the treasury and embodiment of our valuable cultures and strength. In both this cultural heritage and the reduction of the world to one village, Kiswahili has got no place in Uganda.

To bring to a wholesome end the protracted discussion on the medium of instruction in Uganda's schools and on the official language of Uganda, the new Constitution has eased the situation. Thus reads Article 6 of the new Constitution: 'English is the official language of Uganda."

Education development, 1940-1962

The Thomas Education Committee, 1940

The Thomas Education Committee of 1940 conveniently marks the beginning of the above period. The task of the Committee was to lay down educational targets to be achieved by 1950. Its decisions became law through the Education Ordinance of 1942.

The Thomas Education Committee introduced three important aspects in the administration of education in Uganda. Firstly, it emphasised that education had to be arranged along religious lines. Before the convening of that Committee the government had proposed that the Committee should look into the possibility of establishing boarding secondary schools under the management of the Uganda Protectorate government. Such initial schools would be one in Buganda, one in the Eastern Province, one in the Northern Province and one in the Western Province. The first such school was earmarked to be opened up in Gulu. These boarding secondary schools would be inter-denominational.

This proposal met with a lot of opposition from the Missionaries who realized that their hold on education would start to be invaded by the government. Thus the Committee gave up the idea. To emphasise the determination of the Missionaries and their supporters on the Committee, it concluded this issue as follows:

> We must respect and favour the educational establishments and machinery we find, not because education executed by Missionary Societies may be cheaper, but because the highest public interest demands the inculcation of the Christian values.

Therefore the Roman Catholic Church, the Protestant Church which eventually came to be known as the Church of Uganda and the Muslim religion, all should own their own schools separately. Children who belonged to those religions would attend schools established and run by their particular religions. There should be no mixing children of different religions in one school.

Here the Missionaries showed their determination to keep the government influence in schools down to the minimum. This decision was accepted by the Uganda Protectorate government though one of the purposes for having set up the Thomas Education Committee was to try and weaken the control of education by the Churches and Mosques, and to destroy the denominational nature of education in Uganda.

But that decision was unfortunate due to some of the following reasons. Firstly, it continued to strengthen the suspicion and hatred among the people of Uganda which arose from the political and religious quarrels and wars of the 1880s and early 1890s.

Secondly, there was a duplication of schools in an area. For example, three kinds of schools had to be built: one for Catholic children, another one for Muslim children and another one for Protestant children.

At times one could find that there were not enough children in an area to fill each of the above schools. One school could have been enough for all children of these religions in an area. Consequently, teachers and educational scholastic materials would be under utilised in a school which did not have enough pupils. Also money spent by the Uganda Protectorate government on aiding such schools could have been better used to build two schools in different areas where there was a greater need for those schools.

Thirdly, an arrangement of this nature meant that a pupil had to go past a school nearest to his/her home to a school further away just because it happened to be the one run by the religion to which that pupil belonged. This was unnecessarily tiresome. Perhaps this point does not make much sense today because we have got very many schools in one area which are in the neighbourhood of each other and have got enough pupils. But during the colonial days, schools tended to be few and far apart. Consequently, it was not unusual for a boy or girl to walk six miles to a school and back home; thus walking a total of twelve miles a day.

The second important decision made by the Thomas Education Committee of 1940 was the establishment of a system of Boards of Governors for boarding secondary schools and their equivalent such as the Teacher Training Colleges and Technical Schools. After 1952 the same arrangement was set up by the de Bunsen Education Committee for primary schools. The bodies for the primary schools were named School Management Committees.

This arrangement was introduced to interest the public in the administration of their schools which were managed by European Missionaries. The parents' duty was only to send children to those schools and pay school fees. The public looked at all schools as islands managed by European Missionaries who had introduced them into the country.

The Thomas Education Committee felt that that situation was unhealthy. The public should be brought to share in the administration of the schools and to look at them as the people's institutions. People with developmental ideas began to sit on the Boards of Governors and on School Management Committees which started after 1952, to see how schools were being managed and to give their ideas as to their development. So this is how the present Boards of Governors and the School Management Committees began in our education system. Schools whose members of the Board of Governors or School Management Committees with progressive ideas could and even today can forge ahead far beyond those whose members were or are less forward looking.

Another reason of the government for the introduction of the Boards of Governors and the School Management Committees was to try to lessen the missionary hold on the administration of schools. However, this idea failed to be achieved because Missionaries made sure that they dominated the Boards of Governors and the School Management Committees. They also made sure that Ugandans of their point of view were the ones selected as members of the Boards and of the School Management Committees.

The fourth important decision of the Thomas Education Committee was that the local governments should be responsible for financing primary schools in their areas. Up to that time it was the Protectorate government which was responsible for aiding financially both the primary and the secondary schools and other educational institutions such as the Teacher Training Colleges and the Technical Schools. The Education Ordinance of 1927 had however instituted an education tax to be levied by the local governments in aid of education in their areas. But by 1940 the local governments had suspended such a tax.

By the decision of the Committee, the Protectorate Government would aid secondary schools, Teacher Training Colleges and Technical Schools, while the local Governments would aid financially the primary schools. But of course local governments which would fail to raise enough money from the education tax would be assisted by the Protectorate Government.

The above decision was made again to interest the public in the affairs of their schools. The chiefs would have to work with the Missionaries to plan the establishment of primary schools in their areas and to raise enough money to finance the old and new primary schools. It was also hoped that with time, the local governments might be interested in setting up their own primary schools to run side by side with the missionary primary schools. This stipulation in fact became a reality. From 1945 local governments began to set up their own primary schools. By 1955 they had even begun to promote some of their primary schools to secondary school status. The Buganda Government was prominent in establishing its own schools and from 1955 it had a Minister of Education, Mr. Kassim Male. Because of the keen interest to have its own schools, the Buganda government welcomed enthuasitically the Protectorate government's suggestion that local governments should take over the private schools. The Buganda government took over a number of them as we have already seen in Chapter Seven.

The idea of engaging local governments in education was also meant to loosen the missionary hold on the administration of schools.' However, by 1960 apart from the Buganda government which had a fairly large number of its schools, the majority of local governments were playing an insignificant role in the administration of primary schools and the Missionaries solidly controlled these schools in the country. One reason for this was that "the Missionaries" as Jowitt the Director of Education said in 1951, "had got an honesty and self denial and devoted more time to education than lay people could do. The churches were pouring into education directly and indirectly an amount of money which he was quite incapable of estimating".

The fifth important decision made by the Thomas Education Committee was to suggest that the education of the Muslim children be managed by the Muslim Authority along the management of the Christian Churches. It is out of this decision that the Uganda Muslim Education Association (UMEA) was established in 1948 with plenty of help given to this development by the late Prince Al-Hajj Badru Kakungulu. Haj Ramadhan Gava was appointed the Education Secretary for the Muslim schools at the same status of the Missionary Education Secretaries in the different Christian Dioceses. A Roman Catholic or a Protestant Education Secretary was in charge of the schools in a Diocese, while a Roman Catholic or a Protestant Education Secretary General was in charge of all either the Roman Catholic schools or the Protestant schools. Therefore logically Haj Ramadhan Gava should have held the status of an Education Secretary General with several Education Secretaries under him. But Muslim schools were very few by then all over Uganda and they were not as many as the Roman Catholic or Protestant schools found within one Diocese then.

The quantity of educational development between 1940 and 1952

The educational developments between 1940 and 1952 were not very great. One reason was that from 1939 to 1945 was a period of the Second World War. During the war educational developments and other developments in Uganda and indeed in the rest of East Africa were slow due to economic difficulties. Secondly, even many Missionaries in Uganda left to join their fellow citizens in Europe to fight for their nations. The British and the French were allies in this war against the Germans and the Italians. Consequently, many British and French Missionaries left Uganda for Europe to fight against the Germans and the Italians. The Italian Missionaries on the other hand now known as the Comboni Missionaries who were mainly working in the north of Uganda were interned in Uganda by the British colonial administration. The British took them as their enemies Consequently, between 1939-45, educational activities were curtailed in Uganda.

Some Ugandans participated in the Second World War on the side of Britain. Many were recruited to fight in Burma, Ethiopia and in the Middle East, that is in Iran, Iraq, Lebanon, Egypt, Israel and in other countries of the Middle East. That is how we got a group of men in our society who were known by the following names: "Bakaawonawo" - plural, "Kaawonawo" - singular, or

Education Development

"Baseveni" - plural and "Museveni" singular. Some parents however, who even never fought in that war gave such names to their children born around that time in memory of those gallant Ugandans who participated in the Second World War, 1939-45.

The words "Museveni" and "Baseveni" came from the Kiganda rendering of the 7th Battalion. All men recruited to fight in the Second World War from Uganda, Kenya, Tanzania, Malawi, Zambia and Zimbabwe were put into the 7th Battalion. So on return to civilian life in 1945 after the war they were named as "Baseveni" - plural and "Museveni" - singular, i.e. of the 7th Battalion. "Bakaawonawo", or "Kaawonawo" mean respectively those men or that man who escaped inevitable death in the Second World War.

Thirdly, after the war, Uganda was headed by Governor Sir John Hall up to 1950. This Governor was not keenly interested in the education of Ugandans. He had been disappointed by the attitude of the pupils who went to school for hating to work on the land. He felt that education made those young people who went to school to despise engaging in agriculture. He thus contended:

> Teachers have failed to eradicate the belief that physical labour is socially degrading. Formal primary education makes the youth of Uganda hate to participate in productive work which requires physical exertion, considering themselves to have automatically joined the ranks of those who order others to work'.

Consequently, he was not keen on making large developments in education during his governorship, 1945-50. Rather than concentrating education on agriculture in schools which tended to be purely academic, Hall emphasised out-of-school education through propaganda and extension services and the schools should join in this campaign which would affect both the adults out of school and the pupils within schools which had been already established.

Exercise
1. Find out two ways in which the School Management Committee of a primary school affects the running of a primary school.
2. Point out two bad attitudes which boys and girls get as a result of going to school and suggest ways of stopping those attitudes.

Educational Developments, 1952-1962
Governor Sir John Hall was succeeded by Governor Sir Andrew Cohen in 1951. Unfortunately Sir Andrew Cohen was more known by the Baganda at large for having annoyed them than for the wonderful and tremendous developments which he introduced in Uganda both in education and in other sectors.

Sir Andrew Cohen annoyed the Baganda by deposing and deporting to England their Kabaka, the late Sir Edward Muteesa II in 1953 for having

History and Development of Education

demanded independence of Uganda from the British. However, Sir Edward Muteesa II returned from England as Kabaka in 1955. But the Baganda never forgave Sir Andrew Cohen for the way he had treated their Kabaka. He however, believed in the power of education and was not pessimistic like his predecessor, Sir John Hall. Governor Cohen felt strongly that once the Ugandans were well educated and in quite large numbers, they would bring about remarkable developments in the country. In this he portrayed the attitude of Governor Sir Philip Mitchell who was Governor of Uganda from 1935 to 1940.

The de Bunsen Education Committee, 1952

The development of education brought about by Sir Andrew Cohen is best seen through the de Bunsen Education Committee of 1952. During the year 1951 when Sir Andrew Cohen was appointed Governor of Uganda, the British government in London set up two education Commissions. One Commission was called the Jeffreys Education Commission for West Africa and the other one was called the Binns Study Group for East Africa and Central Africa, that is Malawi, Zambia and Zimbabwe.

At that time Britain felt that there was a need to improve the quality and quantity of education for Africans in these areas. Feelings had begun to advance that in the foreseeable future, these areas would eventually become independent of Britain. Therefore there was a need to increase the number of educated men and women who would take up positions of responsibility when these countries would become independent.

The Binns Study Group examined in 1951 the situation of education in Uganda and recommended to make major changes in the education system to improve both the quality and quantity of education in the country.

On the departure of the Binns Study Group, Sir Andrew Cohen appointed the de Bunsen Education Committee in 1952 to advise the government as to how to implement the suggestions of the Binns Study Group. Therefore the educational developments brought about by Sir Andrew Cohen are better seen through the recommendations of the de Bunsen Education Committee.

The following were the educational recommendations which were made by the de Bunsen Education Committee and which were subsequently implemented:

1. A new structure of education was established. It was as follows:
    i) The Primary school course was to last 6 years with a final examination at the end.
    ii) A Junior Secondary section to last for 2 years, i.e. Junior One and Junior Two. The schools in this section were divided up into two categories. One category was implicitly called academic section. Another section of schools was called practical. These were the Farm Schools, the Rural Trade Schools and the Home Craft Centres.

iii) The Secondary School course O-Level to last 4 years.
iv) The Secondary School course A-Level to last 2 years.
   This section had not been there before in the education system of Uganda.
v) Makerere University College and other Universities abroad.
vi) Teacher Training Colleges Grade II to be joined by candidates from Primary 6 or from Junior Two.
vii) A Government Teacher Training College Grade III to be joined by candidates from Secondary 4. This college was first set up at Mbarara and then transferred to Kyambogo.
   Teachers trained in Grade II Teacher Training Colleges were to teach in Primary Schools. Teachers trained in the Grade III Teacher Training College were to teach in the two classes of the Junior Secondary section.
viii) Technical Colleges for candidates from Junior Two.
ix) Kampala Technical Institute for candidates from Technical Colleges. Graduates from this Kampala Technical Institute would proceed to the Royal Technical College in Nairobi since Makerere did not offer courses in technology. Kampala Technical Institute was at Nakawa and then it was later on transferred to Kyambogo. It is now the present Uganda Polytechnic Institute.

2. The existing primary and secondary schools were enlarged and many more such schools were built to increase the enrolment of pupils and students in schools.

3. The Uganda government was to establish a number of its secondary schools which would be run side by side with the missionary secondary schools.
   As a result of the above recommendation, the Uganda government built the following secondary schools: Ntare School in Mbarara, Kigezi College Butobere in Kabale, Kabalega Secondary School in Masindi, Mvara Secondary School in Arua; Sir Samuel Baker Secondary School (Pongdwong) in Gulu, Lango College in Lira and Teso College Aloet in Soroti. The idea here was to carry educational opportunities outside Buganda and Busoga and also to reduce the denominational idea of education in Uganda.

4. The quality of education at all levels was improved. This was done by providing in schools adequate scholastic materials such as text books and science equipment. Also efforts were made to post qualified teachers to schools, Teacher Training Colleges and Technical Schools.

5. The number of Teacher Training Colleges was reduced and the remaining few Colleges were enlarged and equipped adequately with scholastic materials.

The reduction of these Teacher Training Colleges was necessary for the following reasons: Teacher Training Colleges had been established on the basis of religions. Therefore there were Teacher Training Colleges for the Roman Catholic schools, the Protestant schools and there was a Teacher Training College at Kibuli for the Muslim schools. The result was that there were too many Teacher Training Colleges. Many times each one did not have a large enough enrolment of students. This meant that there was under utilisation of scholastic materials, equipment and the available Tutors.

The remaining few and enlarged Teacher Training Colleges could be improved by posting to them Tutors from the closed ones and by transferring scholastic materials and equipment from the closed ones to the few enlarged ones.
However, these Teacher Training Colleges remained denominational. It is only the government Teacher Training College Grade III at Mbarara which was later transferred to Kyambogo which was training teachers for all the denominations. Yet only teachers from this College who belonged to a particular denomination were posted to the schools of that denomination. For example, Roman Catholic teachers from Kyambogo Teacher Training College were posted to Roman Catholic schools. This was similar for Protestant teachers and Muslim teachers.

Since the grade I teachers ceased to be produced, courses were introduced to upgrade grade I teachers already in service to be raised to the status of gradeII teachers.

6. To give practical skills to pupils who were graduating from Primary six, three kinds of schools to be attended for two years were established all over the country. These were to run side by side the academic two year Junior Secondary schools.
   i) Farm Schools. Students would be taught farming and farm management in these schools. On graduation they were expected to stay in the villages and use the skills learnt so as to be progressive farmers.
   ii) Home Craft Centres. These schools would teach girls all skills necessary in home management and motherhood and wifery.
   iii) Rural Trade Schools. Students would be taught technical skills which a boy especially could use to earn a living in the rural countryside and not in urban areas. He learnt skills of making doors, chairs, beds, bricks, building houses and many other practical skills.
7. Secondary Modern Schools. These were to be joined by graduates from the above three group of practical schools. They were at the level of the academic Secondary Schools 0-Level.

Education Development

8. At each Junior Secondary School of the academic nature, it was suggested that there should be a carpentry workshop to give practical skills to the students.

9. Secondary schools to teach agriculture were proposed to be built. But this never materialised.

The recommendations of the de Bunsen Education Committee improved the quality and quantity of education in Uganda. Until independence these recommendations were still being followed. And by 1962 the number of schools which had to be built as proposed had already been built and the number of students who had been estimated to occupy those schools were already there and even above the estimated number. For example, the de Bunsen Education Committee had recommended that the number of students graduating from the 0-Level course would rise from 250 in 1952 to 500 in 1960. But by 1960 the number had risen to 700.

This meant that after regaining independence, there was need to build a larger number of new secondary schools. In the next Section we shall see how the independent government of Uganda tackled this problem.

Like the Thomas Education Committee of 1940, the de Bunsen Education Committee also raised the issue of denomination schools. Some members of this Committee were even adamant that denominational education should be stopped in Uganda. They gave their reasons that denominational education made children suffer by walking long distances past schools nearer their homes just because they did not belong to their religions.

Secondly, denominational education kept alive suspicion and hatred which had originated in the political and religious wars of the 1880s and early 1890s. Thirdly, they contended that it was wasteful because some schools were under utilized. However, the missionary influence was still so great that the above proposal was not accepted to be implemented by government. The members however, who were in favour of abolishing denominational education produced a Minority Report to demonstrate their conviction against denominational education. They signed their names as Y. Lule who later on became a Principal of Makerere University College and the President of Uganda for two months in 1979, S.W. Kulubya and Ms E. Senkaatuuka.

Exercise
i) Ask some men and women who are over fifty years of age in your area to tell you how the Baganda behaved when Kabaka, Sir Edward Muteesa II was deposed and deported to England by Sir Andrew Cohen from 1953 to 1955.

ii) Try to find out why schools which were teaching practical skills such as the Rural Trade Schools, Farm Schools and Home Craft Centres failed during the colonial period.

The fate of the Farm Schools, Home Craft Centres, Rural Trade Schools and the Secondary Modern Schools

The Farm Schools, the Home Craft Centres, the Rural Trade Schools and the Secondary Modern Schools failed to become popular when they began operation in 1955. Firstly, they were being joined by students who had failed to score high enough marks at the Primary Leaving Examinations. So they could not join the academic Junior Secondary Schools and later on the academic Senior Secondary Schools. Therefore these students went to these schools feeling failures. Even their colleagues who managed to go to the academic Junior Secondary Schools despised them. What used to happen was that many of these students would join these schools and try to work privately to resit the Primary Leaving Examination again and be able to join the academic Junior Secondary Schools.

Secondly, those students who managed to complete the courses in these practical schools, on graduation, went to towns to look for jobs. Yet this was not the intention behind these schools. These schools were meant to give ready practical and technical skills for use in the rural areas on the initiative of the graduates.

In towns, these graduates were competing with graduates from the properly established technical schools. Of course they were disappointed because their skills were below those of the graduates from the proper technical schools such as Kisubi Technical School, Masaka Technical School, Soroti Technical School, Lira Technical School, Gulu Technical School, Mbale Technical School, Mbarara Technical Schools, Fort Portal Technical School, Masindi Technical School, Arua Technical School and others. Therefore the technical skills of the graduates from the Farm Schools, the Home Craft Centres and the Rural Trade Schools found no employer who needed them.

Lack of employment further frustrated the students of this category who looked upon these schools as useless. The result was that candidates hated these schools. Consequently, these schools were failing by 1962 and were being joined by very few students.

Unfortunately also the teachers in these schools were not quite trained in those fields. So they could not give inspiration to the students in these schools. Many times teachers who had been trained in the usual way of teaching academic subjects were the ones who were recruited to teach in these schools which required of them to teach practical skills of a technical nature.

The Secondary Modern Schools fared no better. As a result they were closed together with the Farm Schools, the Home Craft Centres and the Rural Trade

Education Development

Schools by the 1963 Castle Education Commission. Thus died a good innovation in the education system of Uganda which had been intended to give practical skills for use in rural areas on the initiative of the graduates of these schools. But the fault lay with the officers who were responsible for directing the education system. Any schools which are set aside with the idea of being for students who are failures, are not likely to succeed. At the same time any schools which are meant for teaching students practically need to be run by people who have got the technical skills and who believe in the efficacy of these practical skills.

Exercise
1. What work did the British colonial government in Uganda come to do in education in 1925?
2. Name 4 benefits which were the result of the British colonial government in Uganda in entering the field of education.
3. Through what missionary education officers did the Department of Education cooperate with the Missionaries and later with the Muslims in their schools?
4. Why did the pioneers of establishing private schools begin to set up their private schools?
5. State two important things which the 1940 Thomas Education Commitee introduced in the education system of Uganda.
6. Name two developments which the de Bunsen Education Committee brought in the education system of Uganda?
7. What three problems did the private schools face up to 1953?
8. What two factors prevented a more appreciable development of education in Uganda between 1940 and 1951?
9. What was the purpose for the Farm Schools, Home Craft Centres and the Rural Trade Schools which were established by the 1952 de Bunsen Education Committee?
10. Mention three things which were bad for conducting schools along religious lines during the colonial period.

11 Colonial Education for responsible government 1940-1962

Introduction
The period between 1940 and 1962 has been referred to as a period during when the British colonial policies from London and the colonial government in Uganda under the Governors was preparing Ugandans for responsible government.

The above statement however, needs to be seen in the light of the following observations. From 1940 to nearly the end of the 1950's, neither the British government in London and its colonial administrations in Uganda nor the people of Uganda had any idea that Uganda would regain her independence at the beginning of the 1960's. Many British colonial administrators were vaguely putting the date for independence probably during the 1970's. The suddenness of indepenence on the 9th October 1962 made even Sir Andrew Cohen who was a very progressive Governor of Uganda between 1951 and 1956 to exclaim thus, "We thought we had an indefinite time ahead of us". He uttered this on the 9th October 1962 when he had been invited to attend Uganda's Independence celebrations.

Sir Andrew Cohen's exclamation indicates that all what the British colonial administrators were doing between 1940 and 1962 in terms of preparing Ugandans for self government was not hurried most importantly because the date for self government was not imagined or planned to be during the early 1960's. For example, the Colonial Office in London sent in 1951 to Uganda and to the rest of East Africa the Binns Study Group to examine the state of education in Uganda and recommend new gigantic trends for educational advancement. The de Bunsen Education Committee which Governor Sir Andrew Cohen appointed in 1952 to launch a programme to execute the suggestions of the Binns Study Group, recommended that candidates sitting for the "O"Level Cambridge School Certificate Examinations should gradually increase from 250 in 1955 to 500 in 1960. You can imagine this number in terms of qualified Ugandans for the whole country. Today 500 students for O'Level examinations are produced by only one secondary school of Kololo Secondary School.

Colonial Strategies for preparing Ugandans for Responsible Government
With the above observations clearly indicated, there were however, several educational arrangements which were launched to prepare Ugandans slowly for self government between 1940 and 1962.

Colonial Education

The 1940 Thomas Education Committee set up measures which had elements of preparing Ugandans for responsible government. It was set up by the colonial government in Uganda to discuss a ten year development plan for African education.

This education plan set up targets to be achieved in terms of number of Primary schools, Secondary schools, technical schools and teacher training schools. It also mentioned the projected number of pupils and students which by the end of the ten years would be gradually produced through the above categories of educational institutions.

The target however, in terms of the numbers was not achieved by the end of the ten year period for two reasons. Firstly, half of that period was occupied by the Second World War which raged from September 1939 to June 1945. During the war, educational developments like any other developments were quite slow due to shortage of funds and inflation and due to the fact that many British and French Missionaries returned to their respective countries to participate in war efforts against the Germans and the Italians. Also very few young Missionaries were coming to Uganda from Britain and France and Italy. The missionary activities of the Comboni Missionaries then called the Verona Fathers were restricted in Uganda because the British colonial government in the country treated the Italian Missionaries who composed the bulk of the Comboni Missionaries as enemies of the British Empire due to the Italian government's alliance with Germany in the Second World War against the British and the French.

Secondly, from 1945 to 1950, Uganda was led by Governor Sir John Hall. This Governor had been displeased by the attitude which he found prevailing among the students who were joining and attending the schools. They hated any education which was connected with manual labour. And indeed missionary education at that time was predominantly academic. The students who went through it got the impression that they were being prepared for white collar jobs. Especially they looked down upon any work which was connected with tilling the land. Sir John Hall hated this attitude and he was not enthusiastic to see many primary schools and secondary schools built. He rather concentrated on out-of-school education carried on outside the schools and classrooms and given to the masses of adult people through demonstration on their gardens and in their homes and through live films shown to the people at subcounty headquarters.

Thirdly, Governor Sir John Hall had a pessimistic view about the ability of Ugandans to sustain developments once launched with financial assistance from Britain. He was convinced that once such projects were launched, after the British funds would dry up, Ugandans had no ability to sustain them economically. This attitude made Sir John Hall not to take advantage of the funds set aside by the British government after the war for developments in the British Empire through the Colonial Development and Welfare Fund. In terms of education, this made the targets made by the Thomas Education Committee for ten years from 1940 to 1950 not to be fulfilled.

However, in terms of preparing Ugandans for responsible government, the 1940 Thomas Education Committee launched two arrangements which made Ugandans participate in the administration of education and be aware of the implications of developing education in the country. Hitherto Ugandans did not participate in the administration of education. Their job was only to send their children to the schools and left the Missionaries carry on with the job of running the schools.

The arrangement of the Thomas Education Committee called upon Ugandans who were development oriented to be involved in the administration and development of secondary schools and other post primary institutions by being appointed members to their Boards of Governors.

Some Ugandans were to be appointed to the Boards of Governors of those schools. This began a trend of making Ugandans to realise the implications of administering education and the costs involved. The de Bunsen Education Committee of 1952 extended this arrangement to the primary schools by establishing School Management Committees to act like the Boards of Governors for post primary institutions.

The involvement of the local governments in financing primary schools was the second arrangement made by the 1940 Thomas Education Committee. From 1925 to 1940, it was the colonial government which was voting money to supplement missionary funds to run all education efforts in the country. The 1927 Education Ordinance had required the local governments to set up an education tax in their respective areas. But that tax had been dropped by 1940 by the local governments. This made the people to wait for both the colonial administration and the Missionaries to finance education. This robbed the Ugandans who were under indirect rule whereby they involved in administration through their local governments chance to participate in the planning educational developments in their areas and to realize how costly educational developments were.

The new arrangement involved the local governments working hand in hand with the Missionaries in planning educational developments at primary school level in their respective areas and to finance those developments. It was also envisaged that in time, these local governments would wish to start and own their primary schools and secondary schools to run side by side with those of the Missionaries to reduce the missionary predominant position education and eventually also make the Muslim Authority in Uganda to start shouldering the administration and establishing further schools for the Muslim children. This was fulfilled in 1948 when the Muslim Authority set up the Uganda Muslim Education Association. (UMEA).

Towards the end of the 1940's, some local governments had begun to establish and own their own primary schools which they financed together with the missionary primary schools. This development was more prominent in Buganda so much so that from 1955, the then Buganda Kingdom appointed its Minister of Education in the person of Kassim Male.

The establishment of the Boards of Governors and the commitment of the local governments in the involvement of educational developments for primary schools and financing them, were made into law by the 1942 Education Ordiance.

Mass Education in African Societies 1944

Another arrangement in the trend of preparing Ugandans for responsible government came through the British Colonial policy in London called Mass Education in African Societies . This Mass Education Policy meant a movement designed to promote better living for the whole community within each African colony through adult education conducted outside the formal school set up. The Colonial Office in London feared that the colonial administrations locally were concentrating on formal education of the young and leaving the majority of people uninfluenced by Western education.

The memorandum of Mass Education for African Societies of 1944 found quite a favourable atmosphere in Uganda. By the time it came out Governor Sir John Hall had just taken over from Governor Charles Dundas the direction of the administration of Uganda in 1945. He was well disposed towards the kind of education which was being proposed. His line of thought was for reducing drastically formal primary education because he thought that formal primary education which was enjoyed by the majority of children in Uganda made the youth of Uganda to hate to participate in productive work which required physical exertion, "considering themselves to have automatically joined the ranks of those who ordered others to work".

Therefore Governor Hall launched educational public propaganda carried out outside the schools for the illiterate and barely literate adult people to learn proper agricultural techniques to increase crop production. They would at the same time be attending literacy classes outside the schools which classes would be conducted by non paid volunteers at the direction of British officers.

At the same time, Sir John Hall came at the time when Uganda had already been aroused by the return of the service men from the Second World War. The administration of Governor Sir Charles Dundas, his predecessor, had already set up a committee known as the Civil Absorption Committee to facilitate the return to civilian life for the returned ex-service men. These men, the majority of whom were illiterate had enjoyed some higher standards during the war, also their horizons and outlook had been widened. The colonial government wanted to build on their experiences and open mindedness through adult education arrangement. The Department of Education arranged for them technical courses at various places in towns all over the country. Indeed this was in response to the Colonial Office policy which required colonial administrations in Africa to build through adult education on the experiences which those men had gained during the war. These ex-service men were known by the names of "Baseveni" - plural and "Museveni" - singular or "Bakaawonawo" –plural "Kaawonawo" –singular.

As a result of his enthusiasm for out-of-school education, Governor Hall set up the Department of Public Relations and Social Welfare to take charge of, and to coordinate, adult education activities hitherto carried on rather spasmodically by the Department of Education, by the Medical Department and by the Department of Agriculture separately. Then a programme was evolved which this new Department followed throughout the country.

That programme involved the formation of demonstration teams at provincial level. Each demonstration team toured each province in which it was stationed using as its starting base a county headquarters. Its lessons concerned the correct way of planting and harvesting crops for the largest yield, animal care, protection of water supply, digging of latrines to guard against hookworms and bilharzia, soil conservation and the dangers of soil erosion, manuring and sanitary houses, the building of kitchens and animal houses in a home and the preparation of balanced diets. Demonstrations were being augmented through audio visual arrangement by film shows at sub county headquarters. These film shows were very popular and they were being attended by hundreds of people for both entertainment and education.

As a result of this educational propaganda which was meant to lift the whole society, there was remarkable improvement in people's approach to agriculture from which the majority of people earned a living. There was also an improvement in bodily and domestic sanitation and soil conservation. Special grasses were planted such as paspalm and elephant grasses. Trenches to lead rain water through gardens without ruining the soil were taught and dug. Contour formation in hilly areas such as Kigezi, Bugisu and West Nile were taught. Wells for providing clean water for domestic use which before then were not scrupulously cared about.were constructed.

Many homes lacked pit-latrines and kitchens. Many people were using the same sleeping house for kitchen, for domestic animals and fowls, while the walls of the houses were not plastered and they lacked windows. All these evils were attacked effectively through the demonstration lessons of the Social Relations and Welfare Department with the full support of the local administration in each area. After the lessons in which the chiefs figured prominently these chiefs went back from house to house to see that what had been taught was being put into execution. Those people who failed to follow the lessons were charged in local courts if they persistently refused to do so. This penalty device was really very

Colonial Education

effective in making the people observe what was being demonstrated. Above all, famine and economic distress were systematically attacked by the government making sure that each homestead cultivated a prescribed acreage of cotton, cassava, potatoes, maize and millet and that each homestead had a barn for storing food.

Besides the above strategies, the Department of Public Relations and Social Welfare encouraged the formation of clubs in urban and rural areas for people to engage in social meetings and discuss economic, social and civic affairs.

In 1947 that Department inaugurated its mass literacy campaign. The local governments took an active part in this activity, encouraging people to turn up to be taught and in enlisting voluntary teachers.

To help the development of reading habits and the consolidation of literacy, the Department launched the following weekly newspapers: "Mawulire" in Luganda, "Wamanya" in Runyoro-Rutooro, Runyankore-Rukiga, "Samachar" in Lugbara, "Lok Awinya" in Luo and "Apupeta" in Ateso.

The East African Literature Bureau, a High Commission Service formed in 1948 for the whole of East Africa to run Common Services for the region based in Nairobi, was brought in to help produce cheap primers for the mass literacy campaign and help to set up lending libraries all over the country at district headquarters and in towns.

The Department of Education joined in by launching evening continuation classes which began in 1948 in Kampala. The following courses were conducted initially, short-hand, book-keeping, commerce, building construction, carpentry, English, Arithmetic and electrical engineering.

All the above educational measures were carried on to make the whole country to be alert to the duties of a responsible government ahead. The measures were intended to make Ugandans have a strong economic and social base to be better prepared when responsible government would arrive at an indefinite date ahead.

The memorandum known as Education for Citizenship in Africa 1948

The memorandum for Mass Education for African Societies was followed by another memorandum again from London called Education for Citizenship in Africa in 1948. This memorandum was another strategy for preparing Ugandans for responsible government.

Both memoranda originated from the Colonial Office in London and they applied to all colonies in the British Empire. Among other things, the memorandum known as Education for Citizenship in Africa stated:

> His majesty's government has often proclaimed that responsible self-government is the goal at which all Colonies should aim. The central purpose of British Colonial administration was a pledge to guide colonial peoples along the road of self-government within the framework of the British Empire, to build up their social and economic institutions, and to develop their natural resources.

Responsible self-government was the aim which all economic and social development, and especially the development of education should have in view. Education for Citizenship in Africa laid down specific steps to be followed in training Africans for responsible government. At primary school level, the ideals required for Citizenship had to be imparted through the subjects of history, geography and through planning topics by teachers and students together for discussion to assist meaningful discussion of issues pertaining to citizenship.

At secondary school level, there was introduction of democratically run societies to break the autocratically run school administration. Young Farmers' Clubs were introduced. Each school had one large society and several small clubs. The older students had to be trained in the techniques of running societies and were helped to recognise the qualities of character needed for success. Deliberate attempts were made to link the miniature problems of their school society with similar ones in adult local and national life.

Debates at secondary school level were arranged with the view of inoculating the young citizens against the commonest deceptions in argument and propaganda. Examples of such things were exaggerations and the unfair use of written documents which carried emotional content. Examples were being drawn from lessons of the students' own society discussions, their essays, the local newspapers and advertisements and they were contrasted with fair statements.

The teaching of civics was pursued vigorously. The topics in this subject included what the Police do, the Law Courts, the Army, the Post Office, colonisation, the working of local governments and of the Legislative Council and government Ordinances. Also examples of what were being done in other countries in terms of the above topics were discussed for emphasis.

Discussion on character objectives in the modern state, training of supervisory staff, formation of youth organisations, adult education to create social consciousness, were all pursued vigorously under Education for Citizenship in Africa in schools and outside schools.

Opportunities were given to graduates of the schools and Universities to participate in political responsibility through local governments to put ideas learnt through schools into practice. Consequently traditional chiefs in local governments were being joined by educated young men. This trend was followed by the arrangement of direct elections to local government councils in 1958 and to the Uganda Legislative Council which was then the Parliament in Uganda.

Visits to Britain were arranged by the colonial government for trained local government officials and for some members of local government authorities. These visits were also joined by some African civil servants and chiefs. All these people were spending in Britain time ranging between three months and six months and some for a year. Some of these people spent time working with local government authorities in Britain to learn how those bodies operated. Some were

Colonial Education

attending lectures at some British Universities in administration. Also in Uganda, the Extra Mural Department of Makerere University founded in 1953 which now has been termed the Institute of Adult and Continuing Education ran courses all over the country in administration for civil servants, chiefs and local government officials.

A healthy public opinion can only be formed on the basis of ample information by the government so that people can discuss what the government is doing or is intending to do. In this respect, the colonial administration improved the information services and the Press so that the people could know what was being done by the colonial government and what it was intending to do and why.

All the above strategies were launched in Uganda by the colonial government to awaken the Ugandans to the responsibilities which lay ahead of them when they would regain their independence. There was a remarkable eagerness on the part of the public to support these programmes.

Sir Andrew Cohen, Governor of Uganda up to 1956.

Uganda was fortunate to get Governor Sir Andrew Cohen in 1951. He came determined to give a great challenge to Ugandans to develop towards responsible government. He also believed in the ability of Ugandans to participate in developmental programmes initiated by the government and be able to sustain them when the government would leave them to the people to carry on.

Consequently Sir Andrew Cohen combined the programmes which were under "out-of-school education", "Mass Education programmes" and "the Education for Citizenship" into one broad programme with a budget of Pounds 500,000 from 1952 to 1960. He abolished the Department of Public Relations and Social Welfare. In its place he created the Department of Community Development. He spelt out the objective of community development as "to secure the support and active participation of the people in programmes for their social and economic betterment".

To Sir Andrew Cohen, responsible government meant a greater call on people's initiative and readiness to do things and to maintain them for themselves without waiting for a mysterious body called "government" to come and do them. This is why he made the de Bunsen Education Committee to support the private schools and to give them an official standing in the education system because they showed African initiative. He directed that rural training projects should be emphasised to involve nearly every person in the society paying particular attention to the involvement of women through clubs due to their role in the homes.

Through its training centre at Nsamizi which was established in 1954, the Community Development Department conducted vigorous personnel training programmes offering courses to central government staff, local government staff and voluntary workers. Public administration, laws, civics courses were being given to government officials while leaders for rural women's clubs and adult literacy workers were also being given guide-lines of operation. The trainees for voluntary leadership represented the Mothers' Union, the Catholic Action Organisation, the Salvation Army, the Red Cross people and Y.M.C.A. and Y.W.C.A. leaders. These voluntary leaders were responsible for conducting educational courses in rural and urban areas in home crafts, sanitary and agricultural and farm extension techniques.

While the above courses at Nsamizi Training Centre and courses among the general population were going on, the Department of Education was conducting formal evening continuation courses all over the country.

The Binns Study Group which visited East Africa in 1951 from the Colonial Office In London recommended to better the quality of education and to increase the quantity of education to produce a sizeable number of qualified Ugandans who would eventually take on jobs before responsible government arrived and after it had come. The de Bunsen Education Committee of 1952 supported those recommendations and put them into a programme of action from 1953 to 1962.

The 1959 Education Ordiance was also passed in terms of preparing Ugandans for responsible government. That Ordinance allowed Africans to attend Asian schools because if Asians segregated themselves from Africans, they would find it hard to be acceptable as citizens in the independent Uganda.

Colonial Education

In conclusion, all the above educational efforts carried out both in schools and outside schools betweren 1940 and 1962 were put in place to prepare Ugandans for responsible government.

At the threshold of Uganda's regaining her independence, all the people were alert to the great tasks which lay ahead of them and were prepared as never before for those tasks. But despite the active educational efforts between 1940 and 1960 carried out both in schools and outside schools, by the time Uganda regained her independence on 9th October 1962, the country experienced tremendous shortage of trained men and women.

Questions
1. How is the claim that the period between 1940 and 1960 was for preparing Ugandans for responsible government difficult to appreciate?
2. What elements for responsible government did the 1940 Thomas Education Committee put in place?
3. Enumerate three of the educational activities which were carried out through the "Mass Education Programme for responsible government?
4. What was "Education for Citizenship in African Societies" intended to do in terms of preparing Ugandans for responsible government?
5. What were some of the educational activities carried out by the colonial government through the programme of "Education for Citizenship in African societies?
6. How did the presence of Sir Andrew Cohen as Governor of Uganda assist in the acceleration of education of Ugandans for responsible government?
7. Why should we see the visit of the Binns Study Group to Uganda in 1951 in the context of preparing Ugandans for responsible government?
8. How can the beginning of direct elections of members to local governments in 1958 be seen in the context of preparing Ugandans for responsible government?
9. What was one of the reasons for passing the 1959 Education Ordinance?
10. Why did Governor Sir John Hall feel less inclined to develop primary education and prefer to increase out-ofschool education efforts?

12 Development of Education 1962-1990

The challenges which Uganda faced immediately after regaining her independence.
Uganda regained her independence on the 9th October 1962. This brought new challenges in the country and the government expected the education system to help in solving many of those challenges.

The first challenge concerned qualified people. Though the recommendations of the de Bunsen Education Committee of 1952 had doubled the number of pupils and students in schools, still the schools and Makerere University College had by 1962 produced very few qualified personnel. Therefore government departments and companies lacked enough qualified people to work in them. Numerous jobs were created around 1961 and 1962 partly by the departure of European and Asian civil servants and teachers who did not want to be under the leadership of Africans. The other kind of jobs were created by the establishment of many Ministries in the government which had not been there before.

Despite the remarkable education developments carried out as a result of the de Bunsen Education Committee, missionary and colonial education deliberately produced few qualified Ugandans and some kinds of skills were deliberately not produced. The reason for this was that Britain had to send her excessive qualified workers to Uganda and to her other colonies in Africa.

For example, State Registered Sisters for hospitals and Office Secretaries used to be wives of British Officers working in Uganda. Or they used to be British unmarried ladies who could not get jobs in Britain because there were too many of them in Britain. Therefore the above kind of workers were deliberately not produced in Uganda to preserve posts for the excessive British workers. Uganda now after regaining her independence had to produce many such workers.

The second challenge concerned developing economic activities in the country to increase production so that government services could be carried out. Though the economy was not very bad at independence time in 1962, it needed to be developed further and faster. This also required qualified people produced through the education system. The government hoped that by producing many School Certificate holders and many Degree holders, this would help to create economic developments in the country.

A third challenge was the need to give confidence to Ugandans that they were capable of solving their problems and should not feel shy and unequal to the tasks of sustaining their independence. That in discussions with Europeans, they should show that they are people who are capable of thinking and of solving their

Development of Education

problems intelligently. One aspect of missionary and colonial education was that it did not give confidence to its students to stand on their own. They were always being educated to take the positions of assistants to the European and Asian civil servants and teachers but not to be fully fledged controllers of things. Missionary and colonial education was always giving Ugandans the feeling that they were incapable of doing and managing things: it was the Whites who were able to do things and who knew what was the right things to do. So Ugandans had to be in subordinate positions. This kind of treatment must have made Ugandans feel that they were inferior to the Whites and so many of them lacked confidence in themselves.

After regaining independence, the education system in Uganda had to remove this inferiority feeling from the minds of the students. In this effort two important slogans were inaugurated namely "the creation of African identity" and "the development of African personality". Lessons and speeches to students all the time had to hum on these two ideologies. Fortunately, soon Ugandans began to feel confident in their ability to solve their problems and to be quite aggressive in discussions with the Whites and with their educated fellow Africans outside Uganda.

Steps taken through education to solve the above three challenges

In 1963 the Uganda government appointed the Castle Education Commission. The duty of the Commission was to review the education system which was still operating along the recommendations of the de Bunsen Education Committee of 1952. The new recommendations in education would focus on producing enough qualified people to fill all jobs in the country with a view that they could help to boost the economy and also produce people who are confident in themselves as capable and intelligent.

The Castle Education Commission set up a new structure of education which was as follows:

(a) The Primary school course to last 7 years instead of 6.
(b) The Junior Secondary section of two years was abolished. Also the Farm Schools, the Rural Trade Schools, the Home Craft Centres and the Secondary Modern Schools were abolished and turned into academic secondary schools. The above kind of schools had created the impression that they were for failures. The Commission wondered whether the new nation of Uganda would be built on the "backs of young people who have been made to feel as failures".
(c) The Senior Secondary section O-Level to last 4 years.
(d) The Senior Secondary section A-Level to last 2 years.
(e) Makerere University and other Universities.
(f) Teacher Training Colleges for Grade III teachers with O-Level Secondary education, Teacher Training Colleges for Grade II teachers with primary

school education had to be phased out. Also courses had to be mounted to upgrade the existing Grade II Primary school teachers to Grade III status.
(g) Technical Colleges to be joined after O-Level.
(h) Technical institutes to be joined after the completion of the course in the Technical Colleges.
(i) Agricultural Colleges to be joined after O-Level.
(j) District Farm Institutes to be joined after the completion of the course in the Agricultural Colleges.

To defeat the shortage of qualified manpower, the Castle Education Commission recommended a tremendous increase in school enrolment especially at secondary school level. Many graduates from these secondary schools would proceed to do University courses. Those others who would not join University would go and get jobs in offices and train on the job.

Consequently, many new primary schools were built all over the country. The existing secondary schools were enlarged to take in more students. And many new secondary schools were built. The nature of educational expansion between 1962 and 1970 can be shown by the following figures. In 1962 there were 28 government grant-aided secondary schools. By 1970, there were 73 secondary schools. The enrolment of secondary schools at O-Level was 1991 students in 1962. By 1970, there were 29,540 O-Level students. To the above secondary schools were added many private secondary schools built by individual people, which produced very many students. Thus in the respect of producing many secondary school students, the First Five Year Development Plan, 1962-1965/66 had the following preamble:

> The main weight of government expenditure on education must concentrate on Secondary and Technical education, particularly the former, since the present limited secondary school facilities are the bottleneck to the production of Ugandans for higher academic professional and technical education.

Facilities at Makerere University College were increased to take in more students. Similar expansions were made at the University College of Nairobi and at the University College of Dar es Salaam to cope with more students from the three East African countries. Consequently, there was a great increase of Ugandan students doing degree courses at Makerere University College, at the University College of Nairobi, at the University College of Dar es Salaam and at various Universities abroad. Incidentally by 1960, all the above three University Colleges were under the authority of the University of London. In 1963 they all became independent of the University of London and they were formed into the University of East Africa each as a constituent College of the University of East Africa. Students from the three East African countries were free to attend at any of those constituent colleges of the University of East Africa.

Development of Education

In 1970 however, each of the three constituent University Colleges of the University of East Africa became independent and the University of East Africa ended. From then each constituent University College became a fully fledged University. One reason why the University of East Africa broke up was due to the different ideologies followed by the different countries in East Africa and the desire for each to consolidate its separate authority and control.

In terms of ideologies, in 1967 Tanzania inaugurated officially her African socialism by the Arusha Declaration. She called it African Socialism, Ujamaa in Kiswahili. She changed the name of the TANU political party into "Chama Cha Mapinduzi", a revolutionary party. Uganda though capitalistic was contemplating adoption of socialism, while Kenya remained capitalistic. Julius Kambarage Nyerere who was the President of Tanzania then hated capitalism intensely. He called any capitalistic country "man-eat-man-country". With this antagonistic view to capitalistic countries, the University College of Dar es Salaam could not continue together with Makerere University College and Nairobi University College whose countries were practising capitalism. Nyerere wanted to see that Tanzania's University had to sing the African socialistic ideologies. Yet those ideologies were not attractive to both Kenya and Uganda.

Besides, each East African country wanted to have a firm control over its own University without reference to another country. Moreover despite the expansion of facilities at these three University Colleges, they were taking in less students than the demands of each country. So it was felt that each country should have under its control its own University and plan its expansion to take in as many students as possible from its own citizens, though on exchange arrangements, these Universities would continue to enrol a limited number of students from each country.

For example, by arrangement in 1963, there were certain Faculties which were not to be duplicated in the constituent University Colleges. In this respect, the Faculty of Medicine was supposed to be in Makerere University College and no others in Nairobi and Dar es Salaam. The Faculty of Veterinary Medicine was supposed to be in the University College of Nairobi and no others at Makerere and Dar es Salaam. The Faculty of Agriculture was supposed to be at Makerere University College and no others at Nairobi and Dar es Salaam. The Faculty of Law was supposed to be at the University College of Dar es Salaam and no others at Makerere and Nairobi. This was seen by the leaders that it would take a very long time to produce a sizeable number of qualified men and women with degrees in the above specialities. For example, the annual intake of students in the Faculty of Medicine at Makerere was 120. This meant that annually after five years, each East African country would hope to get just about 40 Doctors. This was too small a number for a country.

So it was deemed that by separating these University Colleges, each country could expand the facilities at each University to increase the intake of students in each course comprising of students coming mainly from each country. Also each

History and Development of Education

University was free to have whatever Faculties it desired necessary for the country.

Makerere as a fully fledged University was inaugurated on the 8th October 1970 at a colourful ceremony which was attended by President Jomo Kenyatta then President of Kenya, President Julius K. Nyerere then President of Tanzania, President K. Kaunda of Zambia and President Milton A. Obote then President of Uganda.

To bring about the above educational developments at both secondary and University levels, the Uganda government borrowed money from the World Bank and from the British and American governments, of course with strings

(Left to right) Presidents Kenneth Kaunda of Zambia, Milton Obote of Uganda, Julius Nyerere of Tanzania and Jomo Kenyatta of Kenya. Behind to the right of Obote is Frank K. Kalimuzo the first Vice Chancellor at the inaugration of Makerere University.

attached. For example, the USA government built for Uganda a first class school of Tororo Girls Secondary School. Though the school is just a Kilometre away from the Tororo Cement Industry, all the cement, other building materials, electric wires, bulbs, sockets, refrigerators and type-writers had to be imported from the United States of America. Half the teaching staff and the Headmistress had to come from the United States of America for ten years.

This indebtness also meant that though independent, Uganda had to observe strictly the policies of the countries from which she had borrowed money to build these schools and to expand Makerere University.

To produce men and women who could assist to increase economic developments, practical subjects such as agriculture, woodwork, metal-work, technical drawing and secretarial courses were introduced in some secondary schools. These subjects became examinable at both O-Level and A-Level. Also the teaching of science subjects was stepped up and strengthened in secondary schools.

To create "African identity" and "African personality," subjects began to be taught stressing the Ugandan background and situation. This was known as the Africanisation of the curriculum. For example, during the colonial period, students were being taught the Geography of Britain and of the United States of America. The Geography of Uganda or of East Africa as a whole was not taught. Similarly, History of Britain and of the United States of America was the one which was being taught. The History of Uganda and of other African countries was not being taught.

Likewise, during the colonial days, Science was being taught from the European and American background. For example, in Biology, frogs and cockroaches which were being dissected in the laboratories at 0-Level and at A-Level School Certificate Examinations, were being flown all the way from Britain while such frogs and cockroaches are so much available in Uganda. Mathematics was being taught using Pints, Pounds, Pences and Farthings which we were not using here in Uganda but which were being used in Britain.

All the above teaching during the colonial days was intended to make the Ugandans feel that it were things from the White man's world that had a value and which were worthwhile learning. The end result of this was to create lack of confidence in the feelings of Ugandans and to under estimate the value of African things.

In the first chapter of this book, you read about Ugandan and other African indigenous education before Western education was introduced in Uganda. There was also a reference to the Ugandan indigenous religions before Christianity and Islam were introduced in Uganda. The impression which missionary and colonial education created in the minds of Ugandans was that Ugandans before the colonial days had no education systems and religions which taught that there is one God. All the above was done by the missionary and colonial education to destroy confidence in Ugandans and to make them feel that they were totally helpless before the Missionaries and the colonial administrators began to educate them from the end of the 19th century.

In the drive of Africanising the curriculum, serious researches began to be carried out. This is why for example, we can speak with confidence that before the coming of the Missionaries and the colonial administrators, the Ugandans had education systems through which they educated their young people. Also research was made in the history of Uganda and of other African countries and then new syllabi were written to teach this new revelation to the students.

To create "African identity" and "African personality" in the minds of the Ugandan students, the curriculum from 1964 was designed to create confidence in Ugandans and thereby be proud of their African identity and African personality. The knowledge of one's past and one's situation helps to create pride in one and to have confidence. Consequently, Ugandan history, the geography of Uganda, the sociology of Uganda and similar subjects were researched into and taught to the students. This research is still going on.

The government takes over control of schools: The 1963 Education Act

During the colonial period, some schools were owned and controlled by the Church of Uganda, some other schools were owned and controlled by the Roman Catholic Church, some others were owned and controlled by the Uganda Muslim Education Association (UMEA), some schools were owned and controlled by the Uganda Protectorate Government and by the local governments and a few others were owned and controlled by the various Asian sections such as the Goanese, the Shikhs, the Ismails and the Banyans. Then there were also private schools under the control of one or a number of persons. Though the government through the Department of Education was responsible for the whole education system and for giving financial assistance to those schools except to the private schools, the above groups had a very great say in deciding as to which pupils and students should attend those schools and the kind of ideology they should follow in terms of the groups which controlled the various schools.

For example, each group taught mainly the children of its followers. It was free to deny entry into its schools children who did not belong to its religion. This meant that some children could be denied opportunity of education if there were no places in schools run by other groups. Yet such schools were being financed by the government.

The controlling of schools by the above various groups was realised by the independent government that it would interfere with its plans. For example, it could prevent the production of adequate qualified men and women by refusing children from another group. It could also prevent the government ideology from being given to pupils and students such as the idea of "African personality" and the idea of "African identity." Yet the government was paying a lot of money to run the education system to accommodate as many boys and girls as possible in those schools to give them qualifications and its ideology. By 1970 the government was spending about 28% of the national budget on education. This was quite high in terms of one item only.

Similarly, the government realised that the existence of denominational schools was continuing to keep suspicions and hatred created during the religious and political wars of the he 1880's and the early 1890's. There was need to save the children of this nation from attitudes which had arisen from events which are no longer of importance to us. Prof J.P. Ocitti says,

> ...football matches betweren neighbouring Catholic and Protestant schools were not games but battles of breaking legs among the players and battles of throwing stones among the warring spectators".

Welbourn puts denominationalism in Uganda thus, "Protestants, Catholics and Moslims, educated in separate schools tend to regard one another not as fellow citizens of one nation but as members of different communities each rivalling the other for wealth, power and status.

Also this kind of denominational education was uneconomic and extravagant because each denomination had to build a school in each area to serve the children of its followers whereas the school population did not require two schools or more. This led to under-employment of teachers, of the buildings and scholastic materials and equipment. It also denied schools in places where these denominations did not want to build schools, thus creating unequal development in the country.

There was a need to create a unified teaching service and to accord the teachers the same status as civil servants of the same qualifications. During the missionary and colonial control of education, the Church of Uganda, the Roman Catholic Church, the Uganda Muslim Education Association and the government, each had its own teachers and it treated them under its own terms and conditions of service, many times these terms and conditions of service varied between the above employing authorities and many times teachers did not known their true salaries. Deductions were being made from their salaries without satisfactory explanation being given and suspension from teaching for a period of six months or one year without pay were common.

Similarly, teachers were being treated differently from the civil servants with the same number of years of training and comparable qualifications. Usually the teachers were being paid lower salaries than their counterpart workers in the civil service. Besides, it was generally felt that to leave the control of schools to the Missionaries meant leaving these schools to foreigners and inviting another form of colonialism. In such a situation, it would be difficult to encourage and inculcate national consciousness in children through the school system. The European Missionaries still looked at Africans as unfit for shouldering responsibilities. Then also leaving Asians to control education of their sections meant that they would not allow Africans to mix with them in their schools and they would carry on the same superiority complex which they had over the Africans.

Yet there was another aspect of the issue. The UPC government which was in power knew well enough that the majority of the Roman Catholics were not supporting it, they were supporting DP which was the party in opposition. So to leave the Roman Catholic Church to control its schools would be strengthening the power of the Democratic Party to oppose the UPC government all the more. Moreover that government could not believe that Roman Catholic schools could easily allow to see government measures being carried out in them.

To prevent the occurrence of the above problems, the government passed the 1963 (Amendment) Education Act. This 1963 Education Act put the control of all schools financially aided by the government under the control of the government. This also implied that future schools would be established by the government not by the Churches and Mosques and Asian racial groups. It was only private schools which were not controlled administratively by the government because they were getting no financial assistance from the government.
Moreover these private schools were not discriminating between pupils along religious lines. They welcomed any student who was prepared to attend them and to pay their school fees.

By the 1963 Education Act, the Church of Uganda, the Roman Catholic Church, the Uganda Muslim Education Association and the various Asian communities lost control over the schools which they were formerly controlling. The government took over control and ensured its being in a position to do whatever it wanted in the schools.

However, by the 1963 Education Act, the religious groups and the Asian sections were not entirely excluded from the management of the schools which they had founded. Those groups were referred to in the Act as Foundation Bodies. They continued as they still do today to be consulted on fundamental matters such as to who should be the Headteachers of those schools, members of School Management Committees for Primary Schools and Board of Governors. Up to now the Foundation Bodies continue to have a keen interest in the schools which they founded and those others which they continued to establish from 1964 under the guise of Parents Schools many of which they eventually handed over to the government to get financial support. Moreover these schools continued to be on the land of the Foundation Bodies.

Thus the battle against denomination schools which was started by the Thomas Education Committee in 1940, and continued by the de Bunsen Education Committee of 1952, and by the Uganda Relationship Commission of 1961, alternatively called the Munster Commission, and by the Uganda Teachers' Salary Commission, also known as the Lawrence Commission of 1962, was finally resolved by the 1963 Education Act. Now children join any school without reference to the religion which they follow. Also the Government which the Missionaries had resisted to control schools from 1925 now controlled the schools and the religious bodies were no longer in a position to direct the affairs of the schools as they had been doing during the colonial days.

The take over of the schools which were formerly under the denominations caused a temporary opposition especially from the Roman Catholic Church and the Democratic Party which was in opposition in Parliament. But the Government stuck to its decision and insisted to see that the provisions of the Act were implemented. One of the most important provisions of the Act was the transfer of the Primary schools to the authority of the local governments while the Central government took charge of the secondary schools and other post primary institutions such as Teacher Training Colleges, Technical Schools, Agriculture Schools and Universities.

It has been claimed however, that the take over of the schools from the religious bodies led to the deterioration of effective supervison of school discipline and the desirable behavior among pupils and students in schools. But this view needs verification . The Churches and the Mosques were not entirely excluded from the schools. The former denominational primary and secondary schools and Teacher Training Colleges and Technical Schools continued as they still continue today to be on Church or Mosque land. Even many schools which the government built after 1963 are on Church and Mosque land. Moreover the Churches and the Mosques were still free to continue having Chaplains in these schools to take care of the religious and moral side of the students' lives.

If discipline began to fall in schools which many times was exhibited in strikes especially in secondary schools, this was partly due to an attempt by the government to democraticise the administration of schools. In 1964 the government allowed Secondary Schools, Teachers Training Colleges and Technical Schools to establish students' councils to work hand in hand with the administration. This gave the students a certain kind of boldness to the extent that in many secondary schools students felt that they had been allowed to run the schools themselves in disregard to the real administrators of the schools. And the following English saying could be aptly applied to them that "they came to learn and remained to teach".

Also because many Headteachers wanted to have a free hand from the Church authorities and from the control of the Boards of Governors and the School Management Committees, they tended to disregard them. Because of the desire to be independent of Church control, some newly appointed Headteachers were usually not too keen to work closely with the Church authorities in matters connected with school administration. The government also encouraged this attitude to lessen the religious influence in schools. That attitude gave the Church authorities the impression that they were no longer welcome in matters which concerned education in the schools which they had established. This is one reason why Churches began to encourage the opening up of Parents Schools which were in fact Church private schools but disguised behind the parents who belonged to each individual Church. These church authorities thus began to be less interested in involving themselves in the affairs of those old schools which the government had taken over from them.

The writer interviewed in 1979 the late Emmanuel Cardinal Nsubuga on his feelings about the 1963 Education Act and how it subsequently came to be implemented in the schools. The late Cardinal thus replied:

> The Headteachers and you the lay people did not want us (the priests) in schools. So we left the schools to you. For example, the Headteachers no longer wanted to consult the Parish Priests or even to see them in the schools whereas those schools were on Church land and they were in the wake of the Parish Priests' residences.

One implication from the late Cardinal's words was that Church people had given up temporarily their directing hand in schools especially those which were not being run directly by the lay Brothers and Nuns on the side of the Roman Catholic Church. It would be instructive to read here at length what one Ugandan educationist, Mrs. Margaret N. Nsereko wrote in 1986 in the book entitled *Education Today: A Guide to parents & Teachers in Uganda*.

Firstly, Mrs. Nsereko is a graduate teacher. She was an Education Officer in the then Ministry of Education when the 1963 Education Act was being passed. She was in 1965 appointed Headmistress of Trinity College Nabbingo as the first Ugandan Headmistress of that school. She held that post effectively until 1988 when she retired honourably.

Mrs. Nsereko was one of the top advisers of the late Emmanuel Cardinal Nsubuga on education matters and for a long time she was a key member of the Education Committee of the Roman Catholic Kampala Archdiocese. With other members of the committee, Mrs. Nsereko was behind the policy of the establishment and administration of the Parents Schools on the Roman Catholic side in the Kampala Archdiocese. So what she wrote in the above book is quite instructive on the issue of the position of the Foundation Bodies in terms of the 1963 Education Act. She thus wrote:

> The parish under the jurisdiction of the Catholic Church is the mother of most of these schools, and the parish naturally played a very active role in the running of these schools. In the mid-sixties however, the Uganda Government became more

actively involved in the education of its citizens. Most schools gradually fell into the hands of Government Education Officers and Inspectors. The Parish Priest began treating himself as a visitor in his own schools. He lost sight of the rights he had in those schools, as a leader of the Foundation Body. The Headteacher of a school preferred to kick priests out of the school. The alternative was to start another private school somewhere else which was eventually "lost" in the same way. The Catholic Church in Uganda founded all the necessary types of schools, most of which are now government-aided. Should we grumble that these schools were taken away by the Government? Has the government really taken away these schools?

The Parish Priest is the representative of the Foundation Body on the spot. He should make his parish the centre of attraction to all Catholic Foundation Schools in his area and should take interest in whatever goes in these schools.

The Headteachers, on their part, should note that those schools are not owned by any individual, but belong to the Foundation Body, especially in as much as they stand on Church land, and have a Church background to them.

The education of a child is not a simple matter: it involves a number of parties: the parents, the teachers, the government and finally the Foundation Body. Whereas some of these parties may be concerned with the cultural, political, social and physical upbringing of a child, the Church, through the Parish Priest, would come out very strongly as the party concerned with the most important aspect of man-that is his moral and spiritual upbringing. It is my submission, therefore, that the Parish and the school work hand in hand, in order to promote the welfare of the whole man. Having said that, I wish to conclude by saying that the Catholic Church in Uganda today has a big task to fulfil, and that is, to redirect the minds of teachers and headteachers, in the Catholic founded schools, to impress upon these teachers the fact that she (the Church) is the mother and owner of all these schools.

In recent times the Churches and the Mosques have shown once again a keener interest in wanting to assume a more directing hand in the schools which they founded though however, not in opposition to the Government. One reason for this is that they have realised the necessity of redirecting the moral conduct and discipline of the teachers, pupils and students in schools.

One other reason why there has been a deterioration in discipline and desirable behaviour in our schools should be attributed to the society as a whole. A society's culture of which discipline and desirable behaviour are part, is safeguarded by the society as a whole. Therefore if there are undesirable factors in schools, the members of the society should cooperate to fight against them.

To make this point short, let us take an example from what was happening during the days when the Missionaries controlled the schools. The Missionaries would not accept teachers in the schools who were not socially exemplary. Even the members of society were supporting the Missionaries in this respect. The Missionaries for example, would not allow a male teacher to continue teaching once he was proved that he was in the habit of befriending his female pupils or students. They would not allow a school mistress who would bear children outside wedlock to continue teaching in their schools. They would not tolerate a teacher who would reveal examination questions to the pupils or students. And the society supported the Missionaries in this firmness because such teachers could not be expected to give good examples to the pupils and students and to the rest of the society.

But when the Churches and the Mosques temporarily distanced themselves from the schools from 1963, one began to find many male teachers being accused of defiling school girls. Many unmarried school mistresses began bearing children from a number of men. Some teachers and even Headteachers began to be involved in malpractices in public examinations. What is worse, the above teachers tended to get away with it. The public continued to accept to see that such teachers went on teaching in the schools.

These schools have got School Management Committees and Boards of Governors on which sit serious minded Christian and Muslim people. One would expect that they should be loud and clear in their protestation against such unexemplary behaviour of some teachers and even force them from coming into contact with the nation's children. But the general impression one gets is that they keep a closed eye against such teachers. Yet they are the same people who lament that discipline and desirable behaviour have declined in schools.

Some Headteachers and their teachers have been caught red handed giving answers to their pupils and students past mid night for public examinations which would be sat the following morning. Still society keeps silence and leaves such Headteachers to continue heading our schools and the teachers who assist such Headteachers to continue teaching our children.

One classical example was that of a Headteacher in 1991 who was found by UNEB vigilantes at midnight giving answers to primary school pupils of an examination paper which was going to be sat the following morning. The Headteacher on seeing the vigilantes jumped out of the class-room through a window and left the helpless pupils amazed. The community around the school knew about this incident but kept silence. You can imagine what examples some of our teachers give to our youngsters. Is it any wonder that discipline and desirable behaviour are disappearing from our schools? What more respectability can there be about such Headteachers and teachers in the eyes of the pupils? And how can they enforce discipline and desirable behaviour in our youngsters when the pupils and students know that Headteachers and teachers are themselves corrupt?

Yet society seems to keep a closed eye against all this. Where such incidents are not discovered by the UNEB vigilantes, which incidents may be known by parents, the parents only rejoice that they were too lucky. Their children pass with flying colours.

If society does not go out of its way to fight against these undesirable behaviours in our schools while it still professes Christian and Islamic principles, in days to come, we shall be faced in hospitals with Doctors who passed examinations through cheating. You can imagine what will be the lot of patients who will face such Doctors on the operation tables. Therefore society is also partly to blame for the deterioration of discipline and desirable behaviour in our schools. We need not wait until the Churches and Mosques resume the direction of the schools.

One of the intentions of the 1963 Education Act was to reduce the control of education administration by the religious bodies. The government should have made plans to build future schools on government land and not on church land. But the government ignored to do this. It went on to promote primary schools to secondary schools level the former Church of Uganda and Roman Catholic primary schools. It also went on to have new primary schools, secondary schools and Teacher Training Colleges on either Church of Uganda land or on Roman Catholic Church land.

The trend from the 1980's up to 1993 for the Church of Uganda, the Roman Catholic Church and the Muslim Supreme Council was to increase their powers in the schools of which they were Foundation Bodies in a bid to improve the moral standards of the teachers,of the pupils and of the students and to improve academic standards.

Loss of funds for schools generated by Missionaries was another result of the 1963 Education Act. Up to the time of the passing of the Education Act, Missionaries were spending much money on education. When the Education Act was passed, the Missionaries stopped aiding schools. But the Uganda government was not disturbed by that financial loss because it had plenty of good will from Britain and from the United States of America. As a result it got many soft loans from those countries to finance education. That assistance tapered off in the 1970s' because those countries did not agree with the policies which Idi Amin's government was following. From that time, schools and other education institutions began to face constant shortages of funds coming from the government and it is one reason why Parents Teachers' Associations began to spring up to assist schools.

Loss of effective supervision of schools was also a direct result of the 1963 Education Act. Before the passing of that Education Act, there were two kinds of supervision of schools. One kind was that carried out by the Inspectors of Schools from the Department of Education. The second kind of supervision was that carried out by the School Supervisors of the Roman Catholic schools at Diocesan level, by the School Supervisors of the Church of Uganda schools again at Diocesan level, by the School Supervisors of the Uganda Muslim Education Association schools and by the School Supervisors of the schools under the different local governments.

The 1963 Education Act abolished all the School Supervisors of the above groups. It left only the Inspectors of Schools from the Ministry of Education composed of all shades of men and women.

The above arrangement led to a decrease of supervision of schools because the Inspectors of Schools from the Ministry of Education had no special attachment to schools the way the School Supervisors had. Moreover, since the School Supervisors were at Diocesan level and at local government level, they were closer to the schools and they were visiting them daily. The situation is even worse today. Inspectors of schools have no transport to reach schools.

Recruitment of non-national workers immediately after Uganda had regained her Independence

While all the plans of producing qualified men and women through the schools and the Universities were in progress, the government had to keep the schools running and other kind of work in other government fields. It would take some years before enough Ugandan qualified people were to be produced from secondary schools and Universities.

Consequently from 1962, the government began to recruit workers from Britain, USA, Canada and Australia. It also took back on contract some British civil servants who had resigned on the approach of independence. Some of these British civil servants had feared that under the management of Africans, chaos would come about. They were focussing on the chaos which had resulted after Zaire's regaining her independence in 1960 where the Belgians were chased out of the country and many of them lost their lives and property. Other British civil servants simply did not want to be under the direction of Africans. Those with the fear of chaos ensuing and those who did not want to work under the Africans definitely left the country before or soon after Uganda had regained her independence and they were not among those who became re-engaged on contract.

In terms of the education system, the country got the following category of teachers. One category consisted of those who had just finished their A-Level education in the USA and Canada. Those from the USA came under the scheme called Peace Corps and those from Canada came under the scheme known as Volunteer Service Overseas (VSO). These young men and women taught in our secondary schools on a two years basis after which they left for their countries to pursue further studies in Universities and other tertiary institutions. However, they were not trained teachers. They were also not getting salaries from the Uganda Government except that they were being given accommodation and some money for maintenance. The governments of Canada and the USA paid them their dues in a spirit of assisting Uganda.

The second category of teachers consisted of graduates from Britain, USA, Canada and Australia. These did a Post Graduate Diploma in Education course at Makerere University for one academic year and they would go to teach in secondary schools as qualified teachers. They were free to stay as long as they wanted. But by 1974, most of them had left Uganda.

The third category of teachers consisted of already qualified and experienced teachers from Britain, USA, Canada and Australia. These came as experts and they taught in Teacher Training Colleges, Agricultural Colleges, Technical Colleges, Technical Institutes, Secondary schools and at Makerere University, and some also worked in the Ministry of Education as advisors.

All the above three categories of teachers did commendable work and they helped our schools and other educational institutions to get going while our education system was trying to produce enough graduate Ugandan teachers. Incidentally, the above category of teachers also worked in Kenya and Tanzania. After Idi Amin had expelled the Asians from Uganda in 1972, there was another sudden shortage of teachers in our secondary schools. The government made arrangements and imported some 500 graduate teachers from Ghana. These worked in Uganda for about two years and left for their country. Then the government of Idi Amin recruited many graduate teachers for our secondary schools and Training Institutions from India, Bangladesh and Pakistan.

Implications of employing non-nationals after Uganda had regained her Independence

There were about four serious implications arising out of Uganda employing a large number of non-nationals between 1962 and 1975. First, there was constant discontinuity and interruptions of programmes and projects. These workers were usually on contracts of between two and three years. At the departure of one group, another group would also come. Many times this caused discontinuity and interruptions of projects and programmes. This means that there must have been some loss of money in one way or another.

Secondly, at the time of Uganda regained her independence, there was need to create confidence and pride among Ugandans as people who had taken their rightful place among the peoples of other independent nations of the world. This was one reason why there were such ideologies as "creating an African identity" and "creating an African personality". But employing a large number of non-nationals especially in schools affected the effectiveness of these ideologies. Such people had no belief in those ideologies and one could not expect those non-nationals to promote confidence and pride in the feelings of the Ugandans. Many of them still felt that they had come to teach ignorant Africans as the Missionaries had thought at the turn of the 19th century.

The impression those who were working with the young teachers from Britain, Canada, USA and Australia got was that they felt that they were still on a mission to civilise the backward Africans. So whatever claims we made that we had also taken a rightful place among the peoples of other independent countries in the world, did not make any impression on them. They were the people who knew the right things which should be said and done even in an African situation about which they had no experience.

Thirdly, the government of Uganda had to treat these teachers and other workers in its other Ministries and Departments as a special favoured category of people. The government feared that once they or their countries got annoyed, they could leave the country in its problems. Those African officers who were heading departments were constantly telling their fellow Ugandan workers where privileges were in question, that the "expatriate workers were entitled to those privileges while the Ugandan workers were eligible". This expression meant that those expatriate workers had to be given treatment comparable to what they had left back in their countries. Some of the old teachers still remember that the best houses in a school had to be given to expatriate teachers and the African graduate teachers were being given the rather dilapidated old small huts in a school. When they pointed out the anomaly, the African Officers in the Ministry of Education told them that "the expatriate teachers were entitled to those gorgeous houses and the African teachers were only "eligible". This kind of retort frustrated the African employees and worked against their confidence.

Fourthly, we must appreciate that first class qualified people are few in every country. This is the same even in Britain, Canada, USA and other countries. This means that no country can easily leave its best teachers of Physics, Biology, Chemistry, Mathematics, Agriculture, Geography, History and of other subjects to go and teach in another country. This also applies to other qualified men and women in other fields. Even the first class qualified men and women cannot risk leaving their countries to deprive them of their vital services and risk their lives in unknown countries. Moreover countries go out of their way to treat their qualified workers in such a way that they find it hard to leave their countries. Consequently, normally those workers who go to work in other countries are those whom their countries can dispense with. And the receiving country cannot expect to get the best workers from other countries.

The above point also means that a country should create favourable conditions for its qualified men and women to desire to stay in their country and contribute to its development. Moreover if they leave to work in other countries, the country loses the money it spent on their education. From the 1970's to the present, one unfortunate characteristic of Ugandan qualified men and women has been that many of them leave Uganda and go to work in other countries where they feel that their skills and knowledge are better rewarded as workers. One ironical revelation is that after the departure of many Ugandan qualified men and women, we engage foreign experts whom we pay 45 times more than the same Ugandan qualified men and women who left Uganda for greener pastures. For example, numerous cases have been reported through the Uganda Press where the government has been known to import an expatriate to do a job a Ugandan qualified man could do as ably as the expatriate. Such a Ugandan qualified person is being paid $10 a month while the expatriate expert is paid $6000 a month. This kind of discrepancy must surely discourage the Ugandan qualified people. And it is one reason why many of them leave Uganda for greener pastures in other countries, from where Uganda eventually recruits experts.

Results from the Educational strategies made from 1962 to 1970
One result from the tremendous increase of schools and places in those schools immediately Uganda had regained her independence, was that the shortage of qualified men and women was successfully solved by 1970. Serious shortages were only in a few jobs which needed highly specialised skills in science, technology, medicine and high level teaching such as in the University.

But this increase in qualified people had two disappointments. One disappointment was that graduates from schools and Universities were not job creators but job seekers. Consequently, they could not help to create new jobs and thereby increase the economic development of the country. The economy continued to develop at a very slow pace, yet the government had hoped that by producing very many graduates with secondary school qualifications and University qualifications, it would not only assist in filling up the numerous available jobs but it would also produce many graduates who would assist to create more jobs and thus help to produce further economic developments in the country. But as things turned out, this last hope failed to be realised.

The above disappointment led to the next disappointment. Very many school leavers even University graduates began to roam the streets of Kampala and of other towns in Uganda looking for jobs which were however not available. That was at that time called "the school leaver problem". The implication of this problem was that the curriculum needed to be re-adjusted. The changes which had been made on the curriculum since 1962 had been only grafted onto a system left behind by the British, which no longer suited the Ugandan situation. The re-adjustment aimed at teaching practical skills which gave the graduates the ability to act as job creators on leaving schools and University, especially when they failed to get already created jobs.

Unfortunately there was a feeling among school leavers to avoid the land. Yet very many jobs could be created on the land if these school leavers had the training and interest to stay there. Therefore even the attitude of the boys and girls needed to be changed. However, the curriculum was never drastically changed though the attitudes of the students and of the teachers were constantly subjected to the public outcry that education should produce "job creators and not job seekers".

Due to the realisation that education in primary schools, secondary schools and even in the Universities was giving only literary skills to most of the students, many educationists in Uganda from the 1970's to the present have opened up and continue to establish vocational institutions under various names such as polytechnics, business schools and vocational institutes.

The intention is to take on graduates of primary schools, secondary schools and Universities and give them technical practical skills which they can readily use when employed or when they choose to initiate their own employment.

The imparting of practical skills to many children along the above lines has eased the traditional rush of academic graduates to government and company offices to seek jobs. Usually such academic graduates from Primary Schools through Universities, have got only the skills of reading, writing and solving mathematical numbers. The difference is only in the progressive complexity as one climbs higher the educational ladder up to University.

But the balance between teaching academic knowledge and teaching practical skills has not yet been established in the curriculum. Uganda's education is still mainly academically oriented. One needs to see the academic stuff which pupils cram to pass the PLE Examinations. One wonders what use it is to nearly 80% of them who do not even join any post primary institutions but stay in the rural areas. This has been made more difficult by the shortage of science materials and equipment so much so that even science subjects being taught lack a large measure of practicability.

The need for teaching practical skills to pupils and students in both Primary and Secondary schools, was realised by the members of the Uganda National Education Policy Review Commission of 1987 chaired by Prof. W. Senteza Kajubi. The members were loud and clear in their recommendation which they expressed in the term "Basic Education for National Development-BEND".

The idea behind BEND gives the challenge to the educationists who have got to reform the curriculum in such a way that there is a fair balance in Primary and Secondary schools between the academic subjects and the practical subjects. The aim should be to produce students at all levels who will be able to create their own jobs especially if they fail to secure already created jobs.

To the failure to produce job seekers and not job creators through our schools, is added the problem of the shortage of school places for Uganda's children. It is estimated that about 55% of children of primary school age attend primary schools today. Yet there are not enough school places to accommodate adequately even this small percentage. However, the shortage of primary school facilities is found mostly in urban areas where there is a concentration of population. Again this shortage is aggravated by the fact that there is a certain number of schools which are preferred by parents because they have got a high rate of passing pupils in the first grade in the PLE, which gives a great chance to the pupils to easily get places in the first class secondary schools in the country. But the solution here is simple. Let the teachers in the primary schools which are at the moment less favoured by many parents, endeavour to improve the methods of passing pupils highly in their PLE. This is possible and between 1970 and 1990 many Primary schools raised their standards to levels which made parents flock to them for placing their children.

About 8% of the primary school leavers get places in the secondary schools because there are no enough places at that level to satisfy all graduates of primary schools. At University level and other tertiary institutions, the shortage of places is also very great. Yet the government spends nearly 28% of the National Budget on education for so small a school enrolment.

The result is that though Uganda has not yet achieved universal primary education, even those children who are willing and capable to attend school at various levels cannot do so because of the shortage of places at those levels. This is very similar to the situation which existed during the colonial days. And it is one reason why private schools developed and became successful in the country despite the initial missionary opposition to them. It is encouraging however, to note that though the "school leaver problem" is still great in Uganda, that is, many of those who graduate from schools do not get jobs, parents still have got a belief in the usefulness of education and they continue to send their children to schools in great numbers.

The cry for secondary school places has been answered by the Government, Churches, Mosques and private people by establishing secondary schools nearly in every parish. This aspect became very hectic during the 1980's when Members of Parliament in Obote II regime joined the activity of establishing secondary schools in their constituencies. They wanted to show themselves as supporters of education with a view of being re-elected. Many of these secondary schools however, were relatively ill equipped to offer secondary courses. Many of their buildings, usually former primary schools, left a lot to be desired. They also lacked qualified teachers especially the science teachers. This period saw the rise of what has been termed "Third World Secondary Schools".

One other disappointing aspect which appeared in the education system was observed from the 1970's. Education from that decade started to get less value in the thinking of some parents and children. This was because during the colonial days and from 1962 to 1970, education was a means to getting easily highly paying jobs in offices. The colonial administrators were deliberately producing a limited number of African qualified men and women to avoid having workers whom they could not give jobs while at the same time they had to give jobs to excessive workers from Britain.

But from the 1970's jobs were few in government establishments. Moreover those few available jobs were no longer paying due to the continued inflation which reduced the value of money paid in fixed salaries. Yet adventurous boys and girls many of whom were semi-literate, could easily engage in trade and make much money. Consequently, education began getting a diminishing value in the eyes of some easily discouraged parents and children. The diminishing value for education in the estimation of the above people has been made even worse by such people as primary school teachers, secondary school teachers and University

Professors who cannot live on their salaries for a week. When many people see such a phenomenon, they wonder whether it pays to attend schools at all.

Fortunately the government is aware of the financial condition of teachers and it has promised to do all it can to improve their salaries. Also wise parents have got faith in education and they encourage their children to go to schools because they know that an educated person will always be in a better position to manage life. This is why the demand for school facilities has not abated. The government aided primary schools now in 1993 stand at 8,300 as opposed to 2,000 in 1962. The government aided secondary schools as a result rose from 120 in 1980 to 508 in 1986. The number at the time of writing in 1995 is 630. This number does not include private secondary schools which is close to 400.

The Military Regime of Idi Amin 1971-79

The period between 1971 and 1980 experienced several dramatic incidents in the education field. First of all, many educational programmes and projects which were going on during the 1960's ceased. These programmes and projects were being supported by Britain and by the United States of America. But these countries lost faith in the military regime of President Idi Amin. For example, late in the 1960's there was started the International Development Agency (IDA) Project for improving teaching in all spheres of education by providing improved teacher education and scholastic materials. This Project is still going on in other African countries. By 1971 the IDA Project had only reached stage three as the 3rd IDA Project and it stalled for some time. It was only picked up towards the end of the 1970's. It is now at stage five as the 5th IDA Project while other African countries are at stage ten as the 10th IDA Project.

The 1960's saw a concentration on secondary school education in the drive of producing qualified Ugandans to work in government departments and in other fields. Consequently many secondary schools were built rising from 28 in 1962 to 73 secondary schools in 1970. During the 1970's very few secondary schools were built and yet there was an increase in primary schools during the 1970,s. This meant that there was a bottleneck at secondary school level. Therefore many pupils who were graduating from primary schools could not be absorbed in secondary schools because there was no comparable increase in secondary school facilities. Building of secondary schools only resumed in the 1980's with the result that by 1995 there were nearly 630 secondary schools in the country.

The Churches especially the Roman Catholic Church took advantage of the relaxation in the enforcing of the provisions of the 1963 Education Act and the 1970 Education Act passed by the Obote I regime to drastically reduce the influence of the religious bodies in education. The Roman Catholic Church built many Parents Schools. This in a way compensated the schools which that Church had lost to the control of the government by the 1963 Education Act.

Development of Education

During the 1970's there was an upsurge in Muslim education. The Amin regime offered many opportunities for the employment of Muslims in government and in parastatal bodies. But many jobs in those spheres needed specialised skills acquired through the education system and many Muslims did not have those skills so they missed such opportunities. Therefore Muslims realised the need for school education and there was an exceptional enthusiasm for Muslim parents to send their daughters and sons to schools. Also the Uganda Muslim Supreme Council which was created by Idi Amin for the unity of Uganda Muslims took a forward plunge in establishing schools and in encouraging Muslim parents to send their children to schools. This enthusiasm has been kept up to the present time assisted by funds from the Arab World.

During this same period of the 1970's, Uganda experienced a sharp decline in foreign exchange partly as a result of foreign countries withholding aid to the country, because they did not trust enough the military regime of President Idi Amin and partly because in 1972 that regime dismissed Asians from the country in the drive of getting the economy in the hands of Ugandans. These Asians were the controllers of the commercial and industrial activities in the country. They knew how to manipulate foreign exchange. It would take some time before the Ugandan African business men and women and industrialists would adequately learn the intricacies of attracting foreign exchange into the country.

The result of this shortage of foreign exchange in terms of education was that it became progressively difficult to import into the country scholastic materials, science materials and science equipment. Even Longman, the famous Publishing House of Britain which had long established a firm branch in Uganda closed it. All this led to a very great shortage of text books, other scholastic materials, science materials, equipment and it affected education adversely in the country.

However, on a positive note, this shortage of scholastic materials such as text books, made Ugandans to improvise. Many Ugandan writers came out to meet the challenge and began to produce text books through the system of duplicated manuals. Text book writing by Ugandans which is booming today had its origin in the 1970 s. This praiseworthy effort has however been frustrated and hindered by the darth of Ugandan Publishers otherwise the text book industry would have been already captured by Ugandan authors.

During this same period there was wanton destruction of valuable scholastic materials in libraries and schools all over the country. Money became short and many irresponsible people began looting books in libraries and institutions which they sold either to veranda book vendors or to market men and women for wrapping in tomatoes, oranges, pan-cakes and the like. Thousands of valuable books, magazines and journals were lost.

This same trend saw the looting of office files in government offices and educational institutions. This rendered the keeping of valuable records difficult because even confidential official letters were finding their way in markets daily, for wrapping merchandise.

1978 and 1979 were years during which Tanzanian soldiers combined efforts with Ugandan guerrillas to overthrow Idi Amin and his government. These Tanzanian soldiers and the Uganda guerrillas together with Amin's soldiers destroyed much property of the schools because all groups used to camp in schools. They were using books from libraries for lighting the fire, and desks and tables for cooking and for camp fires. This trend was repeated in 1985 and part of 1986 during the war which overthrew both Obote II and Okello Lutwa regimes. By the end of all these wars, many schools in areas in which the major fighting took place had lost books, desks, tables, doors, windows and beds in the case of boarding schools.

Due to the insecurity during the 1970's and due to the desire to look for greener pastures outside Uganda, the 1970's saw the first serious brain drain ever experienced in the country. This was serious and unfortunate because from 1962 to 1970, government effort had been concentrated on producing highly qualified men and women through the secondary schools and Universities in East Africa and abroad. But insecurity to life and the desire for looking for greener pastures attracted thousands of qualified Ugandans to leave the country and go to work especially in Kenya, in Central African countries and countries in Southern Africa and far beyond in Europe, USA and Canada.

The Amin administration resorted to attracting Bangladesh, Pakistani and Libyan nationals to work in Uganda as teachers, lecturers, doctors, engineers and other workers in different fields, of course at higher salaries than those which were being paid to Ugandan qualified men and women. In 1972 Asians were dismissed from Uganda. This left schools without qualified teachers in Kampala and in other towns in which Asian children formerly studied. The schools were now left to African children to fill but without enough qualified African teachers.

However, Makerere University and Kyambogo stepped up their intakes for undergraduate teachers and Post Graduate Teachers and they managed to keep the education system supplied with qualified teachers at the secondary school level. But the problem was that it was difficult to retain the qualified graduate teachers when across the border in Kenya, there was a great shortage of graduate teachers too and security and salaries were very attractive. Very many Ugandan graduate teachers went to teach in Kenya schools and they left an indelible mark on the Kenyan education system for their devotion to duty, efficiency and effectiveness as professional teachers, a sign of Uganda's soundness in her education system.

Therefore nearly half the qualified teachers produced every year by Makerere University and Kyambogo for Secondary schools were leaving the country. The

Development of Education

further implication of this brain drain abroad was that Uganda was training many high level qualified men and women at a great cost in many fields out of whom it gained nothing. Qualified graduate teachers, doctors, engineers, lawyers, accountants and seasoned Civil Servants were constantly leaving the country. This trend of brain drain is still going on today not so much for insecurity, but for seeking greener pastures outside the country. Consequently many resources of the country are lost in this drain of graduate qualified manpower on which the country spends tremendous resources.

Exercise :
  i) Why did many educational projects get suspended between 1971 and 1979?
  ii) Why was there an increase in Parents' Schools built by both the Christian Churches and the Uganda Muslim Supreme Council during the 1970's?
  iii) Why was there a large number of Ugandan text book writers during the 1970's?
  iv) Why did the brain drain abroad begin in Uganda during the 1970s and what has Uganda lost in this phenomenon?

The Education structure proposed by the Senteza Kajubi Education Commission, 1987

In 1978 an Education Policy Review Commission was set up to study and make recommendations on the education system of the country. The outbreak of the war in 1979 which drove away Idi Amin from power rendered the work of the Commission incomplete. In 1987 the NRM government felt the need to set up a new National Education Policy Review Commission and it set it up under the Chairmanship of Professor W. Senteza Kajubi. That Commission presented to the government its recommendations in 1989. One of the most important recommendations regarded the structure of education which differed drastically from that set up by the Castle Education Commission in 1963 which was still being followed by 1995.

The following is the structure proposed by the Senteza Kajubi Education Commission.

Primary School Education: 8 years
  1 (a) Lower Primary: Primary 1 to Primary 4. The medium of instruction will be the mother tongue of the area where the primary school is. The emphasis here will be on the acquisition of reading, writing, numeracy and some science basic principles.
  (b) Upper Primary: primary 5 to primary 8. The medium of instruction will be English. There will be an emphasis here on practical subjects so that a

pupil can acquire practical skills for use in life even if he or she does not continue to the secondary school section of education.

2(a) General secondary schools: These will be similar to the majority of the present academic secondary schools, offering a course of 3 years.

(b) Comprehensive secondary schools: These will offer a multi-purpose curriculum comprising of both academic and vocational subjects. Each comprehensive secondary school will offer a minimum of four vocational subjects and a whole range of academic subjects for 3 years.

(c) Vocational secondary schools: These will be similar to the present technical schools and they will offer a 3 year course.

3. Advanced level secondary education of two years after the Uganda Certificate of Education (UCE) leading to the Uganda Advanced Certificate of Education (UACE). The course to last 2 years.

Tertiary level
This level will be joined after A Level. It will consist of courses at Universities, polytechnics, all types of colleges and specialised training institutions.

Imparting practical skills from primary five to the end of the secondary stage is implied in this structure. **The structure as it is, is quite good. Eight years of Primary education mean that in this respect a child who joins Primary one at the age of six years, will be 14 years by the end of Primary eight.**

At the age of 14 years such a child can work usefully if he or she does not continue into the secondary school section, provided that he or she has been given effective practical skills in the Primary section. The provision of comprehensive secondary schools means that this kind of secondary schools will teach both academic subjects and practical skills all in one package. Also students who will graduate from these comprehensive secondary schools and do not continue into the next stages, will be able to employ themselves usefully or to be employed by other people.

The above is the same for the provision of the vocational secondary schools. Students in these vocational secondary schools will be even more grounded in the practical skills. Another positive point about the comprehensive secondary schools and the vocational secondary schools is that capable students can work their way up to University and to other tertiary institutions along practical education.

An observation from History in terms of practical education
Similar attempts for teaching practical skills have been made in our education system ever since the government in 1925 became a partner with the Missionaries in the education field in Uganda. For example, from 1925 to 1952, the curriculum

of the primary schools included a strong element of practical skills through the subject of hand-work in which agriculture skills and handcrafts were being taught. From 1930 to 1937, there were Junior Secondary Schools called Central Schools. These schools had a minimum amount of academic work and a great amount of practical education. From 1952 as a result of the recommendations of the 1952 de Bunsen Education Committee, there were instituted practical junior secondary schools known as Rural Trade Schools, Farm Schools and Home Craft Centres plus Modern Secondary Schools at the senior seconday level. That education Committe proposed that a number of senior secondary schools teaching agriculture should be set up under the government. Ntare School in Mbarara and Sir Samuel Baker in Gulu had been originally proposed to be agricultural senior secondary schools.

But when the first Headmasters were appointed to run the above schools as agricultural senior secondary schools they did not run them as such. They decided to run them on the some basis of the already famous secondary schools such as St. Mary's College Kisubi, King's College Buddo, Mwiri College, Nabumali High school, Gayaza High School and others of like manner.

The practical Namutamba Project which was inaugurated in 1977 for primary schools and teacher training colleges failed to bear fruits.

Several factors in the past played a role in reducing the effectiveness of practical education in Uganda's education system.

The attitude of parents and students played a great role in minimising the effectiveness of this kind of practical approach to education. Thus Eric Hussey, the first Director of Education commented on this attitude in 1925:

> To most of the children who go to school, the learning of a little English is the coveted goal and the motive behind that desire is that they might escape from the ranks of a manual worker and fit themselves for some kind of clerical occupation, which they believe to be dignified and less arduous.

In 1928, one Church Missionary Society educator T.C. Vincent of Bishop Tucker College Mukono summed up nicely the feelings of students about practical education thus:

> Parents send their children to mission schools with the hope that they will escape from the routine of village life to which they themselves were subject, and not that they may return to it with new knowledge and ideas that would make that life acceptable and of worth to them.

During the same year at a conference at Namirembe, one son of Sir Apollo Kaggwa remarked that.' The chiefs sent their boys to high schools not to learn to drive bullock wagons and to look after cattle, but to learn to be fitted for posts of high standing" . He alleged that Canon H.M. Grace, then Headmaster of Buddo was trying to educate them for slavery work.

Fortunately today, the attitude of both the parents and the students is ready for this kind of practical approach to education. Both of them want the kind of education which will enable the recipients to be employed by other people and if they choose to initiate their own employment they should have the skills to do so.

The Department of Education which is today's Ministry of Education and Sports tended in the past to treat practical education as a field for the less able students. This made the students who went through this practical kind of education to feel failures and rejectees.

It is here that the Ministry of Education and Sports will find a very big challenge. The Ugandan society hopes that especially the vocational secondary schools and the comprehensive secondary school will not be for those candidates who will have scored lower marks in their PLE. Once there is a tendency towards selecting seemingly less academically capable students to join these schools, that will be the beginning of killing these schools. This is what ruined the Central Schools of the 1930s and the Farm Schools, the Home Craft Centres, the Rural Trade Schools and the Secondary Modern Schools of the de Bunsen days, 1952-63.

The teachers too have been an obstacle to the effectiveness of practical education in the Uganda education system, this arising from the failure of the Teacher Training Colleges and Makerere to train special teachers meant for teaching practical skills to the students in the schools.

The majority of teachers for the Central Schools of the 1930s and for the Farm Schools, the Home Craft Centres, the Rural Trade Schools and the Secondary Modern Schools, were usually drawn from the teachers who had been trained academically. Consequently, one could not expect such teachers to impart practical skills to the students in an effective manner. Even the attitude of those teachers was not quite positive as regards making practical education strong in the education system.

Thus the Director of Education in his 1950 Annual Education Report remarked on the teachers:

> It has become the custom to read year after year reports from the Provinces as follows: 'No handwork has been done this term owing to lack of materials. The teacher intends to begin handwork lessons soon. Handwork periods have been used for extra cultivation or cutting the grass in the compound'. Some schools in the country have specialist carpentry teachers on their staff, but it is strange with the regularity that has been reported, that the carpentry master was not seen or that carpentry had to be stopped because the tools had been stolen.

So the teachers took a *laissez faire* attitude to the teaching of practical skills. This can only be blamed on the way the teachers had been trained in their Teacher Training Colleges.

If we want to see a wholesome change, courses in the teacher education institutions need to be overhauled. The present courses and the approach to training teachers today cannot produce teachers who will teach effectively the practical skills in the schools. We need also to retrain the serving teachers now.

From the 1940s to 1960, St. Mary's College Kisubi, Namilyango College and St. Peter's College Tororo were running Commercial courses together with academic courses. But students from those Colleges with this practical bias had no opening in Makerere College for further studies. Many times students who were taking those commercial courses in the above secondary schools were despised by their fellow students who were following purely academic courses with Makerere College in view. This created a stigma on practical courses since Makerere which had been established in 1922 unconsciously dominated the Uganda system of education as far back as the first year of junior secondary education .

Fortunately by the arrangement of the Senteza Kajubi Education structure, candidates with a bias to practical skills especially from the Vocational Secondary Schools can also join Makerere University. Makerere University runs such courses now in its Faculty of Technology.

The Uganda society needs to realise now that it will have to meet higher costs of running a heavily practical education system. Schools will need tools to use. For example, if students have to learn carpentry in one lesson in a school, they will require hammers, sews, screw drivers, planes, measuring tapes and several other tools. They will also need wood and other materials to practise on.

If after the carpentry lesson students have to learn bicycle mechanics in the next lesson, they will also need to have special tools for this kind of lesson. For example, they will need a supply of new and old bicycles to practise on. The list of practical subjects is a long one and each subject requires different tools and different materials on which students will have to practise. What all this means is that the Uganda society needs to be prepared to find the money to meet all the above expenses. Besides the costs on materials and equipment, there will be need to build workshops and laboratories. All these require quite a large outlay of money. The high running costs of practical education influenced school managers in the past to run academic education in their schools and also reduced the effectiveness of conducting practical education in the Uganda education system.

Therefore the present plunge into providing a large dose of practical education in the education system needs to find a way of removing the above kind of obstacles which bedevilled the efforts in the past.

Question
1. Give two reasons why there was a shortage of qualified men and women at independence in 1962 in Uganda.
2. Give two things which the Uganda government hoped to achieve by expanding greatly the secondary school educational facilities after 1962.
3. Why was there need to create in Ugandan children at school the ideas of "African identity and African personality" after Uganda had regained her independence?
4. What do you think was the intention of colonial education to teach things from the European and American background during the colonial period?
5. What indigenous names were river Nile and lake Victoria called by Ugandans before Europeans came to Uganda?
6. Give two benefits which the Uganda government hoped to bring in Uganda by the 1963 Education Act.
7. How did the 1963 Education Act still safeguarded the interests of the Churches and Mosques in schools?
8. What two disappointments did the Uganda government get by 1970 from the greatly expanded educational facilities?
9. What is the background to "Basic Education for National Development"(BEND) which was proposed by the Senteza Kajubi Education Commission of 1987?
10. Why did the value of education begin to decrease in the estimation of some Ugandan parents and children from the 1970s?
11. What traumatic incidents disturbed the Uganda education system between 1971 and 1980?

13 Effects of some Education Ordinances, Commissions, Committees and Education Acts on the Education System of Uganda

Introduction
Governments time and again appoint education commissions and committees to examine either a particular aspect in the education system or to review the whole education system. The purpose for this is to get recommendations for readjusting a particular aspect of education or the whole education system to achieve better results. For example, the government may set up an education commission or committee to review the curriculum in the Teacher Training Colleges, to review technical education, to review the trend of University education at one University as it did in 1987 for Makerere University, or to review the whole education system in the country as it did in the same year through the Uganda National Education Policy Review Commission chaired by Prof. W. Senteza Kajubi. The recommendations of education commissions and committees are given to the government which takes them to Parliament to be debated on by the Members of Parliament. After being considered by Parliament usually with some amendments, the recommendations are passed. Then Ordinances or Acts are enacted to make the recommendations legal. After that, the government implements those recommendations through the Ministry of Education and Sports.

The Phelps Stokes Commission, 1924-25
The Phelps-Stokes Commission visited Uganda from the United States of America towards the end of 1924 and stayed in Uganda for a short time at the beginning of 1925. It was invited by the British government in London to examine the state of education for Africans in Kenya, Tanzania and Uganda. Its recommendations would assist the British colonial administrators in Kenya, Tanzania and Uganda to develop education for Africans in these three countries along progressive lines.

In terms of Uganda, the Phelps-Stokes Commission recommended that the colonial administration should participate fully in the educational activities of Uganda. It should not leave those activities to the Missionaries who had started them during the last quarter of the 19th century. Those Missionaries had little money and they could not coordinate and supervise the educational system all over the country. The Commission also criticised the Missionaries for running a curriculum which did not teach practical subjects such as agriculture and technical skills. The curriculum was mainly teaching reading, writing, numeracy, history, geography, some physical sciences and Christian education.

The colonial government in Uganda accepted the recommendations of the Phelps-Stokes Commission. It subsequently established the Department of Education in 1925 on Makerere hill. The colonial government used this Department of Education to direct and finance the educational system in Uganda. The Missionaries however, were not stopped from administering their schools and from building new ones nor from directing the teaching in those schools.

The work of the Department of Education was to lay down the policies regarding education in the whole country. It had to develop the syllabi and to supervise how they were being followed in schools. It was responsible for awarding different education certificates. It had to make the annual estimates for education and to distribute the money voted by the government to the different missionary groups through their education secretariats. This Department of Education had also to make arrangements to build government primary schools and teacher training schools for the Muslims because they had no Missionaries to build schools for their children.

The influence of the Phelps-Stokes Commission was quite great on the development of education in Uganda. It emphasised that the government of a country was duty bound to take the top responsibility for the education of the children of that country. Before 1925, the colonial government in Uganda had left the duty of education to the Missionaries. It was only giving them some money on request to assist them, but without being committed to financing fully the education system and to the direction and supervision of education in the country.

The 1927 Education Ordinance

From 1925 the colonial government in Uganda accepted the responsibility of directing and financing the education affairs of the country. To make its position legal, the then Parliament of Uganda known as the Uganda Legislative Council passed the 1927 Education Ordinance. This Education Ordinance spelt out the powers and procedures in the education system by the government.

The de La Warr Commission, 1937

The de La Warr Commission was sent to East Africa by the Colonial Office in London on the suggestions of Sir Philip Mitchell who was the Governor of Uganda from 1935 to 1940. The Commission's work was to examine the state of higher education in East Africa.

Makerere College which had been established in 1922 by the Uganda colonial government was by 1929 admitting students from Kenya and Tanzania, besides those from Uganda. The de La Warr Commission recommended that Makerere

College should be developed with a view to becoming a University in due course, to serve the whole of East and Central Africa.

In 1949 Makerere College was turned into a University College under the direction of the University of London. It then began to offer degree courses from 1950. The first group of students to get degrees graduated in 1953.

The recommendations of the de La Warr Commission for developing Makerere College to become a University in future meant that several secondary schools had to be developed all over East and Central Africa to feed Makerere College. Consequently, the recommendations of the de La Warr Commission affected the number of secondary schools in this region and their quality. The governments and the Missionaries endeavoured to increase secondary schools and to put them at a standard required to produce candidates for joining Makerere College.

The Thomas Education Committee of 1940

The Thomas Education Committee was appointed to review the education system in Uganda since 1925 when the Uganda Protectorate government had joined the Missionaries in the education field, and to recommend new developments and strategies. It was also specifically requested to examine the issue of starting non-denominational schools under the government.

This committee recommended two important things among others. Firstly, it recommended the system of Boards of Governors for secondary schools, Teacher Training Colleges and Technical Schools. Secondly, the committee recommended that primary education should be financed by the local governments. The purpose for these two recommendations was to draw the community in closer connection with the administration of schools in Uganda. Hitherto the concern of the community was to send children to schools and leave the Missionaries to educate them. In a way, the establishment of the Boards of Governors and the involvement of the local governments in financing primary schools were intended to gradually lessen the missionary predominance in education administration. However, by 1962 this wish had not been achieved. The Missionaries still dominated the administration of the education system. This same committee emphasised the administration of education along religious lines which already existed. It refused to accept building non-denominational schools under the government. To stress this point it thus wrote in the report:

> We must respect and favour the educational establishments and machinery we find, not because education executed by missionary societies may be cheaper, but because the highest public interest demands the inculcation of the Christian values.

The 1942 Education Ordinance

The 1942 Education Ordinance made legal the recommendations of the Thomas Education Committee of 1940.

The Binns Study Group, 1951

By 1950 Britain was thinking of giving independence to its colonies in East, Central and West Africa. Consequently, she wanted to raise the level of education in those colonies before they regained their independence. In order to do this, in 1951 Britain appointed the Jeffreys Education Commission to visit West Africa and the Binns Study Group to come to East and Central Africa. The mission of these two Commissions was to examine the situation of education in these areas and make the necessary recommendations to the British government in London for improving it and for increasing enrolment of students in the schools.

The Binns Study Group in terms of Uganda recommended a great increase of schools to enrol more pupils and students and the raising of the level and quality of education. Its recommendations were partly put into reality by the de Bunsen Education Committee. We need to realise that by 1951 secondary schools in Uganda were producing 250 students annually for the O-Level Cambridge School Certificate. The Binns Study Group pointed out that this number was too small. The de Bunsen Education Committee recommended that this number should rise to 500 candidates by 1960 - still a very small number for a whole country.

Further, the Binns Study Group suggested a new trend in education which was however, not implemented by the de Bunsen Education Committee of 1952 but which the Senteza Kajubi Education Commission of 1987 attempted to recommend. The Binns Study Group realised that the attitude of parents, students and many teachers was not favourable to practical education. And the already famous secondary schools such as King's College Buddo, St. Mary's College Kisubi, Namilyango College, Busoga College Mwiri, Nabumali High School, Nyakasura School and St. Henry's College Kitovu, were giving the impression that only academic secondary education led a student to glory.

The Binns Study Group proposed that the way to break this state of affairs would be to run these schools and others like them and the future ones to be established, as comprehensive secondary schools. All those schools would run a curriculum which would comprise both academic and technical practical subjects. This way the parents and the students would not have purely academic secondary schools to compare and contrast with practically oriented secondary schools and post primary technical schools.

But there were odds against producing a curriculum along the lines suggested by the Binns Study Group. Firstly, the preoccupation of the time was to produce students with academic qualifications in rising numbers to take up many jobs in government departments. So to start experimenting with a new curriculum would retard developments in this trend.

Secondly, when the colonial government on the recommendations of the de Bunsen Education Committee established secondary schools such as Ntare School, Kigezi College, Sir Samuel Baker, Teso College and Lango College, the people among whom these secondary schools were established looked forward to seeing those secondary schools to run along the basis of the already famous secondary schools mentioned above. Even the British headmasters who were appointed to head these new secondary schools were out to emulate the record of the old secondary schools and achieve similar status which those old secondary schools had already achieved. And indeed they managed to do this so that by 1962 a student who was attending these new secondary schools under the colonial government did not feel to have missed anything for not having attended the old traditional secondary schools under the Missionaries.

What the de Bunsen Education Committee did was exactly what the Binns Study Group foresaw as likely to make students and parents hate practical education. That committee recommended the establishment of separate practical post primary schools known as Rural Trade Schools, Farm Schools, Home Craft Centres and Secondary Modern Schools for those students who had failed to score high enough marks required by the academic junior secondary schools leading to a full secondary course.

What the Binns Study Group foresaw was exactly what happened. The above schools were hated by parents and students and therefore they failed. They were turned into academic secondary schools by the Castle Education Commission of 1963 to avoid a situation of producing students who would be in society with lack of confidence in themselves.

The Senteza Kajubi Education Commission of 1987 nearly going along the idea of the Binns Study Group, recommended a section of secondary schools run as comprehensive secondary schools but still left the traditional academic secondary schools in existence which it called General Secondary Schools and created a third group of secondary schools called Vocational Secondary Schools which would have a predominance of practical technical courses.

Still the above recommendation did not remove room for comparing academic secondary schools with practical secondary schools by parents and students. But the attitudes of parents and students have changed much since the 1950s when the Binns Study Group last visited Uganda such that there is an enthusiasm for students to join these schools and if these practical secondary schools can produce students who can be job creators rather than job seekers, then we shall see a revolution in Uganda's education where practical secondary schools will be preferred to academic secondary schools and the fear of the Binns Study Group will be disproved. Parents and students alike will have realised that going to school and getting out of it without tangible practical skills which one can use readily on one's own, is a luxury, a waste of much scarce resources of time and money.

The de Busen Education Committe, 1952

Sir Andrew Cohen who had become Governor of Uganda in 1951 appointed the de Bunsen Education Committee in 1952. The committee was chaired by the then Principal of Makerere University College, Sir Bernard de Bunsen. The duty of this education committee which is also called the de Bunsen Education Committee was to consider how best the recommendations of the Binns Study Group would be implemented. We have already discussed the changes brought in education by the de Bunsen Education Committee, pp. 146-149.

The Educations Ordinance of 1959

From the beginning of the establishment of Western education in Uganda, education was administered along both racial and religious lines. The European children had their own schools, the Asian children their own schools and the African children their own schools. Children of a different race were not accepted in the schools which were not run by its race. However, because there were no white settlers in Uganda, the children of European government officers attended their primary education in Kenya and their secondary education either in Kenya or in Britain.

Education was also run along religious lines. The Asian community had Hindus, Muslim Ismailis, Sikhs and Roman Catholic Goanese. All these different Asian groups had their own schools along religious lines. Then some of the Ugandans were Roman Catholics, others were Protestants while others were Muslims. Each of these three religious groups had its own schools. From 1925, some Ugandans began to establish private schools. The beauty about these private schools was that they did not discriminate against children in terms of race and religion. They accepted any pupil or student as a person without referring to his or to her race or religion. The de Bunsen Education Committee of 1952 recommended that this racial and religious segregation in schools should start to be eased up. This was necessary among other reasons because there was need to emphasise unity in Uganda in view of independence which would come at some future date.

By 1959, political parties had been formed starting from 1952. In 1958 general elections had even taken place in the country along political parties and people were looking forward to independence in the near future. One step towards unity in 1959 was considered to be the easing up of racial and religious segregation in schools.

Consequently, the government passed the 1959 Education Ordinance. The Ordinance allowed any child regardless of his or her race and religion to attend any school in Uganda. The ordinance was more aimed at Asian schools because the Asians despised the Africans and they were quite opposed to seeing any African child attending their schools or their children attending African schools.

Education Ordinances

Asians treated Africans as their servants and they saw it as infradig to see their children mixing with African children.

Because the Asians had become aware that independence was soon coming and the Africans might be opposed to the Asians continued stay in Uganda, they began allowing into their schools a few African children, normally of highly placed persons in the country.

The 1959 Education Ordinance was also aimed at curbing the rapid increase of private schools which were being opened without regard to education standards and health provisions of the school plants. The ordinance required that any private school to be operated had to be first allowed by the Director of the Department of Education and to adhere to the education and health standards approved by the Department of Education. However, the full integration of races and religions in education had to wait for the 1963 Education Act. Also the proprietors of the private schools ignored the ordinance and continued to run their schools as they saw fit since they realised that the government attitude to their schools was more negative than positive.

The Castle Education Commission, 1963

The government of independent Uganda appointed the Castle Education Commission in 1963. Its duty was to review the education system in order to meet the challenges in independent Uganda. We have already discussed the recommendations of this Education Commission, pp. 164-165.

Similar Education Commissions were appointed by the governments of independent Kenya and Tanzania immediately after regaining independence. The intention of those governments was also to meet the challenges created by independence. As a result of those Commissions, Tanzania passed the 1962 Education Ordinance and Kenya passed the 1965 Education Act.

The 1963 Education Act

This Act was passed to put the control of all grant-aided schools under the government. So the racial groups and the religious bodies were excluded from controlling the schools as it had been during the colonial days. This was done mainly for three reasons. Firstly, there was need to create unity in Uganda. Schools administered along racial and religious lines were dividing the people. They were also continuing to strengthen the hatred among people which originated in the political and religious wars of the 1880s and early 1890s. They were also making pupils avoid schools next to their homes just because they did not belong to their religion. Denomination schools were also duplicating schools in an area where there was no need for several schools, which led to under employment of teachers, facilities and educational materials.

Secondly, the government was fighting through schools to produce enough qualified Ugandans to take up jobs both in government and in companies. If the schools were under the control of religious and racial groups, the government's targets of producing these qualified men and women could be frustrated. Some schools could refuse to enrol pupils and students who did not belong to the racial or religious group which ran particular schools whereas there were places in them, yet while the schools of their racial or religious background did not have places in them.

Thirdly, the government wanted every pupil and student to get its ideology especially that of "African identity and African personality". It feared that if schools were left in the control of racial and religious bodies, the administrators could ignore passing over to the pupils and students this ideology especially as these schools would continue to be under many European and Asian administrators who had been masters during the colonial period and who did not subscribe to these ideologies. The African politicians had dismissed the Europeans from the political field so if these Europeans were left to control the schools, this would look like another form of colonial dependency on White Missionaries and the Asian business community.

The 1970 Education Act

The 1970 Education Act was introduced by the government to put order in the opening and operating of private schools in Uganda and any school by the Uganda Government. The Act streamlined the channels through which a person or groups of persons or a religious body would pass to establish a private school and run it.

The need to pass the 1970 Education Act arose for four reasons. Firstly, due to the great demand for education in Uganda while there were relatively fewer facilities for students especially at secondary school level, some money minded persons were opening up secondary schools which were not up to standard. Such people advertised themselves widely and began to get students. The students would pay their fees and after those greedy persons got the money, they would disappear from the so-called schools. The students would be left stranded. Or such people established private schools but their buildings and the entire school plants fell below the standard of proper schools as prescribed by law.

The second reason why there was need to pass the 1970 Education Act was that some church organisations had begun to open many private schools. They were calling these schools "parents' schools". The government at the time feared that the denomination schools were coming back into the education system of Uganda. This state of affairs had been curbed by the 1963 Education Act which gave power to the government to take over control of all schools which were being financially supported by the government. Consequently, through the 1970 Education Act, the government wanted to curb the building of denomination schools.

Education Ordinances

Thirdly, Asians had begun to establish their own private schools to replace their schools which the government had taken over by the 1963 Education Act. So the government wanted to curb the re-establishment of racial schools in the education system of Uganda.

The 1970 Education Act put all powers in the Chief Education Officer now called the Commissioner for Education regarding the opening up new schools or closing down the already established schools which he or she may deem to be bad elements in the country. In fact this Act made it a bit difficult for an individual person or a group of persons or a religious body to open up and run a private school in Uganda. Thus the bit on opening private schools ran:

> Any person desirous of establishing a private school shall first apply to the Chief Education Officer to be approved as a suitable person to establish a private school, that is to say, that he is of good repute and has the necessary funds to manage the type of school he proposes to start.

Fourthly, there was a need to put all teachers under one authority. During the colonial days when education was being run along denominational lines, teachers were under the authority of each denomination. Consequently, teachers teaching in the schools of the Church of Uganda, were under the authority of the Church of Uganda. Teachers teaching in the schools of the Roman Catholic Church were under the authority of that Church. Teachers teaching in the schools under the Uganda Muslim Education Association were controlled by that Association. Then there were also schools under the government and local administrations. Teachers teaching in those schools were under the government and the local administrations.

The 1970 Education Act created the Unified Teaching Service (UTS) and all teachers had to belong to one authority which is the Teaching Service Commission as the Civil Servants belong to the Public Service Commission. This was intended to better the conditions of service for the teachers.

But the 1970 Education Act was soon followed by the overthrow of Obote's government by Idi Amin on 25th January 1971. The effect of the Act especially as regarded the establishment of private schools was not felt and enterprising people went on opening private schools without Idi Amin's government enforcing the spirit of the Act. The Roman Catholic Church especially stepped up its building of schools under the title of Parents Schools. But unlike during the colonial days, these schools endeavoured to be non- denominational.

The Uganda National Education Policy Review Commission or the Senteza-Kajubi Education Commission, 1987

The Uganda National Education Review Commission of 1987 was set up to review the whole education system of Uganda and to recommend adjustments and new trends in the education system. You need to know that from 1963 to 1995, the educational system of Uganda was running according to the recommendations of the Castle Education Commission of 1963, a total of 32 years. This is a long time for an education system to remain unreviewed because the situation in a country changes constantly and the education system needs to be reviewed at least every ten years for it to meet the changed situation.

For the foreseeable future, the recommendations of the Senteza-Kajubi Education Commission will operate beyond AD 2000. One of the recommendations which will soon affect the teaching in primary and secondary schools is expressed in the words: "Basic Education for National Development- BEND". This idea calls for a drastic approach to the curriculum, teaching methods of students, the examination system and selection to post primary education institutions. Also the new education structure is quite a drastic one especially for secondary schools. One intriguing question will regard the basis for selecting students who will join the comprehensive and the vocational secondary schools. However, this point about selection has been eased because the Government White Paper on Education decided that eventually all Secondary Schools in future would eventually become Comprehensive Secondary Schools.

The Senteza Kajubi Education Commission Report is quite large and full of interesting and challenging ideas about the trend which education should take in Uganda and so is the Government White Paper which reviewed the report in April 1992. It is advisable that student teachers and practising teachers especially, should endeavour to read this report and the Government White Paper on the report. The administration of each school should secure a copy for easy access by its teachers.

The Significance of Education Ordinances and Education Acts

Education Ordinances and Education Acts are the framework of the laws under which an education system in a country is administered. They state the laws and the procedure of applying those laws. They bind the government and the citizens. They are the basis under which the Attorney General of Uganda or an individual person can be taken to court if he breaks one or more of them.

Uganda's education laws therefore began with the 1927 Education Ordinance. From time to time as the situation may require, the government may amend the laws within the Education Ordinances and Education Acts by adding onto them more laws or by abolishing some of them which may no longer be applicable.

Questions
1. What two important things did the Phelps-Stokes Commission, 1924-25, point out to the colonial government in Uganda about the education system?
2. What was the importance of the 1937 de La Warr Commission in the education system of Uganda regarding the development of secondary and higher education?

Education Ordinances

3. Why did the British Government appoint the Jeffreys Commission and the Binns Study Group in 1951?
4. Why did Sir Andrew Cohen appoint the 1952 de Bunsen Education Committee? Mention three important things suggested by that committee.
5. What duty did the 1963 Castle Education Commission have to do and what two recommendations did it give to the government?
6. What powers did the 1970 Education Act give to the Chief Education Officer, now the Commissioner for Education as regards the opening up of private schools?
7. What are schools in your district doing to implement the idea of "Basic Education for National Development-BEND?"
8. What was the purpose for the 1959 Education Ordinance?
9. What is the importance of Education Committees and Education Commissions in the education system of Uganda?
10. Mention the importance of the 1963 Education Act.

14 Some Crucial Issues in Uganda's Education System

The Teaching Profession
When the Missionaries began teaching Ugandans along the lines of Western education from 1877, it was necessary that they should make arrangements to train Ugandan teachers. This was for two reasons.

Firstly, the teachers who were so many in the Ugandan indigenous education systems could not teach in the new schools because what was being taught in those schools was no longer familiar to them. For example, in the Ugandan indigenous education systems, teachers taught history by referring to their origins, their heroic leaders and how their economic, social and political systems had been developed. Now the schools for example, were teaching in history how the Vikings in Europe had invaded Britain from the north, the travels of Christopher Columbus to America and how the British people had gone to America and conquered and nearly exterminated the Red Indians who owned the continent. All this was unfamiliar to the Ugandan teachers who had been used to their history in the indigenous education systems.

In Geography, the teachers in the Ugandan indigenous education systems were for example, teaching their rivers, lakes, the seasons of the year in their respective areas and the native names of the days and months in the year. Now in the schools, the children were being taught river Mississippi in the United States of America as the longest river in the world. They were being taught Lake Superior in the United States and Canada as the largest fresh water lake in the world. They were also being taught the four fantastic European and American seasons in the year. These are Spring, Summer, Autumn and Winter. The days of the week and the months were being taught using Western names such as Sunday and Monday and January and February respectively. All this content was quite unfamiliar to the Ugandan teachers who had been familiar with the geography of their areas as taught through their indigenous education systems.

Secondly, the Missionaries needed to produce Ugandan teachers because they were too few to teach both Christianity and other kind of knowledge all over the country. The first teachers whom the Missionaries produced were called pupil-teachers. These were the pupils of the Missionaries who learned faster what the Missionaries were teaching. When these pupils had mastered it well, the Missionaries made them to teach it to their friends some of whom were slow at learning while some others had just joined the reading and writing classes. So at one time these pupil - teachers were pupils of the Missionaries. At another time

Crucial issues in Education

they took time off to teach their colleagues what they themselve had already mastered. It is of these pupil-teachers that Bishop Alfred Tucker wrote thus:

> No sooner was the first chart of reading mastered than they clamoured for another one. It was a pleasure to see that the pupils who were under a missionary early in the morning, were by the middle of the day teaching others what they had learned and they had a group of their colleagues surrounding them.

Incidentally, with the knowledge of the ages of the pupils in Uganda today, one may wonder how some pupils during the 1890s could become teachers and even go into the country side to establish new schools. These early pupils had ages ranging between ten years and forty years. Therefore some were already married men and women and fathers and mothers of children, much like the disciples of Jesus Christ. For example, St. Peter was approaching fifty years of age and he was head of a family and a fishing enterprise.

From 1898 formal teacher education classes were to be established at particular schools then called Central Schools where those intending to become teachers were trained in a class of their own. Eventually separate teacher training schools were set up. Thus the C.M.S. set up Mukono as their first teacher training school and the Mill Hill Fathers set up Nsambya, the White Fathers set up Bikira near Kyotera in Rakai District and the Verona Fathers set up Gulu. By 1920 teacher training schools similar to the above had spread to many parts of Uganda.

In 1930 the Uganda Protectorate government established Nyanjeeradde Teacher Training School for producing teachers of Kiswahili in schools. Nyanjeeradde is now what is called Makerere Primary School on the top of Makerere hill. However, this Nyanjeeradde Teacher Training School closed in 1937 because Kiswahili had been opposed by the people in the southern part of Uganda as we have already seen. Moreover teachers produced at Nyanjeeradde had no support by the respective missionary groups who had their own teacher training schools. They wanted teachers whom they had themselves produced along their point of view. It was only then that those Missionaries would be sure that their teachers taught the point of view of those different missionary groups.

The Uganda Protectorate Government similarly established a teacher training school for Muslim schools at Kasawo in Mukono District after the closure of Nyanjeeradde. This teacher training school was eventually transferred to Kibuli during the 1950s by the Uganda Muslim Education Association.

At first, the teacher training schools of the Missionaries were called Normal Schools, a term borrowed from the French education system. In France such teacher training schools were called *Ecoles Normales*.

The 1940 Thomas Education Committee changed the name of these teacher education schools from Normal Schools and called them Teacher Training

Centers. The de Bunsen Education Committee of 1952 again changed that name to Teacher Training Colleges because this name gave these teacher training schools a more respectable status.

The training of teachers has passed through various stages up to the present time. Up to 1940 graduates from primary four could train as teachers. From 1940 only graduates of primary six could train as primary school teachers. From 1955 only graduates of junior secondary two could train as primary school teachers. From 1963 only holders of the 0-Level School Certificate could train as primary school teachers.

The stepping up of the academic qualifications of primary school teacher trainees was due to the standards in schools which were rising up gradually. This necessitated the teacher to have higher education qualifications. The stepping up of the academic qualifications of the above grades of teachers necessitated each time to set up up-grading courses so that the already trained and practising teachers at a lower status could be raised to a higher grade.

Those teachers who were teaching in secondary schools were required to hold Diplomas and Degrees. Makerere University College played a big role in producing teachers for junior secondary schools and senior secondary schools. But the production of secondary school teachers by Makerere University College was not large enough to satisfy the secondary schools. Up to nearly 1968, teachers at this level were coming from Britain and the United States of America. But due to the efforts which the government took after Uganda had regained her independence to produce highly qualified people, by 1968 the number of Ugandan teachers holding Degrees and Diplomas had increased greatly. Now British, American or Asian graduate teachers are rare in the Ugandan secondary schools.

At present, we are training and producing the following categories of teachers:

(a) Teachers for primary schools. These have got an O-Level School Certificate. They train in Primary Teachers Colleges (PTCs, for two years. On qualification they are called Grade III Teachers.

(b) Teachers for secondary schools. These are produced at three levels. There are those who are trained at the National Teachers Colleges (NTCs) for two years. These have got A and O Level qualification. On graduation they get a Diploma in Education. Then there are those who are trained at Universities after getting A-Level qualification. At the Universities there are two undergraduate courses. One course is called B.A with Education and B.Sc with Education. It lasts for three years. At the end of the course one graduates as a teacher. The second under graduate course is called B.Ed (Bachelor of Education). At the end of the course, one also qualifies as a teacher. There is the post graduate Diploma in Education (PGDE Course)

The status of teachers

From the very time the Missionaries began producing Ugandan teachers, the teachers have held a respectable status in our society. They have been leaders of opinion in society and setting a good example to be followed by their students and by the rest of people in all walks of life. Teachers should endeavour to keep this status whatever their problems may be.

But from the 1940s to the present, teachers have faced the problem of financial discomfort. This has been mostly due to the decreasing value of the Shilling which has been due to the constant world inflation. Consequently, teachers' salaries have been subjected to a terrible devaluation.

However, since the 1940s to the present the teachers have been fighting this financial problem at various levels. Between 1941 and 1944 the teachers formed the Uganda African Teachers Association. This name was changed in 1957 to the present Uganda Teachers Association (UTA). This was because it was seen as necessary to include also Asian and European teachers in it who would want to join it.

By 1940 many teachers had been produced in Uganda by the C.M.S. Missionaries for their schools, by the Roman Catholic Missionaries for their schools and by the colonial government for Muslim schools. Each of the three groups employed its teachers according to its own terms, salaries and manner of treatment and it dismissed any teacher who did not follow the particular requirements of the different Missionaries. For example, in Christian schools, a teacher was supposed to lead prayers in Church on Sundays, he was supposed to get Holy Communion every Sunday, he was supposed to marry in Church and to have only one wife. If he did not behave in the above manner, he was dismissed from the service, because he did not practise the missionary moral code.

An unmarried woman teacher was dismissed with disgrace if she became pregnant. If she was married and became pregnant, she was suspended from teaching for nearly two years. All the above was done in an attempt to make the teacher behave like a Christian and to be a good example for the community in which he or she lived.

This kind of treatment had by 1940 ceased to be relevant in the estimation of many teachers. They felt that they were not clergy men and clergy women. Once a teacher did his or her work dutifully and behaved gentlemanly like a normal sensible person, there was no need for his or her employer to probe into his or her personal and private life.

As a result of this, the teachers decided to form an association regardless of the missionary group which had produced them and which was employing them. This is the association which in 1957 got its present name of the Uganda Teachers Association (UTA). The teachers demanded that they should all be the employees of the government like the civil servants. The government should draw up a document which stated the conditions of service under which they were being employed, salaries, accommodation and retirement benefits. The situation which prevailed by 1940 regarding the above items depended upon the whims of the employing Missionaries and government officers.

It was not however, an easy task for the Uganda Teachers Association to get accepted by the missionaries and by the government. When the Uganda African Teachers Association was established between 1941 and 1944, the Missionaries viewed it as an association of disgruntled teachers. The Missionaries tried to weaken it by each missionary group trying to group its own teachers in some kind of association controlled by the Missionaries. The most prominent such association was formed by the Roman Catholic Missionaries in the Lubaga Diocese. It was known as *Agali awamu* but it eventually became weak because the Roman Catholic teachers soon realised that it wanted to distract them from their fight for better conditions of service and for better pay.

Again the work of the Uganda Teachers Association was made difficult in the early 1960s, by some teachers within its ranks forming a splinter group known as the Uganda Teachers Union led by Ssemirembe. The grievances of the Uganda Teachers Union were two. Firstly, by the early 1960's, the Uganda Teachers Association looked like an association of graduate teachers because they led the association. But their salaries and conditions of service were quite better than those of the primary school teachers and of the junior secondary school teachers.

Secondly, the members of the Uganda Teachers Union were primarily teachers of primary schools and junior secondary schools. They were more in number than the graduate teachers and their living conditions at these schools were very inferior and poor and their salaries were also quite low. Consequently, they felt that the Uganda Teachers Association was not interested in their welfare. They wanted to use their union as a trade union thereby using the tactics of striking to force the government to better their conditions of service and their salaries.

But eventually the Uganda Teachers Union was weakened because of its stand to call its members to strike. Many other teachers saw this trend in the education system of Uganda as unhealthy. As professional men and women, the majority of teachers felt that the children of this nation should not be punished for the failure of the government to redress the grievances of the teachers and by 1970, the Uganda Teachers Union had sunk into oblivion.

The duty of the Uganda Teachers Association (UTA) has been and still is to negotiate with the government for reasonable wages or salaries for teachers and for reasonable conditions of service as the situation of the country changes. It also seeks to redress wrong done to individual teachers by headteachers and by the government education officers. It also enables teachers to improve professionally.

But to be an important force which can impress the government, the Uganda Teachers Association needs to be joined and supported by all teachers in the service. Then they will speak with one voice with emphasis. This way, the government will listen to the teachers' demands better because they will have a strong body to act as their spokesman. For example, all the teachers of Kenya are united in the Kenya National Union of Teachers (KNUT). This union is very strong and it has managed to get reasonable salaries and conditions of service from the government for the teachers. It also assists to get their wrongs redressed if their headteachers and the government education officers have wronged them. The Kenya National Union of Teachers goes even further. It lends money to teachers to assist them in their endeavours in self developmental projects using their accumulated monthly subscriptions. The teachers of Uganda of all categories should join the Uganda Teachers Association (UTA) and make it as strong as the Kenya National Union of Teachers (KNUT). They will be the gainers for this especially they will accumulate much money through subscriptions which they will be lent to them to better their financial position.

Historically however, from 1944 to nearly 1965, the Uganda Teachers Association (UTA) was being enthusiastically supported by nearly all teachers in Uganda. It had a loan scheme for teachers and the teachers contributed to a general fund for running the services of the Association. Teachers also had an insurance scheme and it is even from the funds of the subscriptions and of the insurance scheme that the Uganda Teachers Association managed to put up a modern building in Kampala in the Bat Valley area. This building houses the headquarters of the association. The rest of the offices are lent out to business firms to raise money for running the affairs of the association. The Uganda Teachers Association also used to run refresher courses for teachers and to arrange promotional courses for some teachers to better their standing in the profession within Uganda and abroad.

Teachers today need to find out the cause why their Uganda Teachers Association lacks enthusiastic support and dynamism at the moment and remedy the situation. All over the world, each country's teachers are organised in either associations or unions which fight for their welfare and also arrange ways and means for bettering their financial situation through loan schemes and to uplift their academic standing in the profession through refresher courses and promotional courses. The Uganda Teachers Association is quite aware of this fact because it is in collaboration with all Teachers' Associations and unions in the world.

Another level at which teachers are fighting financial hardships is by being adventurous. They engage in a number of financial activities to supplement their wages or salaries. For example, they engage in market gardening, farming, keeping poultry and swine, trading activities, writing books and in many other financially profitable activities. Being members of Credit Savings Societies is another level at which teachers are fighting financial hardships. These Credit Savings Societies are scattered in all districts. One of the most famous ones which serves all districts in Buganda is called the Mengo Teachers Cooperative Savings and Credit Society.

Every teacher should make arrangements to belong to these Credit Savings Societies. They are very helpful in many respects. A teacher should always look for ways and means of supplementing his /her wages which are paid to him/her by the government. These wages will never be adequate to solve all his/her needs which require money. Teachers also need to realise that the inflation has affected and continues to affect civil servants with whom they get comparable salaries. Therefore they are not the only ones who are afflicted by this phenomenon. The only difference is that teachers are bound to stay engaged all day long taking charge of their pupils and students in the schools.

Moreover a teacher should always try to be economically progressive so that he/she can buy a piece of land, build his/her own house and have a project which gives him/her money regularly. He/she cannot do all the above unless he/she belongs to a credit savings society which can lend him/her money regularly to develop himself or herself. There is nothing wrong in engaging in such gainful financial activities by teachers. The teachers however, need to be careful to see that these activities for self improvement do not prevent them from doing effectively and efficiently their teaching duties.

Raising their academic qualifications has been another channel through which teachers have been and are trying to raise their financial status. A good example of this is that there are men and women teachers who qualified as primary school teachers. But through following part-time courses or private studies while they are at the same time teaching, they have even managed to become University Professors lecturing in Uganda and abroad.

The government also at various times conducts up-grading courses and refresher courses for teachers. These courses have not been intended only for bettering teachers' financial standing but also for improving their proficiency in the teaching profession as teachers and administrators.

At the moment, one of the problems which is facing the education system of Uganda is the presence of so many untrained teachers especially in the primary schools all over the country. These teachers are called "Licensed Teachers". The explanation for the presence of untrained teachers in the primary schools is that there is a decreasing number of young men and women who want to join the teaching profession especially at the primary school level. Secondly, those who join the teaching profession without a teacher's qualification do so because they do not want to give up their other activities.

This shortage of primary school teachers raises our concern as to how they will be obtained in large enough numbers when primary education becomes universal by the year AD2003.

The presence of a large number of untrained teachers also raises concern when we talk about "Basic Education for National Development - BEND". These untrained teachers will continue to teach in the same academic way they were themselves taught when they were still at school. They will have no methods of teaching practical skills. The result will be a failure of BEND to produce the desired results.

The nation needs to look into the problem of why there is a decreasing number of young men and young women who want to join the teaching profession especially at the primary school level. Indeed one of the reasons is the unattractive salaries and other conditions of service for the primary school teachers. Unless these two obstacles are removed, the country will continue to experience a great shortage of primary school teachers.

At the moment the Ministry of Education and Sports in collaboration with a number of NGOs, has launched some projects for training "licensed teachers" on the job. It is expected these projects will give professional courses to the "licensed teachers" while they continue to teach in their respective schools. We wait to see how effective such programmes as MITEP, NITEP, LITEP, UPDMS and the Primary Teachers Colleges will be.

Exercise
1) Do you know where the headquarters of the Uganda Teachers Association (UTA) are located in Kampala?
ii) Is there a contact office of the Uganda Teachers Association (UTA) in your district?
iii) Make an effort to visit the offices of the Mengo Teachers Cooperative Savings and Credit Society in Kampala and talk to the officials there about saving money with them.

Cost sharing in education

"Cost sharing" in education simply means that the parents and the rest of the Uganda society should meet the expenses of the education of the Ugandan citizens together with the government. This financial burden should not be left entirely to the government.

"Cost sharing" in education as a catch expression was first pronounced publicly by the Uganda National Education Policy Review Commission of 1987 which idea was adopted from the Makerere University Visitation Committee of the same year. At that time it was directly pointed towards University and other tertiary education institutions. At University and at other tertiary institutions, the government was giving to students money for transport from home to the education institutions and back home. It was also giving them pocket money known as boom, free text books plus other scholastic materials and free stationery for writing on. At the same time it was giving free accommodation to those students, feeding them and teaching them free of charge.

The argument for the Uganda National Education Policy Review Commission was that both the parents and the government should share the above financial burden for these students which hitherto was being shouldered by the government alone, hence the term "Cost Sharing". The money which the government would save, would be used towards providing the projected universal primary education in this nation so that each child should get a chance of attending primary school, to get the basic knowledge and the basic skills to assist himself or herself and the nation as a whole, in national development.

Indeed the suggestion of "cost sharing" in education according to the above explanation was not liked by students who were getting the benefits and those who were hoping to get them when their turn would come, and to many parents. When "cost sharing" began to be implemented in 1990 it caused a strike by some Makerere University students first in May 1990 and then in December 1990. The strike of December 1990 left two students shot dead by the Uganda Police on 10th December 1990 infront of the Main Building. The University was closed and only re-opened in May 1991.

The history of "cost sharing" in education however, is as old as the history of Western education in Uganda. From the very beginning, the Missionaries practised "cost sharing" in education. The parents offered free land on which schools were built, they offered free labour in building the schools, they gave financial donations to the Missionaries to run the schools and they were paying school fees for their children in schools. All the above contributions of the parents supplemented the financial expenditure of the Missionaries to the establishment and running of schools. Thus in 1913, the CMS Board of Education stressed:

> Schools have to be built with money from school fees or from gifts from chiefs. Church funds will not be drawn upon for the purpose of building schools and running them.

By the 1920s many elaborate schools had been established by the above means. They were also assisted by the donations of the friends of the Missionaries both in Europe and America. The Phelps-Stokes Commission which visited Uganda in 1924-5 praised this "cost sharing" venture thus:

> Practically every school in Uganda is a gift from the native community. Education in Uganda is being financed by the fees of the people and missionary financial sacrifice to a degree not visible any where in Africa.

It is the colonial government which wanted to ease the burden of the parents in "cost sharing" when it began to participate in education. When it established Makerere College in 1922, the parents were dispensed from "cost sharing" in that College. The students were being taught free, they were being accommodated and fed free, they were given pocket money, free text books and other scholastic materials. On top of that, they were given money for transport between their homes and the College. This practice was extended to Teacher Training Colleges, to Technical Schools and to tertiary institutions.

One reason for the colonial government's behaving thus was to encourage Ugandan students to engage in higher studies. By the time the parents had engaged in "cost sharing" up to the end of secondary education, the government felt that their financial resources would have been exhausted especially those of the relatively poor parents. We need to realise however, that the colonial government in Uganda was assisting quite few students in the above institutions because the colonial policy was for producing quite a few qualified Ugandans.

From 1991 the argument of the Uganda goverment was that the burden of the parents should be eased at the primary school level. The government would aim at providing enough primary schools at reduced school fees to accommodate all primary school age children by reducing its munificence on higher education. The first things to go in this respect were: pocket money, transport money and money for books, writing paper and other scholastic materials. The students would continue to be taught free of charge, they would be accommodated and fed free of charge and they would be provided with text books which they would share in common. This way the parents would continue in "cost sharing" with the government for students at this higher level.

The trend of things is that eventually most of the students' costs at University and other tertiary institutions will be shouldered by the students themselves. A loan scheme is being consindered to assist the students in this respect.

The rise of the Parents Teachers Associations (PTA)

The origin of the Parents Teachers Association (PTA) was a result of the 1963 Education Act. By that Education Act the Uganda government was given power to take over control of the management of all grant-aided schools from the Christian Churches, the Uganda Muslim Education Association (UMEA) and from the different Asian organisations. It was only the private schools which were left out firstly because they did not discriminate against students in terms of their religions.

Secondly, the private school proprietors did not present a threat to the newly independent government as did the European Missionaries who were seen as perpetuating the authority of the colonial masters whose power had been taken over by the Ugandan politicians. The private schools were under the management of Ugandans.

One of the reactions of the Christian Churches and the Uganda Muslim Education Association to the 1963 Education Act was to start opening up private schools especially on the side of secondary schools called Parents Schools. These schools were being maintained by both the religious bodies and by the parents in terms of the religions to which those parents belonged.

To maintain these schools especially at secondary school level was quite an expensive affair. In the course of time, they were gradually handed over to the government to get financial assistance and to enhance their status because then they began to be called government schools. The religious bodies however, remained as Foundation Bodies in terms of the 1963 Education Act regulations.

But before those Parents' Schools were handed over to the government, the religious bodies and the parents wanted to have the support of the teachers who were teaching in those schools to appreciate their financial difficulties. The teachers then would be closely connected with the administration of these schools instead of behaving as mere employees. Consequently, the religious authorities and the parents formed the Parents Teachers Associations (PTAs).

The originators of the Parents Teachers Association (PTA) had the following original ideas which in time were lost. The parents of students at a school would tax themselves for a year or two by paying some money above the school fees. That money would be used to start money generating projects. These projects would generate money to assist in the following ways. Firstly, some of the money would be used to build new classrooms and to maintain the old ones. Secondly some of the money from the projects would be used to boost the teachers' salaries. Thirdly, some of the money would be used to subsdise the school fees payable by the parents. Eventually the parents would be paying decreasing school fees if not that, the school fees would be kept constant without being raised every term. This would also endear these schools to parents. The writer is so clear about the original ideas for starting the Parents Teachers Associations because he was one of the members for some long time of the Kampala Archdiocese Education Committee of the Roman Catholic Church, 1969-1980.

The success of the Parents Teachers Associations was at once realised in two respects. One respect concerned the support which the teachers gave to these Parents' Schools by being sympathetic and contented with the small salaries they were being paid. They treated the schools as theirs. Another aspect was financial. The parents, through these Parents Teachers Associations, began to cooperate and to solicit for money from parents of children who were attending the individual schools. This money was being contributed by every parent who had a child in a particular school by paying a certain amount of money above the school fees without feeling annoyed. These Parents Teachers Associations arranged other various channels through which they raised money for these schools. There were fund raising activities arranged through public markets, through money generating projects and through soliciting for funds directly from different kindly bodies.

They were using the money so raised to maintain and improve the schools and to supplement the salaries of the teachers without raising the school fees.

By the 1970s some of the Parents Teachers Associations were handing over their schools to the government to be able to get government financial assistance as already pointed out and to enchance their status for being called government schools. But the institution of the Parents Teachers Association was not abolished in those schools handed over to the government. The institution continued to work in those schools. The combination of government financial assistance with the financial assistance from the parents known as PTA contribution, made these schools quite viable. Yet at the same time the financial assistance from the government was not all much while the costs of running these schools were rising almost daily due to inflation of the 1970's. The PTA contribution and money raised from generating projects assisted them very much to balance their budgets.

The financial assistance from the government for the schools which it had taken over by the 1963 Education Act and which it built from then was diminishing and therefore inadequate in the face of rising costs of running the schools. The Boards of Governors for secondary schools and the School Management Committees for primary schools of these government schools, also decided to establish Parents Teachers Associations in those schools. Those PTAs would help in raising funds for the same purpose as the "parents' schools" which had initiated the idea of these Parents Teachers Associations.

Now the Parents Teachers Associations (PTAs) are an established institution in the educational system of Uganda though some schools have not yet established these Parents Teachers Associations. The PTAs are part and parcel of the idea of "cost sharing" in education. These PTAs have proved a very valuable element in assisting schools to run and to develop.

For example, the PTAs assist to put up new buildings, to repair the old ones, to provide new desks and text books, to establish money generating projects for schools and to top up the salaries of teachers. The following example in respect of teachers' salaries is instructive. In 1990, the monthly salary of a Primary school teacher was 2,000/=. But due to the assistance of the PTAs, many Primary schools in Kampala were paying a Primary school teacher 30,000/= per month.

However, in some quarters there is an outcry that the Parents Teachers Associations are burdening the parents with large school charges. Some people are of the view that the PTAs should be abolished. But the fact is that whatever financial contribution the government will give to the schools, that assistance will never be enough. If the Ugandan citizens need to see the progress of education in this country for their children, they must be prepared to foot the rising costs for education. For example, if in 1990 the government could afford to pay only 2,000/= per month for a Primary school teacher's salary, how on earth could any reasonable parent expect a Primary school teacher say in Kampala to live on that salary for a month when a bunch of matooke was costing 2,000/= and above at the time? These same parents who are blaming the PTAs for raising money to assist the teachers are urging the teachers to stay on their job to educate their children effectively from 8.00 a.m. to 5.00 p.m. Surely a teacher and his/her family cannot live on just one meal a month and then you expect him/her to concentrate on the welfare of one's child. You are only forcing him/her to be less effective because whatever you will say, he/she will be obliged to look for alternative ways to supplement his/her salary away from the care of your child.

The alternative to the Parents Teachers Associations is for the school administrations to sit alone without the parents and demand the same charges which the PTAs solicit from the parents. But this is undesirable. It destroys the partnership between society and the school administrators and the idea that Uganda's schools belong to the Ugandan community. The existence of the Parents Teachers Associations assists to make the parents realise the cost of education for running their schools and that cost must be met by themselves. Before the 1940 Thomas Education Committee, schools looked like islands managed by Missionaries. The duty of the parents was only to send their children to those schools and pay the school fees. This was felt to be unsatistactory. That is why that committee initiated the Boards of Governors for secondary schools and in 1952 the de Bunsen Education Committee established the School Management Committees for primary schools so that members of the society should participate in the administration of their schools. That way they would be in a position to realise and appreciate the cost of running schools. Now the institution of the Parents Teachers Associations has come to complete the picture of bringing the parents face to face with the financial realities of educating the citizens of this nation.

But when the above is said and done, the writer feels that in their present form, the Parents Teachers Associations (PTAs) can be dispensed with unless they return to the original ideas of their founders. Those original ideas were that parents of a school should be taxed for a year or two and the money so raised should be used to start money generating projects. The money so raised from those projects should be used to assist in maintaining the schools, in boosting teachers' salaries and in eventually reducing the school fees payable by parents at a school or by keeping the fees constant.

But those original ideas have been abandoned. What the PTAs are doing is to charge parents directly ever increasing amounts of money because this does not involve the PTA Executives in planning money generating projects and in raising money from them. One would wish to see that if the annual estimates of a school are 300/- million shillings and from its revenue items the school can raise only 200./- million shillings. The PTA should go to its account which consists of money from the money generating projects and assist the school by 100/- million shillings instead of asking the parents to contribute that money directly in school fees.

If the PTA charges parents directly, it helps nothing. The Board of Govenors for a secondary school or the School Management Committee for a primary school can easily charge the parents because these are the official bodies which administer schools on behalf of the Ministry of Education. Looked at from the above point of view for failure to maintain the original ideas of the initiators of PTAs in the country, the present PTAs need not exist. They are now taking on the duties of the Boards of Governors and of the School Management Committees. Therefore PTAs would do well if they reverted to the original ideas of the initiators of the institution.

The education of girls in schools

Baptism and Catechism lessons were being given to both boys and girls universally from 1877. But when formal schools began to be attended from 1898, the number of girls attending formal schools was far below that of boys.

For the above state of affairs, the following were some of the pertinent reasons. Firstly, school education was initially seen as preparing young men to become future catechists, teachers, clerks in offices and interpreters for the British officials when addressing the Ugandan citizens, the majority of whom did not know English. Consequently the majority of parents for a long time felt that there was no need for sending girls to schools once they had been baptised and confirmed in their respective Protestant and Roman Catholic faiths. To send girls to schools was seen as wasting resources. After all girls with their indigenous education still made good wives when grown up without having gone to schools.

But the Missionaries from the very beginning realised the importance of educating girls in schools because once educated, they would play a very important role in influencing the men who had been to schools and those who had not done so, and in moulding their children in the new Western point of view.

In this respect, the Missionaries were persuading parents to send their daughters to schools. When the Mill Hill Fathers established Namilyango High school in 1902, they also established Nsuube School for the girls in the same Mukono District. Similarly, when the White Father Missionaries established St. Mary's High School at Lubaga in 1908, they also established Bwanda School in Masaka District. St. Mary's High School was in 1926 transferred from the bustle of Kampala to Kisubi on Entebbe Road, 24kms away from Kampala as Kisubi College. The CMS Missionaries establish in 1905 Buddo High School for boys and Gayaza High School in the same year.

The intention was that young men from Namilyango High School would get school educated future wives from Nsuube School, young men from Buddo High School would get school educated future wives from Gayaza High School and young men from St. Mary's High School would get future wives from Bwanda School.

The Missionaries were quite determined on this and they used to arrange formal marriages for young men of destiny who had graduated from the above boys' schools with young ladies who had graduated from the above girls' schools especially to ward off un-schooled young men from these young ladies whom the Missionaries had scrupulously educated with a mission to accomplish.

The above boys' and girls' schools were at a higher level. But all the headteachers and teachers of all elementary schools encouraged girls to attend those schools. Most of the CMS elementary schools were co-educational, that is, they taught both boys and girls together. But the Roman Catholic schools especially those under the White Fathers, separated the boys from the girls so that in each parish there was a school for boys and a school for girls. These Roman Catholic authorities thought that this approach was more conducive to morality. It also encouraged the girls better to compete among themselves rather than to compete with boys. But still quite a few girls were attending these elementary schools of both the CMS Missionaries and of the Roman Catholic Church because their parents still thought that school education entitled its recipients to doing the above kinds of jobs already mentioned which were at that time seen as men's jobs.

This point of view began only to diminish when girls began to be educated to become teachers and nurses by 1910. These jobs continued for a long time to be the only ones open to school educated girls and women.

Secondly, it took some long time for many men to realise that it was becoming for a woman to go to school. Such men originally felt that the woman's proper place was in the home and not away in working places. So once a girl was baptised and confirmed in her Church, perhaps with some knowledge of reading the Prayer Book, that was all she needed for her station in life. Therefore there was no need to spend money on the education of a girl who was at the same time badly needed to do domestic chores such as assisting her mother to look after her young brothers and sisters and to help her mother in collecting fire-wood, fetching water, washing plates and preparing and cooking food. In the view of many such parents, school attendance for girls robbed the home much of this labour which was mostly assigned more to girls than to boys. Moreover by participating in these chores, a girl was being properly being educated in preparation for her eventual marital life.

Thirdly, many men wanted women to keep a low profile in society. Many such men felt that a woman who had attended school while still a girl was not amenable enough as a wife. She was prone to showing off due to her knowing a bit too much. We have got even two sayings to that effect in Luganda which developed by 1910 namely, *"Nnakapanka, ng'omukazi asoma ebbaluwa"* and *"Atijjanga Maria omubatize"*. (A school educated girl or woman is presumptuous).

Fourthly, nearly up to the 1950s, schools were few and therefore at fairly long distances from the majority of people's homes. Besides, the age of both boys and girls attending primary schools were a bit high and parents feared that unscrupulous young men could entice such daughters on these daily long travels to and from school and force them into acts of immorality.

Because boys and girls up to the 1950s used to attend primary schools at fairly an advanced age, some girls used to become pregnant inadvertently while still in primary schools. This discouraged many parents and made them either to keep their daughters for a very short time in schools or not to send them to the schools at all. Usually once girls appeared to have reached marriageable age, their parents would cut short their stay at school and begin to look for young men to marry them off. All this made the parents to feel that sending girls to schools was a waste of much needed resources. So when a father had less money and had to choose between sending his son or his daughter to school, he chose to send the son and leave the daughter to stay at home doing domestic chores and being educated through the African indigenous education.

Fifthly, there was a wrong feeling among many men that girls did not have the stamina to study hard enough. This feeling will die hard because even today some men still feel that girls cannot study as hard as boys. This feeling is also extended to certain subjects such as mathematics, physics, chemistry and technology. Unfortunately, even some girls have tended to succumb to this discouraging attitude of some men. And it has tended to make girls not to pull their full strength while studying those subjects feeling that such subjects are men's subjects. This is of course an erroneous point of view which should be disregarded by the girls.

For all the above reasons, the population of girls in schools was very small up to the 1950s. It was usually the fairly rich parents, Protestant clergymen, teachers and chiefs who were generally keen on sending their daughters to schools without giving a preference to boys. Also many other girls were encouraged to go to schools and to stay in them by the Missionaries who were keeping them in their parishes as their benefactors and paid their school fees while those girls worked for them.

But the Missionaries and the colonial government officials encouraged the education of girls very much and they took several measures to achieve this. One of the measures was for girls to study free of charge in primary one and two and to pay quite reduced school fees thereafter. Another measure was to encourage parents to send their daughters to school from the age of six years. This would help the girls to stay a full length of the primary and junior secondary courses when they were still fairly young and less susceptible to the idea of being befriended by men, which would either lead them to becoming pregnant before completing their courses or to wish to stop schooling before completing their courses and go to get married.

History and Development of Education

Another measure was to set up many girls' primary schools because in these primary schools girls could compete more easily with their fellow girls while in co-education schools many would tend to be discouraged by the chauvinistic ideas of the boys. This increase in the number of schools for girls also helped girls to walk shorter distances from home to school and back again.

From the 1950s, girls' education began to rise. This was for several reasons. Firstly, the parents began to heed sending their daughters to schools at an early

Prof. Josephine Nambooze graduate of Namagunga College, the first Ugandan woman Doctor (left) and Geraldine N. Bitamazire, graduate of Nabbingo College the first Ugandan woman Minister. She became Minister of Education in 1979.

age. This helped because girls could complete their courses at school while still fairly young without being distracted by the lure of marriage or being befriended by young men. Secondly, Missionaries and local governments established many primary schools. This reduced the anxiety of parents who used to feel uneasy at risking their daughters to walk long distances. Thirdly, very many parents began to realise the importance of school education for girls especially when there appeared many opportunities for women employment. However, even if such daughters did not get jobs after school, it was realised that in a progressive society, women as married wives needed to be able to read and write so that when they got letters from friends, they would not need to look for other people to read those letters for them, or when they needed to write letters themselves to other people, they would not require to look for other people to write them for them.

Crucial issues in Education

Fourthly, mothers who had been to schools themselves saw it necessary that their daughters also went to schools and not only their sons. Moreover many such mothers began to have independent sources of earning money and they would spend some of their money on the education of their daughters even when their fathers would rather want to concentrate their money on sons.

Fifthly, parents began to realise that school educated daughters, once employed, they helped their parents quite substantially in terms of services, money and material goods.

Sixthly, men's ideas that it was preposterous to marry school educated women began to wane apace. Many young men who had been to schools began to prefer marrying young ladies who had been to school like themselves rather than marrying young ladies who had been brought up solely through the African indigenous education system. The former ladies would easily appreciate the point of view of their husbands when progressive ideas were being discussed and introduced in homes. Also such wives would fit more easily in the wider society when out at social gatherings with their husbands. They would also talk at the same brain wave length with their husbands and with other men and other ladies who had attended schools.

At present, parents send both their sons and daughters to schools as a matter of course without discriminating against their daughters. It is interesting to note that in some schools which are attended by both boys and girls, the population of girls is either equal to that of boys, or it exceeds that of boys, or it is fast catching up with that of boys. For example, Makerere College School is a case in point. This school which was once dominated by boys from its foundation in 1945, now its population of girls at 0-Level exceeds that of boys though not at the A-Level.

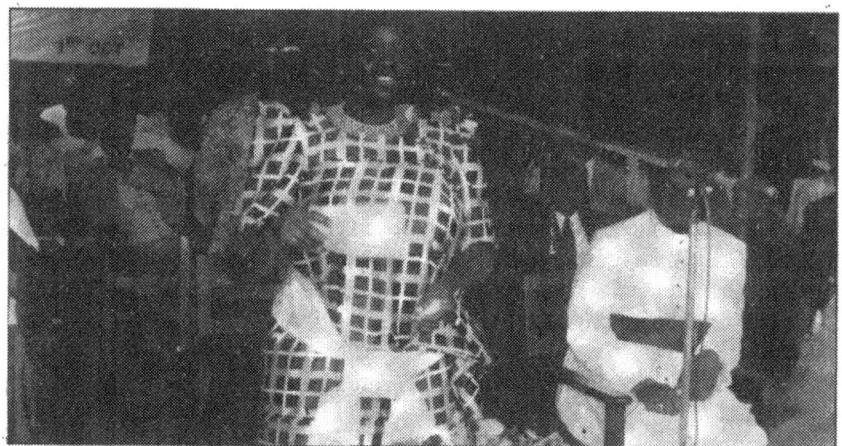

Specioza W. Kazibwe graduate of Namagunga College Uganda's first woman Vice President.

Therefore girls' school education which for a long time lagged behind that of boys, is now catching up with that of boys. The fall in girls' age at which they start schooling, the change of attitude in parents towards their daughters' school education, the availability of school facilities nearer to the homes of parents, the changed attitude of men to school educated girls when they become wives and the numerous opportunities for women employment in many jobs which require specialized skills acquired through schools, have all played a role in bringing about this desirable and wholesome change.

At the moment, school educated young ladies and middle aged ladies are found in very many jobs which require a woman to have attended school and acquired specialised skills. Now the sky is the limit for school educated women's opportunities especially now that even the clergyship has been thrown wide open by men to women in some churches. We shall eventually have women archbishops.

Questions
1. Mention three ways in which the PTA financial contribution should best be used in a school.
2. Why were there very few qualified men and women to take up jobs immediately after Uganda's regaining her independence in 1962?
3. What two things did the rulers of independent Uganda hope to gain out of the expanded educational facilities.
4. Why did the Uganda government take over the full control of the grant-aided schools by the 1963 Education Act?
5. What were the efforts to Africanise the curriculum intended to achieve?
6. How did "the school leaver problem" arise by 1968 in Uganda?
7. What has been the traditional status of the teacher in Uganda and what has been a danger to that status?
8. Name three things which teachers can do to supplement their salaries without necessarily neglecting their teaching duties?
9. How did the Parents Teachers Associations begin and what contribution have they made in the Ugandan educational system?
10. Suppose that the government suspended paying tuition fees and costs for accommodation, feeding and scholastic materials for the University students in Uganda. Suggest new strategies which the government could put in place for the University students to meet the above costs.
11. Why did for a long time the school education of girls lag behind that of boys?
12. Why is the school education of girls catching up rapidly with that of boys now?

15 A Historical Perspective of Basic Education for National Development (BEND)

Introduction

BEND is one of the catch terms in the revitalisation of education as declared by the 1987 Uganda National Education Policy Review Commission. This term is the abbreviation of Basic Education for National Development. The idea behind BEND is to impart practical skills at both Primary school level and Secondary school level so that the student graduates with tangible practical skills which he or she can readily use to be productive, more so by creating his or her own employment after completion of school.

The idea of teaching practical skills in Uganda for personal and national development to the students however, is as old as education itself. Therefore it did not begin with the Uganda National Education Policy Review Commission of 1987. What is new however, is the great concern and vigour with which it has been taken up by the government. One implication of this is that all past efforts of imparting "Basic Education for National Development"-BEND, have failed to be as effective as they were desired to be so that it required the above Commission to seek ways and means of emphasising it.

Production learning

The African indigenous education which was replaced by the present school education, emphasised basic education for national development for every young person in every society in Uganda. That universal education endeavoured to impart basic practical skills and basic knowledge to every child so that on graduation such a person would be capable of creating his or her own employment using the practical skills and knowledge learnt. This is why the African indigenous education emphasised the fact that a person learned as he or she produced materials and services. Thus it made sure to see that the basic practical skills so taught were really mastered by the learner being visibly seen to produce materials and services for the home and for the society. That approach to education can be termed **production learning.**

The result was that the people who passed through the African indigenous education systems were able to develop themselves and their societies. Hence today's catch term "BEND" suited this approach to teaching and learning.

When the Missionaries introduced in Uganda the Western type of education from 1877, there was however, a temporary break from the idea of Basic Education for National Development-BEND. Thus in the 1925 annual report of the Department of Education, the CMS Board of Education reported nearly 50 years since 1877 thus:

> The idea that dominates our school system may be summed up clearly and concisely first and foremost that the spiritual interests of the child are paramount to every other matter, and these divine interests are supreme.

Hence the major aim of missionary education from its introduction in Uganda from 1877 to nearly 1925 was to establish Christianity and its practice in the country and to convert as many people as possible to that faith. Other educational aims were secondary. In fact they were only by-products of the teaching of Christianity and its practice. For example, reading and writing came as a result of Missionaries wanting the Ugandans to read Bibles, Prayer Books and books on meditation to refresh their minds on religion when the Missionaries and the African teachers were not around.

However, in terms of BEND, these early Missionaries taught those attending their schools some simple skills in agriculture and technology. Thus planting of crops using modern methods such as cotton and skills in carpentry, brick making and brick laying were taught. But these skills were taught more for the benefit of the Missionaries than for the benefit of the individuals though as a by-product, the individual also benefited and the country likewise. Thus those who learnt the skills of agriculture tendered the plants of the Missionaries. Those who learnt carpentry and building were employed by the Missionaries in building the churches, schools and mission houses and also in making furniture for them.

Education For Adaptation To The Environment

It is the 1925 Phelps-Stokes Commission which visited Uganda from the United States of America to examine the situation of education in Uganda that pointed out to the Missionaries and to the then Uganda Protectorate government that education as carried out by the Missionaries then was devoid of Basic Education for National Development-BEND. The Commission introduced a new term of BEND known as "Education for Adaptation to the Environment". It thus pointed out:

> The Missionaries have failed to relate their educational activities to the community needs of the people by concentrating on literary education and nearly neglected the teaching of agricultural and technical skills.

On the departure of the Phelps-Stokes Commission in 1925, the Uganda Protectorate government assumed responsibility of directing the educational policies of Uganda. In terms of Basic Education for National Development-BEND, the government declared thus:

Historical Perspective of basic Education

The aim of education will be to promote the advancement of the community as a whole through the improvement of agriculture and industrial skills in schools.

In the same trend, to combine teaching of practical skills in agriculture with technical skills in the spirit of giving Basic Education for National Development, the Protectorate government established the teaching of agriculture and technical skills in the following arrangement in primary schools. Agriculture was daily taught theoretically in the classroom and practically in school gardens. Technical skills were taught through the practice of making handcrafts such as mats, stools, baskets, brooms, carpets, chairs, beds, doors, windows and embroidery for girls.

The inclusion of agricultural and technical skills in the primary school curriculum came to meet the criticism labelled by the Phelps-Stokes Commission against missionary education which had not put into prominence Basic Education for National Development-BEND when they had replaced the universal African indigenous education with Western education. Thus that criticism of the Commission ran:

> With all the wealth of agricultural resources in the Protectorate, there is not a single agricultural school to prepare the natives to take advantage of their wealth. This extreme neglect is almost equalled as regards industrial training.

In the drive of giving agricultural and technical skills to the students in the spirit of BEND, from 1930, the Junior secondary schools were divided up into two separate sections. One section was called the Middle Schools and were intended to give a purely academic course leading to a full secondary course. The other section was called the Central Schools running a practical course consisting of academic content subjects and agriculture, carpentry, pottery, iron work, brick making, building, tailoring and typing. In the spirit of the 1987 Uganda National Education Policy Review Commission, we could call the Middle school General Secondary Schools and the Central Schools, Vocational Secondary Schools.

In his inauguration of the Middle Schools and the Central Schools, the Director of Education then E.G. Morris said:

> Our education system should not prepare the majority of the pupils for benefits that do not exist in real life. The alternative would be to have an increasing number of misfits who would have gone so far on the road to higher education and yet could get no benefit out of that education in real life.

In his 1931 Education Annual Report he reiterated the same idea thus:
> A policy which tended to give a purely literary education to the masses in order to serve a small minority which may benefit by higher education and qualify for semi professional careers, if persisted in could only lead to the creating of a discontented

community divorced from its own heredity and environment with no outlet for its energies but political intrigue and the flouting of authority.

The Missionaries who had given less emphasis to the idea of BEND supported wholeheartedly these efforts of teaching agriculture and technical skills in their schools. In this drive, Canon H.M. Grace, then Headmaster of King' College Buddo opened up a section of Central School at Namutamba with the following intention:

> The boys who are less academically inclined at Buddo will work out their own salvation, depending on their initiative and enterprise.

Other Missionaries also acted like Canon Grace of Buddo. They turned many of their schools into Central Schools to teach practical skills.

For some time, these Central Schools were making a favourable impression on the society of Uganda in terms of BEND. Thus in his 1933 Annual Education Report, the Director of Education pointed out:

> Central Schools are producing excellent material for training in the Technical Schools and in the Teacher Training Schools.

The optimism of the Director of Education however, was short-lived. The Department of Education, today's Ministry of Education and Sports discontinued the Central Schools in 1938 and turned them into purely academic junior secondary schools to run pure academic courses like their counter parts called the Middle Schools.

One reason for their discontinuation was because they were attracting fewer students every year. The majority of students preferred the Middle Schools which were running purely academic courses. Thus the Missionary Education Secretaries of the C.M.S. and of the White Father Society commented in 1935:

> Central Schools with their somewhat experimental curriculum and vague status offered little attraction to pupils leaving lower schools. The effort made to stimulate interest in these schools is meeting with scanty support from both teachers and students.

Another reason why these Central Schools were closed was because Sir Philip Mitchell who became Governor of Uganda from 1935 was not interested in vocational oriented post primary schools. He wanted academic secondary schools to produce Ugandans who could take up junior administrative posts in the civil service to assist the British officers.

Thirdly, the teachers had not been properly trained to run a practical cum academic course in these Central Schools. The old type of teachers who were accustomed to teaching purely academic courses in the post primary schools were the ones who were assigned to the Central Schools with the hope that they would run practical courses. Thus the C.M.S. Education Secretary wrote:

> It is to be regretted that the Central Schools have not functioned according to syllabus because of the lack of suitable staff, the schools having remained largely academic.

The Director of Education joined the C.M.S. and the White Fathers Education Secretaries in lamenting the inability of the teachers to run a practical course in the Central Schools and he reported thus:

> The Central Schools for the most part continue to disappoint because the masters have failed to assimilate the ideals and aims of the syllabus. Similarly, their attitude to imparting practical skills is negative.

Therefore the Department of Education had established the Central Schools without having first taken steps to train the teachers who would run them along the vocational skills which were needed and it did not also take care to re-orient their attitude towards these practical skills.

Fourthly, society did not like these practical oriented Central Schools. It preferred the Middle Schools which were running an academic course. The attitude of the society was epitomised by the remarks of one of the sons of Sir Apollo Kaggwa, former Katikkiro of Buganda at an education Conference at Namirembe. He thus burst out:

> The chiefs send their boys to high schools not to learn to drive bullock wagons and to look after cattle, but to learn to be fitted for posts of high standing. Canon Grace, Headmaster of Buddo is trying to educate them for slavery work by running a side show at Namutamba for Buddo students who were supposedly less academically able.

When the Central Schools were closed in 1938, the primary schools however, continued to run the academic and practical side in agriculture and handcraft skills to give the students practical skills which they could use readily after primary education in terms of BEND. But the idea of adaptation to the environment ceased with the closure of the Central Schools. Africans felt that an inferior kind of education was being subjected to them.

Practical skills for academic failures

The next important phase of cementing Basic Education for National Development-BEND, was ushered in by the de Bunsen Education Committee of 1952. This Committee removed the agriculture and handcraft lessons from the primary schools to a new kind of schools. One reason for this was that pupils were too young to gain from the teaching of practical skills in agriculture and handcrafts at that level.

The new kind of schools which were set up to teach agriculture and technical skills were to be joined after primary six for two years. One category was called Farm Schools to teach practical skills in agriculture and farm management. The second category was called Rural Trade Schools to teach practical technical skills. The third category was called Home Craft Centres to run practical courses for girls in home management. The above schools ran side by side with the two year academic Junior Secondary schools. The graduates from the Farm Schools, the Rural Trade Schools and the Home Craft Centres were supposed to join the Secondary Modern Schools as senior secondary schools but running practical skills.

All the above schools however, were very unpopular for the following reasons: Firstly, the teachers for them had not been properly trained to run practical courses. Nor was their attitude prepared to like these courses. The teachers had been picked up from those who were running formerly the academic courses in the Junior Secondary Schools and in the upper section of the Primary schools.

Secondly, parents and students preferred the academic Junior Secondary Schools. Thirdly, the Department of Education which is today's Ministry of Education and Sports treated these schools as meant for those pupils who had scored lower marks at the end of the Primary six section. So they were looked at as schools for the failures; students who could not cope up with academic subjects.

Moreover on graduation, those few boys who had gone through these schools had no easy opportunity for getting paid employment. Indeed the idea behind these schools was to give practical skills to their students to employ themselves usefully in rural areas and not to go to towns to look for jobs. But because a paid job is very attractive, on graduation, these students used to go to towns to look for paid employment swinging their Certificates to possible employers. But their skills were inferior to those of the graduates who had gone through the proper technical schools. So the graduates of the Farm Schools, Rural Trade Schools, Home Craft Centres and Secondary Modern Schools failed to get jobs. Consequently, parents and students viewed these schools as useless. So by 1962, they were lacking students and the Castle Education Commission of 1963 turned them into purely academic secondary schools with a question mark, "shall we build this nation on the backs of people who have been made to feel as failures?"

BEND in limbo

Though the Castle Education Commission of 1963 had one of the aims of education in Uganda as for preparing the pupils to live in their communities and serve them productively, the trend of the curriculum at both Primary and Secondary School levels was to prepare pupils and students academically to get the numerous white-collar jobs which were so much available during the decade which followed 1962, the year Uganda regained her independence. The abundance of these white-collar jobs had been brought about by the departure of many British Civil Servants and due to so many Ministries which had been created.

Basic Education Integrated Into Rural Development – BEIRD or the Namutamba project

By 1968 the jobs which had been so much abundant immediately Uganda had regained her independence and a few years afterwards, became filled up and the economy was developing at a very slow pace, so the creation of jobs in the private sector did not match the pace at which the schools and the Universities were turning out academically oriented graduates. The result was the appearance of the "School Leaver Problem" which began to spread to University graduates especially on the Arts side. Students from primary schools to A-level Secondary schools had been produced in very large numbers yet without any tangible practical skills to create their own employment.

The phenomenon of producing through schools students who had no practical skills led to the leaders at that time to start preaching the Gospel known as "Back to the land" in the spirit of BEND. But unfortunately the graduates from the schools had no tangible practical skills to use on the land. This also led to the then President of Uganda, Dr. Apollo Milton Obote to declare thus in 1969:

> In this spirit of reorganising the curriculum and changing the attitude of those going to secondary schools, our education system will have to be tailored in future to our national needs and geared to the production of faithful and competent servants of Uganda and not to the multiplication of the elites and the gentry.
> The curriculum and syllabi will therefore have to be revised accordingly.

In pursuance of this idea, the government invited a UNESCO expert to start the project known as Basic Education Integrated into Rural Development-BEIRD, based at Namutamba. Consequently, the Project came to be familiarly known as the Namutamba Project.

The Namutamba Project produced an academically and technically integrated practical curriculum for both primary schools and Teacher Training Colleges which produce teachers for the primary schools. By 1977 after experimenting with this curriculum for ten years, the experimented curriculum was completed and declared viable. Then it was inaugurated by the Government to spread into all primary schools and Teacher Training Colleges in Uganda.

But the enthusiasm with which the Namutamba Project was inaugurated was not accompanied by the same enthusiasm for its execution and implementation in the Primary schools and in the Teacher Training Colleges. The curriculum in the Primary schools and in the Teacher Training Colleges continued to be heavily academic. The pre-occupation in the Primary schools continued to be as it does today, that of preparing primary school pupils to enter the academic secondary schools by passing the PLE in the first grade. Therefore the Namutamba Project remained on paper. One of the reasons why the Namutamba curriculum failed was the failure to get financial support in the primary schools and in the Teacher Training Colleges to implement that curriculum.

While the Namutamba Project was being experimented out at Namutamba Teacher Training College for ten years, there was enough money supplied by UNESCO to meet all the necessary costs to buy the required equipment. But once that money stopped to flow after the experiment, there was no money coming from the government for buying equipment in primary schools and in the Teacher Training Colleges to sustain the practical curriculum. This same fate of the absence of money may befall any practical curriculum designed to achieve the aims behind Basic Education for National Development: BEND. Therefore we need to watch against it.

According to statistics from the Planning Unit of the Ministry of Education and Sports, we all know that about 10% of the graduates from Primary schools get access to the secondary schools and to some other post primary institutions. The 90% stay within the rural areas to look after themselves the best they can with no tangible practical skills to use. It is this state of affairs which must have alarmed the 1987 Uganda National Education Policy Review Commission and led it to declare the need to inaugurate the policy of Basic Education for National Development-BEND for the next reorganisation of the Uganda National Education System.

Reflection on Basic Education For National Development -BEND

The above exposition shows that at various times in the development of education in Uganda, the idea of Basic Education for National Development-BEND, has been tried. What is now new is the catch term of BEND. However, it is fortunate to be launched when there is a historical legacy behind for us to look at. This raises the big question why BEND did not become effective in Uganda's education system during the colonial days and why it also failed to take root when the heavily internationally funded and internationally publicised Namutamba Project was inaugrated in 1977.

If we can answer the above question we shall be able to launch BEND when we have tried to remove those obstacles if they may still exist today. The following were the major obstacles to BEND:

Historical Perspective of basic Education

Firstly, the attitude of society and of the students was opposed to an education which was not literary. Having been conditioned by the people who introduced Western education in Uganda, the Uganda society believed that it was the academic education which led to glory. This arose from the very way Western education had been introduced into this country and continued to be carried on. The famous schools which gained prominence from the very beginning of this Western education added to this fever for academic education. Such schools were Namilyango College, King's College Buddo, St. Mary's College Kisubi, Gayaza High School, Busoga College Mwiri and Nabumali High School. Nyakasura School however, escaped this legacy, thanks to the efforts of Commander Calwell, its founder, who from the very beginning in the 1920s started it and ran it along an integrated course of academic and practical subjects. Makerere College which was established by the government in 1922 added to this fever for academic education in the country and outside it because it unconsciously dominated the Uganda system of education as far back a the first year of Junior secondary education.

Speaking about the fever for academic education, the first Director of Education in Uganda, Eric Hussey wrote the following in the 1925 Education Annual Report:

> To most of the children who go to school, the learning of a little English is the coveted goal, and the motive behind that desire is that they might escape from the ranks of a manual worker and fit themselves for some kind of clerical occupation, which they believe to be dignified and less arduous'

In the same vane a C.M.S. educator T.C. Vincent of Bishop Tucker College Mukono declared at an education Conference in Britain in 1928 thus:

> Parents in Uganda send their children to mission schools with the hope that they would escape from the routine of village life to which they themselves were subjected, and not that they might return to it with new knowledge and idea that would make that life acceptable and of worth to them.

Throughout the colonial period and decades after Uganda had regained her independence, parents and students were convinced that it was only a graduate of literary education who stood a greater chance to get a white-collar job and thereby get a respectable status in society. The teachers and the school curriculum also emphasised this fact as they continue to do today and indeed the parents and the students cannot be blamed for this.

In our endeavour to cement Basic Education for National Development-BEND, we need to answer the question whether the attitude of the Uganda society and of the students has changed to make it smooth for BEND to succeed. If this attitude has not yet changed, the educationists have got to find ways and means of changing this attitude. Therefore research in this attitude of society and students is necessary at this initial stage of implementing BEND.

Secondly, the teachers themselves were an obstacle to the full realisation of BEND historically. The administrators of the education system failed to produce a cadre of teachers who could teach effectively the practical skills and who at the same time had the right attitude towards those skills. Consequently, even when the practical aspects of the curriculum were being taught, they had a great bias towards academic education.

Thus the Binns Study Group from London remarked in 1951:

> For the most part, the missionary teachers had been required to possess University degrees. Many of them had been more familiar with town than with country life and their own education had its emphasis more on literary than on practical education. Consequently, with this kind of background, the European missionary teachers had brought that limited experience into schools and teacher training colleges in Africa, preparing pupils and teachers for primary schools mostly in rural areas.

Speaking about the attitude of teachers in terms of imparting practical skills, the same Binns Study Group pointed out further:

> Realising the need for education in Uganda to be related to rural life, the authorities have from time to time prescribed a period of practical work to be done in all schools, and the schools have done their best to comply with the instructions thus given, in spite of the opposition of some of the African staff and pupils.
> We have seen children marched to a store and told to draw hoes from it and then go and dig the ground rather aimlessly while the teacher kept one eye on the clock and every body obviously hoped for the end of the lesson. This same observation applies equally to the teaching and practising of technically oriented practical skills in schools in Uganda.

Therefore there is now a need to review the curriculum of the Primary Teachers Colleges and methodology in the School of Education at Makerere University and at other Universities in Uganda and at the National Teachers Colleges (NTCs) and at the Institute of Teacher Education Kyambogo (ITEK) so that teachers produced will have a positive attitude and practical skills to be able to teach those practical skills in the schools. The present teacher education courses in the above institutions and the way they are taught cannot achieve what BEND stipulates to achieve. The teachers who are being produced are generally fit to teach in the General Secondary Schools which are similar to the majority of the present academic secondary schools.

There is also need to retrain the present teachers who are already teaching in schools so that they can also impart practical skills on the basis of BEND with an attitude which is also positive.

Thirdly, the government's vacillating approach to BEND during the colonial period had also a lot to minimise the impact of BEND. During the term of office of Governor Sir Philip Mitchell, 1935-40, the idea of BEND got into the background in his drive to produce African middle class manpower to work as assistants to the British civil servants.

Similarly, from 1963 to 1969 the prominence by government was given to producing academically qualified man-power to fill up posts left vacant by the departing British civil servants on Uganda's regaining her independence and also to fill up the numerous jobs which had been created due to the establishment of many Ministries.

Again in terms of government, its education system mitigated against the effectiveness of Basic Education for National Development. The emphasis in the curriculum was put on academic education. The examination system emphasised academic education as it still does today. Even if a pupil was quite good at say art and craft lessons and at agricultural practice, these qualities did not count towards his or her final passing say in the P LE. If such a pupil scored very low marks in the academic subjects, he or she was treated as a failure.

Moreover at selection for secondary education, it was the pupils who had scored the lowest marks in the theoretical academic questions at P.L.E. who were selected for such schools as Farm Schools, Rural Trade Schools and Home Craft Centres. Those pupils went to those schools with a deep feeling of failure in their hearts though they might have been first class in the practical subjects. Therefore the examination system also needs to be looked into so that it can give credit to materials and services produced by the pupils through the practical skills in agriculture and other practical subjects. This will also create a change in the methodology of coaching. Coaching would then be carried on more in gardens. The proficiency of the coaching teacher and that of the student who is being coached, would be judged by the plants grown under scientific methods, and one could judge this from large cabbages, tomatoes, greens, potatoes, cassava, simsim, millet and bananas being produced by the student under coaching.

Also coaching would be carried out more in workshops, and the proficiency of the coaching teacher and of the student being coached, would be seen through the ability of the student to repair bicycles, motor cycles, motor vehicles, making machines, making dometic water pumps, making mechanically operated gadgets, making furniture, rat-traps, bricks, making and mending beds and repairing them and making doors and windows, drawing plans for simple houses and engaging in building chicken-houses, hygienic latrines, wracks on which to hang plates and other utensils to dry, plumbing, tinkering with all sorts of technically operated machines and making water reservoirs.

In reference to making water reservoirs, are we aware that we could tap enough rain-water from our houses in the homes to last us from one rain season to the next one? But now we leave all this rain-water to flow away down the valleys, carrying all the top soil from our compounds and gardens. After the rain season water because scarce. If students could be taught the skills of constructing water-reservoirs, each home could have a water-reservoir and there could be several water-reservoirs in each village for public use when there is a prolonged drought. Let the coaching teachers engaged in coaching pupils and students do the above.

Also coaching would be carried out more on farms and the proficiency of the coaching teacher and of the student being coached, would be seen through the ability of the students constructing houses for poultry or for swine, or for rabbits, or for cattle, making manure and animal feeds, looking after animals and birds, and collecting eggs from the poultry house, and milking the cows, and participating in the commercial sale of the same and balancing the books.

All the coaching should show how practical these practical skills are for earning a living. When coaching will be approached in this way, it will stop the practice of making students sit for hours on end in rooms on chairs, copying masses of words and cramming them for reproduction in examinations, when in actual life the majority of these students will never get office jobs where they will be required to sit on chairs doing work daily.

The implication of all this, is that all teacher education institutions need to change their methods of producing teachers and the Ministry of Education and Sports needs to mount refresher courses for the already practising teachers to approach their methods of teaching according to the above point of view. To force teachers to approach coaching and teaching in schools in the above fashion, both the examination system will also need to change to give weight to the practical side of education comparable to that given to the literary side of education. That way, we shall have gone back to the real spirit of the African Indigenous Education which was known as *production learning*. That is, the students learned as they produced materials and services to show how they had mastered the practical skills taught to them.

Fourthly, the cost of running a heavily vocationalised education system needs to be looked into carefully. The cost may easily discourage many school administrators from mounting the teaching of practical skills and this will affect the effectiveness of BEND. For example, if a primary school of 500 pupils wanted to teach carpentry and metal work to each pupil, we need to look into the cost of the workshops, tools, the wood and the metal needed for the pupils to practise on. But such a Primary school will need to teach other practical skills which equally demand that similar outlay of workshops, equipment and materials.

Yet when one is running academic or literary education, one needs only a classroom with a chalk-board, with some desks or without desks, students with or without exercise books, pens and text books. This is the situation which many students today face in Uganda in many schools. In a situation like this, costs of running a school are bound to be lower than in a school where both literary and practical courses are being run for the acquisition of practical tangible skills.

Looked at from the national point of view, by AD 2003 there will be over 10,000 Primary schools in Uganda. If each of those schools were to teach carpentry and metal work, the cost on only those two practical subjects can be imagined. The nation or the citizens therefore must be prepared to pay more money to run a heavily practical education system as suggested by the Senteza-Kajubi Education Commission of 1987. If funds will not be readily forthcoming, the present kind of teaching in primary schools and in secondary schools will continue as of old to the detriment of Basic Education for National Development: BEND.

Finally, a curriculum for vocational education or parts of the curriculum needs to be changed constantly. If this is not done, schools will continue to teach students practical skills when the economic situation no longer requires those skills.

Traditionally, school curricula and syllabuses have got a tendency for being unchanged for years. Syllabuses for vocational education can hardly be useful for more than five years. This then means that the Ministry of Education, through its National Curriculum Development Centre must be prepared financially to review each year the vocational education syllabuses and cause text books to be written for students and feed them into schools.

Conclusion

Basic Education for National Development is not a new idea in the education system of Uganda. What is now new is the term BEND. At various phases of Uganda's development of the education system, it has held the concern of educationists and of the government.

But since Basic Education for National Development has at this moment assumed such concern and prominence, it means that all the previous attempts to impart practical skills to pupils and students through our schools have failed to produce appreciable results.

The urgency of the moment requires us to make research into all the obstacles which prevented BEND from becoming effective and so provide practical answers for the success of BEND. Failure to do so will make the enthusiasm for BEND to produce no better results than those produced in the past.

History and Development of Education

Questions

1. Why was the African indigenous education system called *Production Learning*'?
2. What was the gist in the *Production Learning* of the African indigenous education system?
3. What four significant themes has BEND passed through in Uganda's education system from the pre-colonial days to the present?
4. Discuss four obstacles which have traditionally hindered BEND from producing appreciable results in Uganda's education system?
5. Why is a heavily vocational oriented school curriculum likely to be more expensive to maintain than a heavily academic oriented school curriculum?

Since 1922 Makerere has been the goal for all students with academic ambition. Will it sustain this position in the face of new universities which have sprung up and others yet to come?

Index

Advisory Board of Education, 49, 52, 53, 59
African Greek Orthodox Schools, 108, 124
    Indigenious Education, 4, 8, 10, 14, 17, 21-23, 43 see also Indigenous Education
Aggrey, J.K., Dr, 60
Agricultural Education, 71-83
    Extension, 83
'A' level, 18, 169, 188, 204, 219
Americans, 21, 22, 41
Amin Dada, Idi, 19, 138, 139, 184-187
Arabs, 25, 29, 30, 33, 34
Arusha Declaration, 1167
Asians, 19, 20, 115, 117
Basic Eduction for National Development (BEND), 20, 182, 200, 208, 209, 221-235
Basic Education Intergrated into Rural Development (BEIRD), 227, 228
Bataka Movement, 103, 110
Hesketh, Bell, Sir, 48, 125
Bikira Teachers Training School, 86
Binns Study Group, (1951), 59, 64, 67, 78-82, 91, 97, 114, 123, 136, 137, 148, 154, 162, 194, 195, 230
Bishop Tucker Theological College, 62
British Administrators, 17
Bugema University, 118
Buganda, 8-16, 15, 18, 107
Bunyoro-Kitara, 12, 18, 22, 25
Cambridge School Certificate Examination, 69, 112, 113, 114, 137, 154
Castle Education Commission, (1963), 81, 116, 153, 165, 166, 187, 197, 200, 226, 227
Catholics, 12, 28-30, 32, 35-37, 40, 47, 56, 59, 95, 97, 99-104, 116, 119, 126, 128, 130, 143, 144, 146, 171, 173, 177, 199, 205, 212
Catechist Schools, 40, 53
Central Schools, 41, 61, 63, 73, 76-78, 85, 86, 100, 135, 203, 223-225
Christians, 12, 13, 39, 119
Christianity, 12, 29, 32, 36, 39, 124, 130
Church in Education, 52-58
Church Missionary Society (CMS), 3, 27-29, 33, 34, 42-46, 48, 54, 55, 62, 64, 73-76, 84, 94, 95, 100-104, 120, 129, 133, 134, 203, 205, 210, 215, 216, 222, 228
Chwa, Daudi, Kabaka, 131
Chwa II Memorial College, 94, 167, 110, 112.
Cohen, Andrew, Sir, 94, 147, 148, 161, 162, 196.
Colonial Education, 154-163
    Government, 43, 47, 49-56, 59-61, 65, 94, 109, 122
Comboni Missionaries, 38, 46, 86, 128, 146, 155
Cost-sharing, 209-211
Curriculum, 2, 8, 13-15, 18, 40, 55, 61, 63, 67, 68, 73, 75, 86, 91, 96, 107, 136, 169, 181, 200, 228.
Daily Telegraph, 26, 27
De Bunsen Education Committee, (1952), 67, 68, 78, 80, 88, 97, 114, 122, 144, 148-153, 162, 164, 165, 172, 189, 194 - 196, 204, 214
De La Warr Commission, (1957), 59, 76, 77, 87, 92, 121, 128, 136, 192, 193
Democratic Party (DP), 36, 107, 111, 172, 173
Department of Education, 52-56, 73, 84, 96, 97
Director of Education, 60 66, 72-76, 89, 96, 99, 100, 102, 104, 105, 112, 113, 119, 123, 134, 158
East African Literature Bureau, 159
    High Commission, 136
Education Act, (1963), 57, 115, 116, 170-177, 185, 197-199, 211, 212, 213
    (1970), 117, 184, 198, 199

Annual Report, (1925), 39, 229
(1931), 224
(1933), 224
(1947), 106
(1948), 96
(1950), 90, 102, 106, 190
(1951), 106
(1956), 123
Education Committee, (1940), 106, 121
development (1940-62), 143-153, 164-190
for citizenship, 159-163
Ordinance, (1927) 104, 120, 121, 145, 156, 192, 200
(1942), 143, 151, 193
(1959), 162, 196, 197
of girls, 215-219
policy, 72, 87
Secretary, 57, 94, 96, 98, 199
Egyptians, 25, 31, 33
Elgon Technical School, 85, 86, 89.
Europeans, 21, 25, 30, 31, 33, 40-42, 144
Farm Schools, 68, 74, 88, 149, 152, 153, 189, 190, 195, 226, 231
Foundation Bodies, 122, 172, 174, 212
Gava, Ramadhan, Haji, 57, 108, 146
Government White Paper, 140
Hall, John, 65, 77, 147, 155, 157
Home Crafts Centre, 68, 88, 149, 152, 153, 189, 190, 195, 226, 231
Hussey, Eric, 52, 60, 61, 81, 99, 119, 120, 135, 189
Imperial British East African Company (IBEA Co.), 36
Imperialism, 49
Indigenious Education, 2, 14, 17-19, 42, 43
Inspectorate of Education, 57, 105
Islam, 12, 25, 29, 32, 36, 47, 129, 169
Jeffrey's Education Commission, 148, 194
Jones, Hesse, Dr, 60
Jowitt, H., 65

Junior Secondary, 54, 100, 119, 152
Kabaka Yekka (KY), 36, 111
Kabalega, Omukama, 25, 35, 48*
Kaggwa, Apollo, Sir, 36, 62, 79, 189, 225
Kakungulu, Badru, Al-Haji, Prince, 57, 146
Kalibbala, Balintuma Ernest, Dr, 94-96, 98, 111
Kanadda Rural School, 86, 96, 107, 117
Kampala Technical Institute, 68, 92, 119
School, 85, 86
Kasagama, Omukama, 131
Kiwanuka, Joseph, Bishop, 103
Koran, 29, 33, 47
Lawerence Commission, 173
Legislative Council, 74, 123, 125, 160, 192
Literary Education, 59-82, 97
Local Government, 89, 145, 156, 157
Lourdel Simon, 28, 32
Lugard Frederick, Capt., 36
Lule, Y.K., 122, 151
Mackay, Alexander, 27, 32
Mahdist Rebellion, 31
Makerere College, 12, 54, 55, 60, 66, 85, 93, 192, 219
University, 53, 54, 79, 92, 151, 164, 166-169, 179, 186-189, 191, 196, 204, 209, 210, 230
Male Kassim, 157
Martyrs, 34
Mau Mau Movement, 111
Middle Schools, 61, 73, 85, 119, 223
Mill Hill Fathers, 38, 44, 45, 48, 55, 86, 130, 133, 203, 215
Minority Report, 122
Mission Schools, 105, 109
Mitchell, Philip, Sir, 65, 76, 86, 87, 120, 135, 192, 224, 231
Mukasa, Ssebbanja, Reuben, 94
Munster Commission, 173
Musa Body University, 118
Muslims, 12, 13, 29-33, 35-37, 47, 56, 57, 97, 99, 119, 121, 143-146, 171, 176, 185, 192, 196, 199

Index

Musoke, Anslem, 86, 95-98, 101, 107, 117.
Muteesa II, Kabaka, 25-35, 89, 102, 111, 132, 148
Mwanga, Kabaka, 34, 35, 48
National Curriculum Development Centre, 59, 233
National Resistance Council (NRC), 139
        Movement (NRM), 139, 187
Native Education, 50
Ndejje University, 118
Negro Movement, 49
Nkozi University, 118
Nkumba University, 118
Normal School (Encoles Normales), 42, 203
Nsamizi Training Centre, 162
Nsubuga, Emmanuel, Cardinal, 174
Obote, Apollo Milton, 108, 138, 139, 168, 183, 184, 186, 199, 227
Ocitti, J. P., 171
Okello, Lutwa, 139, 186
'O' level, 18, 154, 169, 204, 219
Orthodox Church, 94, 110, see also African Greek Orthodox.
Parents Teachers Association (PTA), 117, 211 - 215
Parents Schools, 116, 117, 172, 174, 185
Phelps - Stokes Commission, (1924-25), 44, 50, 59, 60, 71, 72, 125, 136, 191, 210, 222, 223
Political and Religious Wars, 35-38.
Pre-colonial, 8
Primary Education, 17, 18, 54, 57
        Leaving Examination (PLE), 69, 88, 90, 104, 109, 113, 116, 152, 182, 183, 190, 231
        Leaving Certificate, 103, 104
Private Schools, 94-118, 199
Protestants, 12, 27, 29-32, 35-37, 40, 47, 50, 56, 57, 59, 94, 95, 97, 99, 102, 118, 126, 130, 143-146, 171, 215, 217

Royal Commission, (1951-55), 59
Royal Geographical Society, 26, 89
Rural Trade Schools, 68, 88, 117, 149, 152, 153, 189, 190, 195, 226, 231
School Management Committee, 144, 145, 173, 176, 213, 214
        open day, 90
Secondary Schools, 54, 57, 152, 153, 190, 195.
Senteza-Kajubi Education Commission, (1987), 78, 139, 140, 141, 182, 187-190, 191, 194, 195, 199, 200, 233
Spartas, Fr., 94, 96, 101, 107, 108, 124
Stanely, Henry Morton, 26, 31
Swahili Traders, 25, 34, 131
Teaching Service, 202-109
Technical Education, 84-93
        Schools, 42, 54
        Skills, 21
Thomas Education Committee, (1940), 143-147, 151, 155, 156, (1972), 193, 203, 214
Traditional Rulers, 131, 133
Tucker, Alfred, Bishop, 44, 45, 129, 189, 203, 229
Tuskegee Institute, 71, 95.
Uganda Muslim Education Association (UMEA), 57, 97, 108, 146, 156, 170, 171, 177, 199, 211.
Uganda National Education Policy Review Commission, 20, 139, 182, 191, 199, 200, 209, 221, 223,; see also Senteza-Kajubi
Uganda Teacher's Association (UJTA), 205-207
United Nations Organisation, 98.
Vernacular Schools, 40, 41, 54, 127
Verona Fathers, 38, 46, 55, 61, 74, 155.
Village Schools, 40, 41, 54, 127.
Western Education, 17, 18, 21, 25-58, 101, 202

White Fathers Missionaries, 3, 27, 45, 48, 55, 84, 86, 120, 130, 133, 134, 203, 215, 225
Young Farmers Club, 160

www.ingramcontent.com/pod-product-compliance
Lightning Source LLC
Chambersburg PA
CBHW021401290426
44108CB00010B/332